Global Health Economics

Shaping Health Policy in Low-
and Middle-Income Countries

World Scientific Series in Global Health Economics and Public Policy

ISSN: 2010-2089

Series Editor-in-Chief: Peter Berman *(The University of British Columbia, Canada & Harvard University, USA)*

The World Scientific Series in Global Health Economics and Public Policy, under the leadership of Professor Peter Berman, a renowned healthcare economist, public policy specialist and researcher in this field, seeks to fill this gap. It strives to publish high-quality scientific works, including monographs, edited volumes, references, handbooks, etc., which address subjects of primary scientific importance on the global scale, as related to international economic policies in healthcare, social capital and healthcare economics in different global markets, etc. The titles in this series appeal to researchers, graduate students, policy makers, practitioners and commercial businesses, dealing with healthcare economics worldwide.

Published:

More information on this series can also be found at
https://www.worldscientific.com/series/wssghepp

(Continued at end of book)

World Scientific Series in Global Health Economics and Public Policy – Vol. 5

Global Health Economics

Shaping Health Policy in Low- and Middle-Income Countries

Edited by

Paul Revill
University of York, UK

Marc Suhrcke
University of York, UK
Luxembourg Institute of Socio-Economic Research, Luxembourg

Rodrigo Moreno-Serra
University of York, UK

Mark Sculpher
University of York, UK

With a foreword by **Maria Goddard**,
Director of the Centre for Health Economics

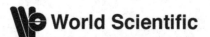

World Scientific

EW JERSEY · LONDON · SINGAPORE · BEIJING · SHANGHAI · HONG KONG · TAIPEI · CHENNAI · TOKYO

Published by

World Scientific Publishing Co. Pte. Ltd.

5 Toh Tuck Link, Singapore 596224

USA office: 27 Warren Street, Suite 401-402, Hackensack, NJ 07601

UK office: 57 Shelton Street, Covent Garden, London WC2H 9HE

Library of Congress Cataloging-in-Publication Data

Names: Revill, Paul, editor. | Suhrcke, Marc, editor. | Moreno-Serra, Rodrigo, editor. |
Sculpher, Mark J., editor.

Title: Global health economics : shaping health policy in low- and middle-income countries /
edited by Paul Revill, Marc Suhrcke, Rodrigo Moreno-Serra, Mark Sculpher.

Other titles: World Scientific series in global healthcare economics and
public policy ; v. 5. 2010-2089

Description: New Jersey : World Scientific Publishing, [2019] |
Series: World Scientific series in global health economics and public policy,
ISSN 2010-2089 ; vol. 5 | Includes bibliographical references and index.

Identifiers: LCCN 2019024363| ISBN 9789813272361 (hardcover) | ISBN 9789813272378 (ebook)

Subjects: | MESH: Global Health--economics | Economics, Medical | Health Policy |
Poverty Areas | Medically Underserved Area

Classification: LCC RA410.5 | NLM WA 530.1 | DDC 338.4/73621--dc23

LC record available at https://lccn.loc.gov/2019024363

British Library Cataloguing-in-Publication Data

A catalogue record for this book is available from the British Library.

For any available supplementary material, please visit
https://www.worldscientific.com/worldscibooks/10.1142/11045#t=suppl

Desk Editor: Jiang Yulin

Printed in Singapore

About the Editors

Paul Revill is a senior research fellow at the Centre for Health Economics, University of York, and is the team lead in global health economic evaluation. He is director of the RCUK GCRF-funded Thanzi la Onse (Health of All) program that aims to support government-led, analytically informed healthcare decision-making in Africa. Paul's research interests revolve around the development of methods and applied economic evaluation to inform resource allocation decisions within healthcare sectors of low- and middle-income countries, particularly in sub-Saharan Africa. The underlying aim of his work is to ensure that resources committed to healthcare are spent in ways likely to lead to greatest improvements in population health and wellbeing, recognizing the complexities of real world healthcare systems. He is a visiting fellow at the Centre for Global Development (CGD) in Washington, D.C. Previously, he was an economist at the Ministry of Health in Malawi.

Marc Suhrcke is Professor of Global Health Economics at the Centre for Health Economics, University of York, where he heads the Global Health Economics team, and Senior Researcher at the Luxembourg Institute for Socio-Economic Research (LISER). The main part of his research revolves around a range of economic and econometric aspects of public health in low- and middle-income countries, which include the micro and macroeconomic consequences of (ill-)health, the economic evaluation of public health interventions, the measurement of socioeconomic inequalities in — and determinants of — health, and empirical policy impact evaluation. Among others he currently directs the NIHR-funded Global Health Econometrics and Economics Group, the focus of which is the evaluation of population and system level interventions using quasi-experimental methods. His work has been funded by the World Bank, WHO, the European Commission, DFID, the Global Fund to Fight AIDS, Tuberculosis and Malaria, the European Centre for Disease Prevention and Control, NIHR, MRC, ESRC, German Research Foundation and others. Previously he was Professor for Public Health Economics at the University of East Anglia, Norwich, and held various research positions in international organizations (WHO, UNICEF).

Rodrigo Moreno-Serra is a Reader (Associate Professor) in Global Health Economics at the Centre for Health Economics, University of York, where he co-leads the Global Health Team. He has previously held academic positions at the University of Sheffield and Imperial College London. Rodrigo has also worked on multiple instances as a consultant for institutions including WHO, OECD, World Bank and the Global Fund to Fight AIDS, Tuberculosis and Malaria. His research interests encompass various topics in health economics, global health and development economics. He has published papers in top academic journals and policy reports dealing with health system financing and the impact evaluation of health policies and programs, among other themes. Rodrigo's research has been recognized through continuous external funding to lead different projects, awards by professional organisations, invitations to speak at international events and press coverage. He is an associate editor of the *Journal of International Development* (Wiley).

Mark Sculpher is Professor of Health Economics at the Centre for Health Economics, University of York, UK where he leads the Centre's Programme on Economic Evaluation and Health Technology Assessment. He is also Co-Director of the Policy Research Unit in Economic Evaluation of Health and Care Interventions.

Mark has worked in the field of economic evaluation and health technology assessment for over 30 years. He has researched in a range of clinical areas including heart disease, cancer, diagnostics, and public health. He has over 250 peer-reviewed publications and is a co-author of two major textbooks in the area: *Methods for the Economic Evaluation of Health Care Programmes* (OUP, 2015 with Drummond, Claxton, Torrance and Stoddart) and *Decision Modelling for Health Economic Evaluation* (OUP, 2006 with Briggs and Claxton).

About the Contributors

Miqdad Asaria: Assistant Professorial Research Fellow, LSE Health, London School of Economics and Political Science, UK; Research Fellow, Centre for Health Economics, University of York, UK

Farasat Bokhari: Associate Professor, School of Economics and Centre for Competition Policy, University of East Anglia, UK

Martin Chalkley: Professor, Centre for Health Economics, University of York, UK

Levison Chiwaula: Senior Lecturer, Department of Economics, University of Malawi, Zomba, Malawi

Karl Claxton: Professor, Centre for Health Economics and Department of Economics and Related Studies, University of York, UK

Richard Cookson: Professor, Centre for Health Economics, University of York, UK

Cristóbal Cuadrado: Assistant Professor, School of Public Health, University of Chile, Chile

Bryony Dawkins: Research Assistant, Academic Unit of Health Economics, Leeds Institute of Health Sciences, University of Leeds, UK

Michael Drummond: Professor, Centre for Health Economics, University of York, UK

Jocelyn Dunstan: Assistant Professor, School of Public Health and Faculty of Medicine, University of Chile, UK

Jeffrey W. Eaton: Senior Lecturer, Department for Infectious Disease Epidemiology, Imperial College London, UK

Tim Ensor: Professor of International Health Systems, University of Leeds, UK

Rita Faria: Research Fellow, Centre for Health Economics, University of York, UK

Yevgeny Goryakin: Health Economist/Policy Analyst, Organization for Economic Cooperation and Development (OECD)

Susan Griffin: Senior Research Fellow, Centre for Health Economics, University of York, UK

Timothy B. Hallett: Professor, Department for Infectious Disease Epidemiology, Imperial College London, UK

Arne Hole: Reader, Department of Economics, University of Sheffield, UK

Pritaporn Kingkaew: Researcher, Health Intervention and Technology Assessment Program, Thailand

James Lomas: Research Fellow, Centre for Health Economics, University of York, UK

Gerald Manthalu: Deputy Director, Ministry of Health, Malawi

Finn McGuire: PhD Student, Centre for Health Economics, University of York, UK

Aurelio Mejia: Deputy Director of Health Technology Assessment, Institute of Health Technology Assessment, Colombia

Andrew J. Mirelman: Research Fellow, Centre for Health Economics, University of York, UK; Technical Officer, World Health Organization, Switzerland

Ryota Nakamura: Associate Professor, Hitotsubashi Institute for Advanced Study (HIAS), Japan; formerly Research Fellow, Centre for Health Economics, University of York, UK

Dominic Nkhoma: Lecturer, Health Economics and Policy Unit, College of Medicine, Malawi

Jessica Ochalek: Research Fellow, Centre for Health Economics, University of York, UK

Andrew Phillips: Professor, Institute for Global Health, University College London, UK

Alexandra Rollinger: Project Manager, Centre for Health Economics, University of York, UK

Sax Sandanam: Director of Health, Kabwe Diocese Health, Zambia

Janet Seeley: Professor, London School of Hygiene and Tropical Medicine, UK

Stella Settumba: Health Economist, National Perinatal Epidemiology and Statistics Unit, University of New South Wales, Australia; formerly Health Economist, Medical Research Council, Uganda

Luigi Siciliani: Professor, Department of Economics and Related Studies and Centre for Health Economics, University of York, UK

Nicolás Silva: Master Student, School of Public Health, University of Chile, Chile

Peter C. Smith: Emeritus Professor, Imperial College Business School, London, UK

Rohan Sweeney: Research Fellow, Centre for Health Economics, Monash University, Australia

Suresh Tiwari: Officer Director, Oxford Policy Management, Nepal

Bernard van den Berg: Professor, Faculty of Economics and Business, University of Groningen, Netherlands

Helen Weatherly: Senior Research Fellow, Centre for Health Economics, University of York, UK

Beth Woods: Research Fellow, Centre for Health Economics, University of York, UK

Contents

Foreword

It is both a pleasure and a privilege to write an introductory note for *Global Health Economics*. The book is a reflection of the efforts of leading experts in the field to study the major health and health care issues facing low- and middle-income countries (LMICs) through the lens of economics. The effective, efficient and equitable allocation of scarce resources is central to the economics discipline and this book demonstrates some of the theories, methods and tools that can be applied in order to progress these aims in the context of global health.

A commitment to developing and applying the discipline of economics to improve health and health care is at the heart of our mission at the Centre for Health Economics (CHE) at the University of York. Founded in 1983, CHE has a long tradition of research and training in global health, dating back to the 1990s and indeed even at that time, involving one or two of the authors featured in this book. However, it is more recently that global health economics has become fully embedded as a major strand of research in CHE, embracing almost all the research themes in our portfolio and involving exciting new partnerships and collaborations with research and policy colleagues across the world, as reflected in the authorship of these book chapters. Through strategic investment and careful planning, we have built on our early foundations, establishing a thriving community of researchers pursuing a wide range of activities in global health economics.

The global health research arena is a crowded one. In finding our niche, CHE's focus is on undertaking excellent research underpinned by sound economics principles. But that is not enough; we want our research to make a difference to society. By working alongside research partners and decision-makers in LMICs, we can agree the priority topics on which to concentrate, coproduce research on these topics, help to ensure the research is used to guide policy and practice and enhance analytical capacity in LMICs. CHE's current research portfolio includes several major research projects which set out to achieve exactly these aims, working with colleagues across the world in the east and southern Africa region (e.g. Malawi, Uganda, South Africa), South America (Brazil, Colombia) and east Asia (Indonesia). We hope this book will provide a useful resource for decision-makers and analysts, putting the latest research findings at their disposal in an easily accessible format.

The case for provision of high-quality, relevant, accessible research that addresses the health systems challenges faced by LMICs is compelling. I am delighted that CHE, along with our partners across the world, is playing a substantial role in delivering such research and with global health economics at the core of our research agenda, we will strive to do so well into the future.

Professor Maria Goddard
Director of the Centre for Health Economics,
University of York, UK

Preface

1. Background

Research in the field of health economics is focused on generating evidence and developing analytical methods and frameworks to support policy and decisions regarding resource allocation to enhance health and well-being. The Centre for Health Economics (CHE) at the University of York has been a leading source of high-quality research in this area for over 35 years. For most of that period CHE has had an interest in research to support policy in many jurisdictions. Given its location in the UK, however, supporting government policy and NHS decision-making in that country has been a focus. This has included, for example, developing the methods of economic evaluation to support the National Institute for Health and Care Excellence (NICE) guidance on new medical technologies and public health interventions, and delivering an analytical framework for how the NHS allocates financial resources across its local organizations.

Over the last five years or so, CHE has invested in the development of a programme of work on health economics to support policy and decisions in low- and middle-income countries (LMICs). Although the aims of delivering high-quality and policy-relevant research remain at the core of this programme, the particular challenges of funding and delivering health-enhancing interventions in resource-poor settings have been a key focus. At their core, these challenges are ultimately one of more severe resource constraints. However, the challenges are manifest in a number of ways — more limited health system inputs, weaknesses in governance arrangements, potential for gaming, highly adverse consequences of inefficient decisions, to name just a few — all of which may affect the conduct of health economic analyses and, to some degree, are addressed in this book. We also recognized the importance of collaboration in developing this programme of research, both with policy-making organizations internationally and with researchers undertaking research in economics and complementary areas such as epidemiogical modelling and public administration.

2. Objectives

- To showcase the research undertaken by CHE and its collaborators across the full range of health economics relevant to LMICs.
- To stimulate interest amongst policy- and decision-makers to use economic evidence and analysis routinely as part of their roles.
- To build collaborations to sustain the value of our research, both with those undertaking research and those using its outputs to shape policy.
- To encourage researchers in LMICs to develop interests in health economics and to consider synergies with the research undertaken in CHE.
- To signpost readers to existing work in the field of global health economics.

The book seeks to be non-technical and accessible to a wide readership. In particular, we are aiming to attract readers working in all areas of government and health systems, analysts and decision-makers working for international non-governmental organizations, as well as academics and others interested in public policy and research to inform decision-making in LMICs.

3. Organization of the Book

The book begins with an Editor's Note by colleagues external to CHE commenting on the importance of health economics in general and CHE's programme of global health economics in particular. The main chapters begin with a consideration of the methods of economic evaluation of policies to enhance health and well-being. These show the importance of using and further developing appropriate research methods, but also ensuring these are tailored to meet the needs of policy and decision-making. These chapters extend beyond standard methods to include a consideration of, for example, how equity can be reflected in evaluation methods and the empirical estimation of cost-effectiveness thresholds. The next set of chapters considers the use of economic methods and tools to address health care system problems. These cover issues such as how incentives can be used to stimulate improvements in population health and well-being, challenges concerning resource allocation in low-income settings and how the success of policy can be assessed through wider measures of health development. The book concludes with a series of case studies which illustrate how the analytical methods that have been developed by CHE and its collaborators can be used in practical, policy-focused research in low- and middle-income settings.

The material covered here does not reflect the entire field of health economics, or even CHE's entire programme of research. Important work with clear policy relevance to LMICs is also being undertaken in areas such as behavioral economics applied to public health, evidence synthesis and cross-sectoral economic evaluation. However, the book reflects important developments in this field which represent a foundation upon which CHE intends to build over coming years, with the enduring aim of undertaking rigorous research to help improve policy- and decision-making to enhance health and well-being.

Paul Revill, Marc Suhrcke,
Rodrigo Moreno-Serra and Mark Sculpher

Acknowledgments

We thank Ruth Helstrip and Alex Rollinger for their invaluable help throughout the development of this book. The authors provided chapters without fees, written in their own time, and their contributions are all greatly appreciated.

A number of people have played important roles in the development of global health research at the Centre for Health Economics (CHE). We have benefitted greatly from the direction, support and leadership of CHE's Director, Maria Goddard.

We also thank external academic collaborators and give special thanks to Prof. Diana Gibb (Medical Research Council Clinical Trials Unit), Prof. Andrew Phillips (University College London), Prof. Tim Hallett (Imperial College London), Dominic Nkhoma (College of Medicine, Malawi) and Gerald Manthalu (Ministry of Health, Malawi).

If there are any errors in the book, we — the Editors — take ultimate responsibility.

1. Funding Acknowledgments

Funding from the following organizations for works presented in this book and for related research is gratefully acknowledged:

- Bill and Melinda Gates Foundation (BMGF)
- Centre for Health Economics, University of York (CHE)
- Global Challenges Research Fund (GCRF)

- Inter-American Development Bank (IADB)
- International Decision Support Initiative (IDSI)
- Medical Research Council (MRC)
- MRC/ESRC/DFID/Wellcome Trust Joint Health Systems Research Initiative
- National Institute for Health Research (NIHR)
- Overseas Development Institute (ODI)
- The Global Fund to Fight AIDS, Tuberculosis and Malaria (GFATM)
- The Newton Fund

Paul Revill, Marc Suhrcke, Rodrigo Moreno-Serra
and Mark Sculpher

Editorial — Global Health Economics Research and Policymaking: A Perspective from a Global Health Think Tank

While the field of health economics thrives, the application of health economics to the policies and programmes of low- and middle-income countries (LMIC), and as practiced by citizens and institutions in those countries, remains woefully insufficient.

Although the developing world is home to 84% of the global burden of disease, not a single LMIC institution is ranked among the top 100 working in the field of health economics.[1] Wagstaff and Culyer (2011) look at the country focus in health economics articles between 1969 and 2009, and find that only India and South Africa appear occasionally in the literature in any significant way, with the field almost entirely dominated by health systems issues in the US, the UK, Canada, Australia and Germany.[2] And historically, it is the spending not the health need that tracks closely to a country's production and use of health economics research. Figure 1 illustrates the inverse relationship between country spending and disease burden.

The need then for applied health economics expertise and input into decision problems in LMIC is an order of magnitude greater in LMIC than

---

[1] https://www.sciencedirect.com/science/article/abs/pii/S0167629612000306
[2] https://www.sciencedirect.com/science/article/abs/pii/S0167629612000306

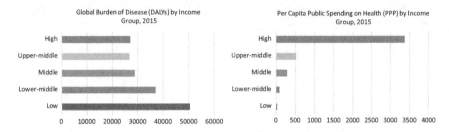

Figure 1. Institute for Health Metrics and Evaluation (IHME).

Source: The graph on the left was created using the IHME data. For the graph on the right, the source was World Bank Indicators Data (https://data.worldbank.org/indicator/SH.XPD.GHED.PP.CD?end=2 015&start=2000&type=shaded&view=map). Both graphs used data from 2015 as this was the most recent year that they had complete data for.

in wealthier countries; issues such as cost-effectiveness and cost–benefit, how demand and supply of health care interact to produce outcomes and affect spending, what influences health outcomes beyond health care, how budgeting and regulation mechanisms affect provider performance and how the whole system is performing on its goals of coverage and quality — all these are at the heart of driving more effective health policy to accelerate gains in health. Particularly where budgets are extremely tight and some analyses find that health spending can be only modestly linked to health improvements,[3] every additional dollar of spending in the health sector requires scrutiny to assure that value for money is maximized. And we know that the different uses of health spending can generate huge differences in the benefits that can be produced by that spending; using Disease Control Priorities data from 2006, Ord (2013) showed how the best of the thousands of evaluated health interventions was 1,400 times as cost-effective as the least good.[4]

In this context, the University of York's Center for Health Economics' (CHE) growing attention to health economics in LMIC is extremely welcome. In its home country, the United Kingdom, CHE has long been engaged in the development of methods and applied work in the service of the government's National Health Service (NHS). The realization that many

---

[3] For example: Filmer and Pritchett (1999); Wagstaff and Claeson (2004); Bokhari *et al.* (2007); Moreno-Serra and Smith (2015).

[4] https://www.cgdev.org/publication/moral-imperative-toward-cost-effectiveness-global-health

of these same methods and approaches can be relevant in LMIC is borne out by the work in this volume. Nakamura *et al.* (2016)'s work to define a more practical definition of the opportunity cost of public health care spending, following on Claxton *et al.*'s (2015) study on the NHS, is a perfect example of how concepts can be applied fruitfully across jurisdictions around the world to generate simple rules of thumb — laid out in the chapter by Revill *et al.* — that would enhance the impact of health spending.

In addition to the contributions of this volume, York CHE is training LMIC students and dedicating a significant share of their work to LMIC issues. Over the past five years, about a fifth of masters and PhD students are LMIC nationals, more faculty are now involved in LMIC topics and more papers are on the horizon.[5]

While still early days, the next challenge is clear — to connect the academic work into policy, reflecting and engaging in the policy process interactively with selected governments and partners in LMIC, as the CHE has engaged with the NHS in England. More coproduction of academic work with LMIC researchers, more responsiveness to policymaker demands, more visibility to the work within the global health community — these are challenges for the future.

References

Bokhari, F. A. S., Gai, Y., Gottret, P. (2007). Government health expenditures and health outcomes. *Health Economics*, 16(3), March: 257–273, https://onlinelibrary.wiley.com/doi/abs/10.1002/hec.1157.

Claxton, K., Martin, S., Soares, M., Rice, N., Spackman, E., Hinde, S., Devlin, N., Smith, P. C., Sculpher, M. (2015). Methods for the estimation of the National Institute for Health and Care Excellence cost-effectiveness threshold. *Health Technology Assessment*, 19(14), February, https://www.journalslibrary.nihr.ac.uk/hta/hta19140/#/abstract.

Filmer, D., Pritchett, L. (1999). The impact of public spending on health: Does money matter? *Social Science & Medicine*, 49(10), November: 1309–1323, https://www.sciencedirect.com/science/article/abs/pii/S0277953699001501?via%3Dihub.

---

[5] Personal communication, Ruth Helstrip, University of York, September 20, 2018.

Moreno-Serra, R., Smith, P. C. (2015). Broader health coverage is good for the nation's health: Evidence from country level panel data. *Journal of the Royal Statistical Society. Series A (Statistics in Society)*, 178(1): 101–124, https://www.ncbi.nlm.nih.gov/pmc/articles/PMC4280714/?tool=pmcentrez &report=.

Nakamura, R., Lomas, J., Claxton, K., Bokhari, F., Moreno-Serra, R., Suhrcke, M. (2016). Assessing the impact of health care expenditures on mortality using cross-country data. University of York, CHE Research Paper 128, April, https://www.york.ac.uk/media/che/documents/papers/researchpapers/ CHERP128_health_care_expenditures_mortality_cross-country_data.pdf.

Ord, T. (2013). The moral imperative toward cost-effectiveness in global health. Center for Global Development, March, https://www.cgdev.org/publication/ moral-imperative-toward-cost-effectiveness-global-health.

Wagstaff, A., Claeson, M. (2004). Rising to the challenges. The World Bank, http:// web.worldbank.org/archive/website01063/WEB/IMAGES/296730PA.PDF.

Wagstaff, A., Culyer, A. J. (2012). Four decades of health economics through a bibliometric lens. *Journal of Health Economics*, 31(2), March: 406–439, https://www.sciencedirect.com/science/article/abs/pii/S0167629612000306.

Amanda Glassman

Executive Vice President and Senior Fellow,

Center for Global Development, USA

Part 1

Health Care Provision and Health

Chapter 1

Assessing the Impact of Health Care Expenditures on Mortality Using Cross-Country Data

Ryota Nakamura, James Lomas, Karl Claxton, Farasat Bokhari, Rodrigo Moreno-Serra and Marc Suhrcke

Abstract

A significant body of literature has examined the impact of public health expenditure on mortality, using a global cross-section or panel of country-level data. However, while a number of studies do confirm such a relationship, the magnitude of the impact varies considerably between studies, and several studies show statistically insignificant effects. In this chapter, we re-examine the literature that identifies this effect using cross-country data. Our analysis builds on the two instrumental variable (IV) approaches applied by key publications in the field — Bokhari *et al.* (2007) and Moreno-Serra and Smith (2015). Using exactly the same data and econometric specifications as the published studies, we start by successfully replicating their findings. However, further analyses using updated data and "streamlined" econometric specifications, plus statistical data imputation and extensive robustness checks, reveal highly sensitive results. In particular, the relevance of the IVs is seriously compromised in the updated data, leading to imprecise estimations of the relationship. While our results should not be taken to imply that there is no true mortality-reducing impact of public health care expenditures, the findings do call for further methodological work, for instance, in terms of

R. Nakamura et al.

identifying more suitable IVs or by applying other estimation strategies, in an effort to derive more robust estimates of the marginal productivity of public health care funding.

1. Introduction

The question of whether, and if so, by how much, public health care expenditures impact on mortality outcomes has occupied and challenged researchers for some decades (Gravelle and Backhouse, 1987). While it is hard to imagine that — if the true relationship were in fact measurable — public health care expenditures would not "buy" mortality reductions, all else equal, in reality there may well be "weak links in the chain" from spending to outcomes (Filmer et al., 2000). Out of the significant body of empirical studies that have attempted to estimate the relationship, some previous studies confirm the expected sign and significance of the relationship, yet the magnitude of the impact varies considerably between studies, and several studies show statistically insignificant effects. For instance, an influential study by Filmer and Pritchett (1999), using global cross-country panel data, found at best a small impact of public health care expenditures on under-five mortality rates, with a 1% increase in spending leading to a — statistically insignificant — reduction in under-five mortality by 0.19% and infant mortality by 0.078%. By contrast, Bokhari et al. (2007) — using a cross-section of data from the year 2000 and an instrumental variable (IV) strategy that broadly follows Filmer and Pritchett (1999) — find that a 1% increase in public health care expenditure significantly (both in statistical and economic terms) reduces under-five mortality by between 0.25% and 0.42%, and maternal mortality by 0.42–0.52%. Those findings have been reinforced very recently by Moreno-Serra and Smith (2015), using again a large cross-country panel analysis with an estimation strategy that allows them to explicitly model the reverse causality from mortality onto spending. Some studies have also pointed to potential nuances in the relationship, e.g. in the sense that public spending matters most for the health of poor people in lower income countries (Bidani and Ravallion, 1997), or that mortality is only reduced in response to public spending when the overall quality of governance in a country exceeds a certain threshold level (Wagstaff and

Claeson, 2004; Rajkumar and Swaroop, 2008). However, while a number of papers do claim to have established a causal relationship between expenditure and mortality outcomes, the magnitude of the impact varies considerably between studies.

In light of these ambiguities, and in order to reflect potential changes in the relationship between public expenditure on health and mortality over time, we revisit the literature that identifies this effect using cross-country data.

Re-estimating this relationship is important for several reasons. To the extent that we are able to derive a robust empirical relationship, this would allow us to capture the marginal productivity of the publicly funded health care system, i.e. the opportunity costs of public health care spending, which in turn would be a crucial element to derive more useful cost-effectiveness threshold estimates than have hitherto been promoted, for instance, in the widely used form of the one to three times per capita GDP rule-of-thumb. This rule was initially proposed by the World Health Organization (WHO) Commission on Macroeconomics and Health (WHO, 2001), and has subsequently been taken up by WHO (2015a, 2015b). From there its use has spread massively, not least for lack of other obvious alternatives. However, the limitations — and potential harms — of this approach have increasingly been recognized (Newall *et al.*, 2014; Revill *et al.*, 2014; Marseille *et al.*, 2015). Recent UK-focused research has shown how cost-effectiveness thresholds can empirically be estimated, starting from rigorous empirical estimates of the impact of spending on health outcomes (Claxton *et al.*, 2015). Subsequent work has produced further within-country threshold estimates in other high-income countries (e.g. Ariste and Di Matteo, 2017; Edney *et al.*, 2018; Vallejo-Torres *et al.*, 2018; Stadhouders et al., 2019). Cross-country-based analysis of the kind presented in this chapter has the potential to inform empirically derived thresholds in countries worldwide, including low- and middle-income countries (LMICs) where the prioritization of health care resources to maximize population health gains is particularly warranted (Ochalek *et al.*, 2018).

In this chapter, we employ an empirical strategy rooted in the literature that has estimated the mortality effects of public health care expenditure using IV strategies — by far the most popular strategy to tackle endogeneity in this literature. While we cannot fully reflect the specific approach taken in every single paper in this literature (see Table A.10[1] for an overview of a select set of studies, and Gallet and Doucouliagos (2015) for a meta-analysis of the broader literature), we first examine the robustness of two exemplary studies — by Bokhari *et al.* (2007) and Moreno-Serra and Smith (2015), henceforth referred to as BGG and MSS, respectively — to new data, while preserving the papers' original model specifications. In the second, major step of the analysis, we then abstract from the two exact specifications to construct panel data models using IVs and covariates taken from our review of the existing literature. In doing so we still preserve the spirit of the two approaches, by applying both a traditional approach to instrumentation (broadly following Bokhari *et al.* (2007) along with an application of Brückner (2013), which is the approach followed by Moreno-Serra and Smith (2015) (discussed further in Section 2). As part of the second step, we also undertake a series of robustness checks, not least to accommodate some other estimation approaches used in the literature (e.g. dynamic panel analysis). Taken together, we argue that following the empirical approaches proposed in these two studies — first literally and then more generally — allows us to capture the currently most promising approaches that have been used in this literature.

We argue that Bokhari *et al.* (2007), apart from having become a highly cited paper in this literature, broadly represents the IV approach adopted in several such papers, starting from Filmer and Pritchett (1999) and Wagstaff and Claeson (2004). Moreno-Serra and Smith (2015), by contrast, offer a different (though also IV-based) approach that, for the first time in this literature, allows for an explicit assessment of the extent of reverse causality, running from mortality to health spending.

By following the above broad strategy, we comprehensively re-examine the robustness of the empirical relationship between public health care spending and mortality outcomes using cross-country data, as it was presented in the main approaches used by the previous literature. Across the two replicated studies, we find that in the majority of replication scenarios, the effect of public health care expenditure on mortality is negative, although qualitative conclusions based on statistical significance vary and the

---

[1] Tables A.1–A.10, B.1–B.3, C.1–C.3, and Figure A.1 are in "Appendix to Chapter 1" which can be found in https://www.worldscientific.com/worldscibooks/10.1142/11045#t=suppl

magnitude of the impact is sensitive to revisions and updates in the data used. New results from our hybrid approach, using a traditional IV approach, are unreliable on account of the chosen instrument (per capita military expenditure of neighboring countries) being found to not be statistically relevant. For another hybrid model, using an identification strategy based on Brückner (2013) and Moreno-Serra and Smith (2015), at least in some cases the estimated effects are broadly consistent with the previous literature, finding that public spending reduced mortality, although at generally lower effect magnitudes and with mixed degrees of statistical significance. Our very mixed findings should not be taken to imply that the conclusions from the previous studies are necessarily invalid, and conclusions need to be seen in the light of the considerable methodological challenges (relating to data and econometric techniques) faced by this strand of research.

2. Methods

Our basic model is specified as follows. We use country-level panel data including low-, middle- and high-income countries. Our primary focus is to estimate the causal impact of public health expenditure on mortality outcomes. To this end, we consider the following simple linear model:

$$\mathrm{MO}_{jt} = \beta_j + \beta_1 \mathrm{EX}_{jt} + \mathbf{X}'_{jt}\boldsymbol{\beta} + \varepsilon_{jt}. \tag{1}$$

MO is mortality and EX is public health care expenditure in country j at time t. The vector X represents covariates. Our main goal is to estimate β_1, which represents the expenditure elasticity when the natural logarithm of MO and EX are used in the regression model, i.e. the effect of a 1% increase in expenditure on the % change in mortality. While health care expenditure may reduce mortality, policymakers may increase health expenditure in response to an increase in mortality, i.e. the idea of reverse causality. Also, mortality and health expenditure may be correlated with a third variable (which is often not observed in the data), which gives rise to omitted variable bias on the estimated coefficients. Given these concerns in this observational setting, we need an exogenous variation of expenditure EX to identify the causal impact of EX on MO (which is represented by the coefficient β_1).

Following both BGG and MSS, we use an IV method. BGG and MSS use distinct IV approaches which differ in their econometric specification and also in their strategy in identifying the causal impact of expenditure. Employing more than one approach allows us to assess the robustness and sensitivity of the estimated impacts to different econometric approaches using the same data. Hence, we start our analyses by replicating the analyses of BGG and MSS, respectively, using their original data as well as our updated data. In order to assess the extent to which their conclusions may be driven by the specific features of the models (e.g. choice of variables and data years), we also construct a hybrid version of the econometric model with our own set of variables (based on a review of the literature), and augment the two distinct approaches to estimate the impact of health expenditure on mortality outcomes.

2.1. BGG model

BGG use a traditional IV approach that may be seen as broadly representative of a range of existing studies published before. However, this particular study uses cross-sectional data from 2000 (as opposed to panel data from multiple years) and also employs a structurally motivated model that investigates the impact of health expenditure as well as GDP per capita on mortality.

The main outcome variables in the BGG model are log of under-five mortality and log of maternal mortality (see Table 1 for descriptive statistics on the data used in the BGG model). There are four key independent variables which are treated as endogenous. The endogenous variables include GDP per capita, public health care expenditure and interaction of public health expenditures with deviation in donor funding on basic health from historical mean and measure of paved roads per unit area in the country (as a proxy of economic development). The model includes the following covariates: log of proportion of non-literate (proxy of education); log of quantity of paved roads per unit area; log of donor funding; and log of proportion of population with access to improved sanitation.

BGG use a number of IVs in their first stage regression with the four endogenous variables. The IVs include the following: (1) log of neighbors' military expenditure per capita, and its interaction with (a) deviation in

Table 1. Descriptive statistics of BGG data (original data and updated data).

	Original data (2000)			Updated data (2000)[a]					
	Mean	SD	N	Mean	SD	N	# missing	Max N	Missing rate
Under 5 mortality	73.49	68.91	127	57.67	58.17	192	44	236	18.6%
Maternal mortality	345.39	425.07	127	264.23	361.86	183	53	236	22.5%
GDP per capita[b]	6962.60	7987.95	127	14396.85	18467.87	185	51	236	21.6%
Public health expenditure[c]	311.21	509.70	127	542.53	866.97	186	50	236	21.2%
Neighbours' military expenditure per capita	161.04	183.22	127	271.48	383.53	222	14	236	5.9%
World Bank CPI on social inclusion and equity	3.63	0.76	127	—	—	—	—	—	—
World Bank CPI on economic management	3.96	1.05	127	—	—	—	—	—	—
Investment–GDP ratio	14.87	8.71	127	22.79	9.92	189	47	236	19.9%
Donor funding on basic health per capita	2.96	6.35	127	—	—	—	—	—	—
Nonliterate rate	21.22	22.15	127	21.32	21.01	101	135	236	57.2%
Paved road rate	31.14	66.63	127	49.37	32.86	169	67	236	28.4%
Sanitation rate	73.98	26.67	127	68.51	31.15	198	38	236	16.1%

Notes: [a]In this column, the analysis includes as many countries as possible (maximum available number of countries is 236) from the updated data sources.
[b]In the original data, GDP per capita using international dollars as of 2000 is used. In the updated data, GDP per capita using constant US dollars 2011 (PPP-adjusted) is used.
[c]In the original data, government health expenditure per capita (international dollars as of 2000) is used. In the updated data, government health expenditure per capita in 2005 constant dollars is used.

donor funding on basic health from historical mean and (b) the quantity of paved roads per unit area; (2) indicators of quality of policies and institutions (based on World Bank's annual assessment of countries), and again its interaction with deviation in donor funding from historical mean and paved road rate; and finally (3) the log of the consumption–investment ratio.

2.2. MSS model

MSS use a more novel IV approach inspired by Brückner (2013), which explicitly takes into account the reverse causality from mortality to health expenditure. In this approach, as the first step, we estimate the reverse causality — the impact of mortality on health care expenditure:

$$EX_{jt} = \gamma_j + \gamma_1 MO_{jt} + \mathbf{X}'_{jt}\boldsymbol{\gamma} + \varepsilon_j. \tag{2}$$

Note that we use the same set of covariates (vector X) in this reverse causality model (see Table 2 for descriptive statistics on the variables used in the MSS model). Once we estimate γ_1 by a panel fixed-effect IV regression, we calculate the following residual:

$$EX^*_{jt} = EX_{jt} - \hat{\gamma}_1 MO_{jt}. \tag{3}$$

Assuming the instruments used in Eq. (2) are valid and relevant, this residual is now orthogonal to the variation of mortality. In the second step, we use this residual as an IV for health expenditure in Eq. (1) to estimate the impact of health expenditure on mortality.

The main outcome variables in the MSS study are under-five mortality, adult female mortality and adult male mortality. MSS specify four endogenous indicators of health expenditure as follows: (a) public health care expenditure; (b) private out-of-pocket (OOP) health care expenditure; (c) expenditure from private voluntary health insurance; and (d) immunization coverage. We therefore estimate Eq. (2) and calculate the residual in Eq. (3) for each endogenous variable separately, but estimate the impact of these variables in one main regression Eq. (1), with four endogenous variables. Since the panel data are clustered at country

Table 2. Descriptive statistics of MSS data (original data and updated data).

	Original data (1995–2008)			Updated data (1995–2008)[a]					
	Mean	SD	N (153 countries)	Mean	SD	N (236 countries)	# missing	Max N	Missing rate
Under 5 mortality	45.68	48.87	1397	52.26	52.93	2618	686	3304	20.8%
Adult female mortality	155.85	114.87	1225	173.97	129.77	2696	608	3304	18.4%
Adult male mortality	226.39	116.92	1225	242.39	123.48	2696	608	3304	18.4%
Public health expenditure (1/100)[b]	5.99	8.43	1397	5.93	10.19	2602	702	3304	21.2%
Privately pooled health expenditure (1/100)	0.59	2.10	1397	2.77	14.27	2602	702	3304	21.2%
Out-of-pocket health expenditure (1/100)	1.88	2.04	1397	0.58	1.93	2233	1071	3304	32.4%
Immunization coverage (1/10)	8.61	1.42	1397	8.43	1.66	2674	630	3304	19.1%
GDP per capita (1/100)[c]	121.15	131.67	1397	148.27	183.98	2578	726	3304	22.0%
Primary education enrollment rate (1/10)	8.61	1.59	1397	8.84	1.54	1477	1827	3304	55.3%
Proportion of population under 14 (1/10)	3.07	1.05	1397	3.19	1.05	2716	588	3304	17.8%
Proportion of population over 65 (1/10)	0.75	0.52	1397	0.70	0.47	2716	588	3304	17.8%
CO2 emission per capita	5.16	6.51	1397	4.79	6.74	2728	576	3304	17.4%
Death by conflict[d]	1.45	25.76	1397	1.12	17.08	3304	0	3304	0.0%

Notes: [a]In this column, the analysis includes as many countries as possible (maximum available number of countries is 236) from the updated data sources. In the original data, government health expenditure per capita (international dollars as of 2005) is used. In the updated data, government health expenditure per capita in 2005 constant dollars is used.
[b]In the original data, GDP per capita using international dollars as of 2005 is used. In the updated data, GDP per capita using constant US dollars 2011 (PPP-adjusted) is used.
[c]In the original data, GDP per capita using international dollars as of 2005 is used. In the updated data, GDP per capita using constant US dollars 2011 (PPP-adjusted) is used.
[d]The variable "Death by conflict" does not have any missing values. The original SIPRI data (see Table A.1) lists the cases of conflicts and the number of deaths where they observed. Following MSS, we assume that there were no conflicts (and therefore no deaths) if the original data do not list any information for a given country.

level, the estimation of the standard errors takes this data structure into account through the use of cluster-robust standard errors.

In the MSS model, the covariates include: GDP per capita, primary education enrolment rate, proportion of population under 14 and proportion of population over 65. Note that, in contrast with BGG, in the MSS analysis GDP per capita is treated as an exogenous control variable. In the following streamlined model, we follow this simplification of the model because our main purpose is specifically to estimate the impact of health expenditure on mortality, which we pursue using a reduced form specification.

2.3. A hybrid model

As described above, BGG and MSS have specific features in terms of data, selection of variables and strategy to estimate causal impacts. For instance, BGG uses cross-sectional data whereas MSS use panel data[2]; they use different set of health expenditure variables (some of which are not our primary interest) and also different sets of covariates. These particular features might have led to different magnitudes of the main estimates or even their conclusions. In order to still follow the spirit of the two approaches represented by these studies without strictly adhering to their specific models, we construct our own specifications (which we refer to as a hybrid model) as described in the following.

---

[2]On the whole, there is good reason to expect that, *all else equal*, using panel data can be more reliable than cross-sectional data as the former allows the researcher to control for unobserved time-invariant factors at country level directly via a fixed-effects estimator. This can be important if such a source of unobserved heterogeneity is both correlated with health spending and mortality outcomes, as it would then reduce the need for finding appropriate IVs for the health spending variable (assuming of course that there is no other source of endogeneity). Alternatively, if the omitted time-invariant variable is not correlated with health spending, one can use random effects models instead of fixed effects for a gain in efficiency. Generally, both types of panel estimators are an improvement over simple cross-sections. The problem, and hence the trade-off in panel versus cross-section data comes from not being able to obtain reliable time series on all variables of interest. This can happen when some of the variables of interest have been provided by data dissemination agencies by interpolating for missing values.

2.3.1. *Data structure*

We use country-level panel data from 1995 to 2011. This means that in applying a traditional IV approach we complement the above-described, cross-sectional BGG analysis by incorporating further, more recent data points, and by allowing for country-level fixed effects in the model and estimate a within-country impact of health expenditure. This will additionally take into account any unobserved, time-invariant country-level heterogeneity. Furthermore, the country-level fixed effect is also likely to account for some of the (unobserved) heterogeneity from factors that vary only slowly over time (and particularly in shorter time series), such as cultural factors and institutional quality. MSS's original study uses data from 1995 to 2008. We therefore include more recent years (up to 2011) in our Brückner IV approach analysis (Brückner, 2013). Descriptive statistics are given in Table 3.

2.3.2. *Outcome variables*

We follow MSS in choosing our outcome variables. We use: under-five mortality, adult female mortality and adult male mortality. However, while MSS uses under-five mortality estimated by the Institute of Health Metrics and Evaluation, we use estimates produced by the United Nations (as in BGG). This is because more data are available in the UN mortality data (up to 2011) than in the Institute for Health Metrics and Evaluation (IHME) data (up to 2010).

2.3.3. *Health care expenditure*

While BGG and MSS specified a number of endogenous variables, in our streamlined model we focus only on public health care expenditure following a reduced form approach. In particular, in line with MSS, in our main model we treat GDP per capita as an exogenous control variable to keep the model parsimonious.[3] Moreover, although BGG include two

---

[3]Table A.9 presents the model where per capita GDP is treated as an endogenous variable. Following BGG, we used the consumption–investment ratio as the instrument for per capita GDP. The estimated effect of per capita GDP is negative and in some

Table 3.   Descriptive statistics of the streamlined model data (1995–2011).

	Mean	SD	N (236 countries)	# missing	Max N	Missing rate
Mortality outcomes						
Under 5 mortality (UN estimate)	51.70	53.78	3264	748	4012	18.6%
Adult female mortality	171.16	128.47	3239	773	4012	19.3%
Adult male mortality	238.45	122.25	3239	773	4012	19.3%
Health expenditure						
Total health expenditure	1085.90	4025.17	3163	849	4012	21.2%
Public health expenditure	631.03	1206.37	3163	849	4012	21.2%
Covariates						
GDP per capita	15234.72	18652.36	3147	865	4012	21.6%
Sanitation rate	69.69	30.77	3299	713	4012	17.8%
Primary education enrollment rate	89.06	14.66	1849	2163	4012	53.9%
Proportion of population under 14	31.38	10.62	3299	713	4012	17.8%
Proportion of population over 65	7.10	4.77	3299	713	4012	17.8%
Paved road rate	53.93	33.04	1621	2391	4012	59.6%
Urban rate	55.46	24.47	3587	425	4012	10.6%
Efficiency of governance	−0.01	1.00	2628	1384	4012	34.5%
Control of corruption	−0.01	1.00	2634	1378	4012	34.3%
Instrumental variables						
CO_2 emission per capita	4.76	6.63	3383	629	4012	15.7%
Death by conflict (per 100,000)	1.00	15.56	4012	0	4012	0.0%
Neighbours' military expenditure per capita	296.13	442.08	3774	238	4012	5.9%
Neighbors' health expenditure per capita	589.29	951.79	3774	238	4012	5.9%
Neighbours' military expenditure (% of GDP)	0.03	0.02	3774	238	4012	5.9%

Table 3. (*Continued*)

	Mean	SD	N (236 countries)	# missing	Max N	Missing rate
Neighbours' health expenditure (% of GDP)	0.04	0.02	3774	238	4012	5.9%
External cause of death						
Transport accident	12.43	6.66	1563	2449	4012	61.0%
Smoke, fire, flames	1.35	1.88	1563	2449	4012	61.0%
Falls	5.55	5.82	1563	2449	4012	61.0%
Drowning and submersion	3.23	3.30	1555	2457	4012	61.2%
Assault	6.70	9.80	1563	2449	4012	61.0%
Poisoning	3.46	6.79	1563	2449	4012	61.0%
All other external cause	9.68	14.17	1557	2455	4012	61.2%

interaction terms involving the rate of paved road and the amount of donor funding on basic health, we drop these interaction terms from our hybrid model because some of the data are not available, and also because these factors are not of primary interest to us.[4] Similarly, we exclude three of

---

cases the effect is statistically significant, i.e. higher national income reduces mortality. The estimated impact of public health expenditure in this model is largely similar to the estimates presented in the main paper. Also, using BGG's original data and following their specification, we estimated the model with per capita GDP treated as exogenous variable. We find that the impacts of public expenditure on the mortality outcomes are largely maintained (the impact is −0.390 (SE = 0.128) for under-five mortality; and it is −0.607 (SE = 0.190) for maternal mortality). These additional results imply that assuming per capita GDP as exogenous should not substantially bias the estimation of the impact of public health care expenditure on mortality outcomes in our data.

[4] Using BGG's original data, we estimated the BGG's model while excluding the interaction terms and also assuming per capita GDP to be exogenous. The impacts of public expenditure on mortality outcomes are qualitatively maintained (the impact is −0.419 (SE = 0.096) for under-five mortality, and it is −0.565 (SE = 0.163) for maternal mortality).

MSS's key explanatory variables, i.e. OOP expenditure, private insurance expenditure and immunization coverage, for the same reason.[5]

2.3.4. Instrumental variables

Based on our review of the existing literature, we use IVs, which have been shown to be relevant in the previous literature, including BGG and MSS papers. However, since we estimate within-country impact by using fixed-effect models, our IVs should vary over time. Therefore, we cannot use time-invariant IVs (i.e. certain dimensions of governance quality and their interactions) in the current specification.

As explained in Sections 2.1 and 2.2, in the traditional IV analysis we need instruments for public health care expenditure, whereas the Brückner IV analysis requires instruments for mortality. In the traditional IV approach, we use neighbors' military expenditure (in % of GDP) and neighbors' public health expenditure (in % of GDP) as IVs (Filmer and Prichett, 1999; Wagstaff and Claeson, 2004).[6,7]

Our instruments in the Brückner IV approach include per capita emission of CO_2 and number of deaths by conflict per 100,000 people,

---

[5] Dropping private expenditure might lead to misspecification of the model and therefore bias the estimated impact of public health care expenditure. However, as shown in Table 4, dropping the private expenditure from the original MSS specification does not affect the impact of public expenditure to a substantive degree. Also, in Table B.1, we estimate the impact of *total* health care expenditure (which includes both public and private expenditure) on mortality, and find that the results are similar to the principal estimation results presented in the main text (Table 6). This might be because public health care expenditure accounts for a majority of health care resources in many (though by no means all) countries and thus the potential bias from omitting private expenditure may be negligible.

[6] In preliminary analyses, we also employed a "just identified" model with one IV, where we used per capita military expenditure of neighboring countries for the single endogenous variable (i.e. public health care expenditure) in the main model. We found this single instrument was too weak in terms of the first-stage F-statistics (F is less than 1 in most cases).

[7] A rationale for the IV is that if neighbouring countries spend more on military equipment and services, the domestic government would increase or decrease military expenditure to maintain the military balance, which would affect the level of health care expenditure per capita. Note that this IV has been widely used in the previous literature — see Anyanwu and Erhijakpor (2009), Bokhari et al. (2007), Filmer and Prichett (1999) and Wagstaff and Claeson (2004). We follow this popular (though not un-contestable) approach in the existing cross-country literature.

following MSS. As a sensitivity check, we also use WHO's data on external causes of death as additional IVs predicting exogenous variations in mortality.[8] Test statistics for the relevance of the IVs are presented and discussed in Section 4.

2.3.5. *Covariates*

Previous studies (including but not limited to the works of BGG and MSS) use a variety of covariates, and there appears to be no common set of covariates that has been applied in all studies. As Gallet and Doucouliagos (2015) point out, the choice of covariates is indeed a significant contributor of the diversity in the estimated impact of expenditure on mortality. In this study, we use the following principle-based selection of covariates. We conduct a literature review of the related, cross-country-type studies. We identified and reviewed 11 studies and recorded covariates from each study (Filmer and Pritchett, 1999; Wagstaff and Claeson, 2004; Bokhari *et al.*, 2007; Rajkumar and Swaroop, 2008; Anyanwu and Erhijakpor, 2009; Gani, 2009; Afridi and Ventelou, 2013; Farag *et al.*, 2013; Hu and Mendoza, 2013; Akinci *et al.*, 2014; Moreno-Serra and Smith, 2015).[9] From the full set of candidates, we obtain a shortlist of covariates in the following way: first, we exclude variables if we decide they can be outcomes of health expenditure (e.g. number of hospital beds), as including those variables would cause a selection bias in the regression (Angrist and Pischke, 2009). Second, we follow Hauck *et al.* (2015) in our selection of further covariates:

(1) We drop a variable if, in the currently available data, more than 60% of observations between 1995 and 2011 are missing across years and countries.

---

[8] External cases of death include: transport accidents, smoke and fire, poisoning, falls, drowning and assault, which largely randomly occur across the population.

[9] These studies were collected using a "snowballing" strategy, in which we started by looking at the reference list of BGG and MSS studies for relevant studies, then once we found a related study (initially judged by title, and then by full text), we included the study in our review and also checked the reference list of the study for further references. We iterated this process for several times, thus converging toward the set of studies included in our review.

(2) In order to avoid multicollinearity among covariates, we calculate the pair-wise correlation between the demeaned candidate variables and drop one of the variables, if the correlation coefficient is above 0.6.[10]

Our final set of covariates is as follows: GDP pc, primary education enrolment rate, proportion of population under 14, proportion of population over 65, rate of paved road, access to improved sanitation, urbanization and two measures of efficiency of governance (government efficiency and control of corruption). See Table 3 for more details.

Finally, in the hybrid model, we use log-scale variables (which are consistent with BGG but not MSS) in order to estimate elasticities, i.e. the percentage reduction/increase in mortality associated with a 1% increase in expenditure.

Following BGG and MSS (and other studies in the literature), all models are estimated via the Generalized Method of Moments.[11] All analyses are conducted using Stata 13 MP.

3. Data

For the original replication of the published results, the authors of the original articles generously allowed us full access to the original data (and codes) that were used for the published results of those papers. When updating the data to include the most recently available ones, we also used, wherever accessible, the sources indicated in the two papers. It should be noted that for most of the variables even the older data are regularly revised in the publicly available data sources, and it is not always possible to obtain older versions of the database.

---

[10] Demeaned variables (i.e. we calculate the mean of a given variable for each country and then subtract the country's mean over the observed time period) are used because we use fixed-effect models, in which demeaned variables are analyzed in the regression.

[11] Table A.10 provides the results of the main streamlined model analysis via Limited Information Maximum Likelihood (LIML) estimation, which could be more robust to weak IVs than GMM or 2SLS. The results using LIML are largely similar to the ones using GMM, but they actually give slightly less-precise estimation. This generally applies to the results presented in other tables in this paper as well as those in Appendix. The full replications of the whole paper using LIML are available upon request.

The majority of our data comes from three widely used sources: World Bank's World Development Indicators (WDI), WHO's Global Health Observatory and the IHME's "Global Health Data Exchange". The sources, definitions and downloaded data of all the variables we used in our empirical analysis study are given in Table A.1.[12]

Tables 1 and 2 give the descriptive statistics of each of the composed datasets we use in our analysis: first, for the original and updated data analysis of the BGG paper (Table 1), and second for the MSS paper (Table 2). In these tables, there are some notable discrepancies between original data and updated data, which could be attributable to data updates by the data providers, or to differences in the exact metric used for a given variable.[13] In Table 1, the original data consist of 127 countries whereas the updated data consist of 238 countries. Similarly, in Table 2, the original data consist of 153 countries whereas the updated data consist of 236 countries. Tables C.1 and C.2 present the descriptive statistics for the subset of updated data using the same set of countries as in the original data. The discrepancies between the original and updated data become smaller. In Section 4, we examine the impacts of using different versions of GDP data on the regression results (see Tables A.2–A.5 for detailed results).

3.1. *Data imputation*

Although we use the most up-to-date data that is currently available in the public domain, significant numbers of missing values do remain. The sample size in different studies (BGG, MSS and others) varies

---

[12] Note that data on mortality are from the World Bank's WDI database (i.e. for adult female mortality rate, adult male mortality rate, maternal mortality rate and under-five mortality rate). The under-five mortality data available in the WDI database are based on United Nations' estimates. IHME has produced alternative estimate of under-five mortality, and it does not appear obvious which one of the two is closer to the truth (Alkema and You, 2012).

[13] For instance, the updated data have GDP per capita based on purchasing power parity in 2011 constant dollars, but MSS used GDP per capita based on purchasing power parity in 2005 constant dollars, and BGG used GDP per capita in 2000 international dollars (also based on purchasing parity). It should be noted that Tables 1 and 2 compare outcomes from different set of countries.

significantly (from around 100 to 150 countries) as a result, depending on the selection of variables and versions of the data source used in their analyses.

Tables 1 and 2 also show the number of missing values in each variable in the updated data, for the replication of the BGG model and the MSS model, respectively. For the BGG data, except for the World Bank in-house data and the data on donor funding on basic health which we failed to obtain,[14] the missing values in the updated data are up to 57% (of 236 countries in the updated data), with the missingness in the illiteracy rate and the rate of paved roads being particularly high. This means that without imputation or without amending the modelling specification we cannot replicate the BGG analysis with a sufficient number of observations. On the other hand, for the MSS data the extent of missingness is relatively moderate: over 15% of observations are missing for all variables (except for "death by conflict"), and more than 50% of "primary education enrolment rate" are missing.

Given the large numbers of missing values in the data (for both BGG and MSS), we decide to implement a standard multiple imputation (MI) by chained equations (MICE) approach, following Hauck et al. (2015), and available as a Stata command ("mi") (StataCorp, 2013).[15] MICE is a regression-based imputation method, in which variables with missing values are regressed on the other variables in the dataset, and then the predicted value of the missing part will be imputed. This procedure is sequentially applied to the other variables with missing values, one at a time. In particular, again following Hauck et al. (2015), we use a predictive mean matching technique (Landerman et al., 1997). According to this technique, a missing value is imputed using non-missing values of samples with a similar predictive mean. In the present study, we use three

---

[14] While in the original BGG data, per capita donor funding for health promotion from the Development Assistance Committee (DAC) of the Organization for Economic Cooperation and Development (OECD) in the year 1998 (which we failed to update) is used. However, we obtained a qualitatively similar data, i.e. data on per capita amount of development assistance for health (DAH), available at the IHME database, which we use in the replication analysis of BGG using data from year 2010.

[15] See also Perkins and Neumayer (2014) for an application of MICE in combination with IVs regressions. The programme package "mi" is a set of Stata's official commands.

neighbors of the predictive mean for the imputation (White *et al.*, 2011). Also, since the data are clustered at country- and year-level, we take this into account in the analysis by including year and country fixed effects in the imputation equations. Throughout this chapter, we replicate the procedure and generate 50 imputed datasets, and hence conduct 50 separate regression analyses at a time, before the estimates are merged into the final estimation result.[16] Finally, if all values of the variables in the regression models are missing for a country, we drop the country from the analysis.[17]

Although in principle, all variables in the regression model should be included in the imputation equation, in the present study we do not impute our IVs in the chained MI. This is because a key condition in an IV approach is that instruments should not be correlated directly with the outcome variable (capturing the exclusion restriction) (Wooldridge, 2010). Imputing the IVs by (partly) using the outcome variable would make it difficult to justify the exclusion restriction. Instead, for the IVs, we impute missing values with the mean of the values from neighboring observations from the same country, i.e. when the value in time t is missing, we impute the mean of the values in $t - 1$ and $t + 1$. If all values are missing in the country, we again do not impute the missing values, and therefore that country is dropped from the final estimation sample.

Finally, we assessed the performance of the MIs. We randomly chose 1000 non-missing observations, and artificially dropped them from the

---

[16] Once the number of replications is specified, this procedure is automatically conducted using the "mi" command in Stata 13 MP. For more detail, see StataCorp (2013). The rule of thumb suggests that the number of replications should correspond to the percentage of missing values in the data. Since less than 50% of the data are missing in our data (Tables 1–3), the number of replications is considered to be sufficiently large.

[17] In the present study, we conduct regression analyses for multiple outcome variables (under-five mortality and adult mortality) separately. However, in the imputation equation we include the other outcome variable, e.g. we use among other variables under-five mortality to impute missing values of adult mortality. Also, in the regression analysis we use the imputed dependent variables. We checked the main regression results by not using the imputed dependent variables but instead using the un-imputed dependent variable, and confirmed that our main conclusion is not affected (details are not reported here).

working data. We imputed the dropped observations (as well as the originally missing observations) using the MICE technique, and then compared the imputed values with the original non-missing values. For all variables used in the streamlined models, the MIs worked well — the mean difference between the original and imputed values was consistently less than one standard deviation point value of each variable.

4. Results

In what follows, we first present the results of the replication exercise for each of the two approaches — BGG (Section 4.1.1) and MSS (Section 4.1.2). Subsequently, we present the results of the hybrid approach — in Section 4.2.1 for BGG and in Section 4.2.2 for MSS.

4.1. *Replication results*

4.1.1. *Replication of BGG*

Table 4 starts by replicating the results of the original approaches used by BGG. Column (1) provides the results as they were given in the original paper. As we obtained the original data (as well as the command files) from the authors of both papers, we then tried to replicate the results using exactly the same specification as in the original specification. The results of this replication correspond exactly to those in the original paper. Table 4 also shows additional test statistics for the first-stage regression for multiple endogenous variables: in addition to the standard F-statistic, we present an augmented F-statistic allowing for multiple endogenous variables (Sanderson and Windmeijer, 2013), as well as Kleibergen and Paap's Wald rk F-statistic for under-identification (Kleibergen and Paap, 2006), showing that the instruments are reasonably "strong" (the rule-of-thumb threshold for F is 10).

As the next step, we replace the original data from the BGG paper by the revised data that is available in the relevant data sources as of August 2015, but for exactly the same year that was covered in the paper, i.e. 2000 (see column (2) in Table 4). This exercise entailed a reduction in the sample size, down from 127 to 66 countries (due to a particularly large number of missing values in the literacy and paved road variables),

Table 4. Replication of BGG analysis.

	Under 5 mortality					
	(1)	(2)	(3)	(4)	(5)	(6)
log public health expenditure	-0.341***	-0.810***	-0.502***	-0.564***	-1.030***	-0.873**
	(0.127)	(0.245)	(0.178)	(0.213)	(0.376)	(0.358)
log public health expenditure X donor funding	0.007**	0.009	0.009**	0.006***	-0.009	0.006***
	(0.003)	(0.007)	(0.004)	(0.002)	(0.009)	(0.002)
log public health expenditure X paved road	-0.000	-0.002**	-0.001***	-0.000	0.001	0.001
	(0.000)	(0.001)	(0.000)	(0.001)	(0.001)	(0.001)
log GDP per capita	-0.404*	0.174	-0.167	0.182	-0.591	0.242
	(0.210)	(0.341)	(0.303)	(0.361)	(0.433)	(0.499)
F for log public health expenditure	10.508	3.337	5.185	5.216	1.525	19.747
F for log public health expenditure X donor funding	135.137	117.490	34.163	23.509	33.040	178.037
F for log public health expenditure X paved road	1407.622	61.444	282.896	100.276	25.112	57.691
F for log GDP per capita	31.596	3.538	4.252	5.281	3.340	7.620
SW-F for log public health expenditure	14.411	4.762	3.538	4.871	3.477	3.094
SW-F for log public health expenditure X donor funding	35.880	10.443	69.138	46.163	5.722	33.189
SW-F for log public health expenditure X paved road	69.637	118.709	52.156	64.920	11.280	28.286
SW-F for log GDP per capita	14.334	4.387	5.508	5.092	3.419	3.409
Kleinbergen-Paap Wald statistics	8.534	2.245	2.012	2.565	1.481	1.55
N	127	66	127	127	44	127

(Continued)

Table 4. (*Continued*)

			Maternal mortality			
	(1)	(2)	(3)	(4)	(5)	(6)
log public health expenditure	-0.519***	-1.274***	-0.769***	-0.641**	-1 729***	-0.883**
	(0.178)	(0.373)	(0.274)	(0.275)	(0.595)	(0.429)
log public health expenditure X donor funding	0.007	0.016*	0.016***	0.010***	0.001	0.006**
	(0.005)	(0.008)	(0.005)	(0.003)	(0.013)	(0.003)
log public health expenditure X paved road	0.000	-0.002**	-0.003***	-0.001	-0.000	0.000
	(0.000)	(0.001)	(0.001)	(0.001)	(0.002)	(0.001)
log GDP per capita	-0.440	0.507	0.099	0.048	0.046	0.236
	(0.272)	(0.484)	(0.457)	(0.438)	(0.705)	(0.641)
F for log public health expenditure	10.508	3.337	5.185	5.216	1.525	19.747
F for log public health expenditure X donor funding	135.137	117.490	34.163	23.509	33.040	178.037
F for log public health expenditure X paved road	1407.622	61.444	282.896	100.276	25.112	57.691
F for log GDP per capita	31.596	3.538	4.252	5.281	3.340	7.620
SW-F for log public health expenditure	14.411	4.762	3.538	4.871	3.477	3.094
SW-F for log public health expenditure X donor funding	35.880	10.443	69.138	46.163	5.722	33.189
SW-F for log public health expenditure X paved road	69.637	118.709	52.156	64.920	11.280	28.286
SW-F for log GDP per capita	14.334	4.387	5.508	5.092	3.419	3.409

Kleinbergen-Paap Wald statistics	8.534	2.245	2.012	2.565	1.481	1.55
N	127	66	127	127	44	127

Notes: Model (1) shows the results as published and replicated; model (2) shows the results from updated data (year 2000) without imputation; model (3) shows the results from updated data (year 2000), imputed using the original data where missing; model (4) shows the results from updated data with MI; model (5) shows the results from updated data (year 2010) without imputation; model (6) shows the results from updated data (year 2010) with MI.

In models (5) and (6), since we do not have access to the World Bank in-house data on quality of governance, we impute the variable using the BGG's original data (as of 2000).

In Table 1, non-literate rate and paved road rate exhibit high rates of missing values in the updated data (81.9% and 47.9%, respectively). Since these variables are not likely to vary overtime, we impute the data for 2000 if there are any information available either in 1998, 1999, 2001 and 2002 (two years before and after 2000). The same imputation of the literacy variable is applied to the updated data from 2010.

*: p-value 0.1 or less, **: p-value 0.05 or less, ***: p-value 0.01 or less.

reducing the comparability of those specific estimates, with respect to the results of the original BGG paper. The reduction in sample size also provides the case for boosting the sample size using imputation methods.[18] We use two different ways of imputation in Table 4 — first, we fill the gaps by using BGG's original data directly, wherever the updated data from readily available sources do not have this information (see column (3)); second, we use a statistical MI method (MICE) to fill the gaps in the currently available data (see column (4)).[19] The results in columns (3) and (4) of Table 4 give outcomes that are qualitatively comparable but quantitatively different from the original research — the size of the impacts of the public health expenditure is remarkably larger in the analyses using the updated data with imputation. For under-five mortality, the original BGG study found that a 1% increase in expenditure will reduce mortality by 0.341% (column (1)). However, when applying MICE to the updated data, the magnitude of the impact is about twice as large as in the original study (the elasticity is −0.564). A similar, but relatively modest increase in the size of the impact is found for maternal mortality (from −0.519 to −0.641). It is important to note that the relevance of the same IVs is now weaker in the updated data, implying the results from the original BGG analysis (column (1)) are more credible than those found in columns (3) and (4).

The BGG original analysis and our replications use data from 2000. In columns (5) and (6) we analyze the updated data for 2010.[20] With and without MIs of the data, the estimated impacts of public health expenditure are greater than the estimated impacts from the 2000 data (in column (6)

---

[18] BGG's original data are manually imputed using similar data sources (e.g. CIA World Factbook), and by using information from adjacent years, where data for the year of their analysis (2000) were missing. By contrast, here we use a statistical method (i.e. MIs) to impute missing values.

[19] We note that the large number of missing variables comes in the readily available data sources, compared to the data used by BGG, is due to extra efforts expended by BGG in filling the gaps manually by using information from other data sources (e.g. CIA World Factbook) and by interpolation, in the case of variables that are likely to not fluctuate much from year to year (e.g. paved roads).

[20] The descriptive statistics of the 2010 data are presented in Table C.3.

with MIs, the magnitude of the impact is about −0.9 for both under-five and maternal mortality).

4.1.2. *Sensitivity checks*

By way of sensitivity checks of the above replication analysis using the 2000 data, starting from the original BGG data, we sequentially update only one variable at a time, in order to assess which variable causes the larges difference. The results are summarized in Tables A.2 and A.3. The size of the impact of public health expenditure displays sensitivity with the impact on under-five mortality now ranging from −0.257 to −0.459 (Table A.3).

4.1.3. *Replication of MSS*

When trying to replicate the results of MSS using the original data (column (1) in Table 5), the model failed to produce the results. By comparing the results to those obtained using an older version of Stata, for which we were able to exactly replicate the original results, it turned out that this significant discrepancy to the original results is the result of an updated version of the Stata code used in the IV fixed-effect estimation -xtivreg2 (Schaffer, 2010; we used the July 2015 version).[21] Therefore, we modified the MSS approach; in that we dropped three of the four endogenous variables, leaving only our key variable of interest — public health expenditure — as the one endogenous variable. Re-running the MSS model, using exactly the same data as in the original paper, we obtain largely similar coefficients on the public health expenditure variable as in MSS (see column (2) in Table 5).

---

[21] The updated code rejects the model as it detects multicollinearity between the four IVs used in the first-stage regression of the MSS model. We used different versions of -ivreg2 and — ranktest — commands which are both used within — xtivreg2 — routine. The analyses presented throughout the present study are based on -ivreg2 — version 4.1.08 26 July 2015 and — ranktest — version 1.3.05 22 Jan 2015. Using older version of the routine -ivreg2 — version 2.2.08 15 Oct 2007 and — ranktest — 1.1.02 15 Oct 2007, we successfully replicate the results published in the MSS study.

Table 5. Replication of MSS analysis.

A: Under 5 mortality

	(1)	(2)	(3)	(4)	(5)	(6)	(7)
Public health expenditure	-13.193**	-13.779**	6.759***	-41.302	-0.486	-4.251***	-0.013
	(0.018)	(5.794)	(1.915)	(37.414)	(0.321)	(1.498)	(0.082)
Out-of-pocket health expenditure	-6.143	—	—	—	—	—	—
	(0.507)						
Privately pooled health expenditure	2.685	—	—	—	—	—	—
	(0.594)						
Immunization coverage	-2.203*	—	—	—	—	—	—
	(0.073)						
1st stage F of reverse causality estimate	3.16	3.070	0.150	0.057	0.770	0.937	1.355
1st stage F of main estimate	—	7.402	21.979	1.285	2630.650	40.332	5.61E+07
Country	153	153	154	159	166	159	162
N	1397	1398	1366	1602	1569	2217	2583

B: Adult female mortality

	(1)	(2)	(3)	(4)	(5)	(6)	(7)
Public health expenditure	-2.583**	-3.957**	12.224**	7.483	0.552	-1.041**	-0.591*
	(0.050)	(1.552)	(5.908)	(4.639)	(0.468)	(0.479)	(0.310)
Out-of-pocket health expenditure	5.153	—	—	—	—	—	—
	(0.161)						
Privately pooled health expenditure	-23.385**	—	—	—	—	—	—
	(0.040)						
Immunization coverage	-9.841**	—	—	—	—	—	—
	(0.030)						

	(1)	(2)	(3)	(4)	(5)	(6)	(7)
1st stage F of reverse causality estimate	7.19	7.341	3.763	2.321	4.195	3.148	4.985
1st stage F of main estimate	—	4857.69	36.830	34.091	71586589.1	226878.2	110959.4
Country	148	148	153	158	165	158	162
N	1222	1223	1359	1677	1562	2203	2699
C: Adult male mortality							
Public health expenditure	-2.210**	-2.944***	8.854**	6.148*	0.646	-0.620	-0.542**
	(0.025)	(1.026)	(3.704)	(3.475)	(0.552)	(0.382)	(0.238)
Out-of-pocket health expenditure	8.731	—	—	—	—	—	—
	(0.172)						
Privately pooled health expenditure	-15.545**	—	—	—	—	—	—
	(0.016)						
Immunization coverage	-7.858**	—	—	—	—	—	—
	(0.020)						
1st stage F of reverse causality estimate	11.60	12.021	2.270	1.487	5.173	1.859	2.615
1st stage F of main estimate	—	13790.4	89.679	52.797	4.216e+08	499648.8	243220.4
Country	148	148	153	158	165	158	162
N	1222	1223	1359	1677	1562	2203	2699

Notes:
- Model (1) shows the results as published.
- Model (2) shows the results (public health expenditure only) from original data using updated Stata 13 (authors' own estimation).
- Model (3) shows the results from updated data (1995–2008) without imputation.
- Model (4) shows the results from updated data (1995–2011) without imputation.
- Model (5) shows the results from updated data (1995–2008), imputed using the original data where missing.
- Model (6) shows the results from updated data (1995–2008) with MI.
- Model (7) shows the results from updated data (1995–2011) with MI.
*: p-value 0.1 or less, **: p-value 0.05 or less, ***: p-value 0.01 or less.

As was done with the BGG analysis above, we then substitute the original data from the MSS paper by the revised data that is available in the relevant data sources as of August 2015, but for exactly the same years as those covered in the papers, i.e. 1995–2008 (see column (3) of Table 5). Following this procedure produces less robust results compared to those based on the original data: the coefficient of interest remains statistically significant but reverses sign, suggesting a counterintuitive relationship between expenditures and mortality rates, i.e. health expenditure *increases* mortality. This is likely the result of the less than ideal instruments for mortality (per capita CO_2 emission and number of deaths by conflict), as suggested by the very low relevance of the instruments in the first-stage regression (F-statistics is less than 4 in all models), reducing the reliability of the estimates.

However, once we impute the data again, first by filling the (now very few) gaps in the data with values from the original MSS data (column (5)) and second by using MI techniques (columns (6) and (7), now with considerably larger sample size), the signs of the coefficients reverse again to the expected direction, but their magnitudes still vary considerably between the specifications, and the instruments for mortality continue to be "weak", i.e. they produce only fairly low F-statistics, according to the benchmarks suggested by Stock and Yogo (2005) and Sanderson and Windmeijer (2013).[22]

4.1.4. *Sensitivity checks*

Similar to Section 4.1.1, we assess which variable is causing the discrepancy between the estimation results using the original and updated data, by replacing every variable in the original data with the corresponding variable in the updated data. Tables A.4 and A.5 show the results. For under-five mortality, replacing CO_2 emission and GDP pc leads to counterintuitive estimates, while for adult female/male mortality, replacing education and public health expenditure leads to counterintuitive results.[23]

---

[22] In the present analysis, we follow Sanderson and Windmeijer's F-statistics for relevance of the instruments. If the endogenous variable(s) are just identified i.e. the number of instruments equals the number of endogenous variables, this augmented F-statistic coincides with the standard F-statistic.

[23] As explained in Section 3.1, the original MSS study uses per capita GDP in 2005 constant US dollars (PPP-adjusted), whereas in the updated data analysis we use per capita GDP in 2011 constant US dollars (PPP-adjusted).

Similar to the BGG analysis, the magnitude of the impact varies considerably upon updating only one variable at a time: the effect estimates range from +1.105 to −14.774 (Table A.5).

4.2. Hybrid model analysis

We use a hybrid approach in which we focus on estimating the impact of public health care expenditure using approaches that are broadly (though no longer literally) in line with those employed in the previous literature, including specifically BGG and MSS.

Table 6 presents the key results of this model, using different strategies to estimate the causal impacts of public health expenditure: fixed-effect IV approach and pooled cross-section IV approach with additional (time-invariant) instruments. Comparing the estimation results with and without the statistical multiple data imputation, we note again the considerable numbers of missing values in the raw data (see Table 3 for more details on missing values).[24]

4.2.1. Hybrid model analysis BGG: The "traditional IV approach"

In the case of the traditional IV approach, using the hybrid model, the results do not confirm the large and significant impacts found in the BGG study. In the first-stage regression, the relevance of the IV (log of per capita military expenditure of neighbouring countries) is too weak to identify the causal effect, and hence the large standard errors of the point estimate, making the model essentially invalid.

4.2.2. Sensitivity checks

Since the results in Table 6 (columns under "Traditional IV") highlight the limitations in the existing instruments with the updated data, we have sought to improve the quality of the predictive power of the instruments

---

[24] The publicly available mortality data are frequently estimated rather than directly observed (Alkema and You, 2012). In order to (partially) avoid the potential problem of serial correlation due to the data estimation, we analyzed the same econometric model with more sparse, 5-year interval data (1995, 2000, 2005 and 2010). The result is presented in Table A.8. The results are qualitatively similar to the results in Table 6.

Table 6. Traditional IV and Bruckner IV approach using streamlined model.

	Traditional IV				Brückner IV			
	Fixed effect		Pooled cross-section		Fixed effect		Pooled cross-section	
	(1)	(2)	(3)	(4)	(5)	(6)	(7)	(8)
A: log under 5 mortality								
log public health expenditure	0.159	0.682	0.683	0.053	0.110**	−0.224**	−0.185*	−0.063
	(0.753)	(0.782)	(0.629)	(0.200)	(0.047)	(0.103)	(0.098)	(0.040)
First stage F of reverse equation	—	—	—	—	1.262	3.707	3.584	2.335
First stage F of main equation	0.245	0.748	0.785	1.761	2323.615	57.13	2413.079	79102.720
Data imputation	No	Yes	No	Yes	No	Yes	No	Yes
Country	100	153	115	148	101	155	105	155
N	661	2601	648	2516	666	2631	634	2631
B: log adult female mortality								
log public health expenditure	0.203	0.293	0.025	−0.033	1.836**	0.100***	−0.063	−0.029
	(1.102)	(0.532)	(0.377)	(0.213)	(0.792)	(0.031)	(0.060)	(0.050)
First stage F of reverse equation	—	—	—	—	0.096	4.408	6.940	4.168
First stage F of main equation	0.108	0.613	0.803	1.728	6.040	1107.273	1424.858	1924.423
Data imputation	No	Yes	No	Yes	No	Yes	No	Yes
Country	99	153	114	148	100	155	105	155
N	642	2560	631	2477	647	2590	618	2590

C: log adult male mortality

log public health expenditure	0.194	0.224	0.147	−0.156	0.337***	−0.144*	−0.037	−0.008
	(1.188)	(0.397)	(0.345)	(0.156)	(0.077)	(0.082)	(0.057)	(0.031)
First stage F of reverse equation					1.293	3.526	8.135	4.827
First stage F of main equation	0.108	0.613	0.803	1.728	82.351	31.314	2050.833	11815.54
Data imputation	No	Yes	No	Yes	No	Yes	No	Yes
Country	99	153	114	148	100	155	105	155
N	642	2560	631	2477	647	2590	618	2590

Notes: The estimates presented in the columns labelled "pooled cross-section" include more time-invariant IVs in addition to original set of time varying instruments. For traditional IV approach, additional instruments for public health expenditure include the legal origin of the country: British, French, Socialist, German and Scandinavian laws (Rajkumar and Swaroop, 2008; Hu and Mendoza, 2013). For Brückner IV approach, additional instruments for mortality include indicators of climate zone based on Kopper's classification and malaria ecology index (Kizsewski *et al.*, 2004; Lorentzen *et al.*, 2008).

by experimenting with different functional forms of the original instruments and by using alternative ones, following suggestions from the literature. The outcome of this exercise is presented in Table A.6 for the traditional IV approach. Despite these efforts, we fail to find results that would confirm our expectations.

Next, in the hybrid model, per capita GDP is treated as an exogenous variable, whereas in the original BGG specification it is endogenous, and there is hence a concern that this could have led to biased estimates due to model misspecification. To examine this possibility, we conduct an analysis that does treat per capita GDP as another endogenous variable. Following BGG, the consumption–investment ratio was used as the additional IV for per capita GDP. Table A.9 shows the results. Although it is interesting to see that the models with the MIs show that higher per capita GDP significantly reduces under-five mortality, we fail to find that public health expenditure reduces mortality outcomes.

4.2.3. Streamlined model analysis MSS: The "Brückner IV approach"

As for the Brückner IV approach, the results using multiple data imputation appear mixed as well, showing the expected negative and statistically significant impacts of public health expenditure in particular for under-five mortality, though less so for adult mortality (see Table 6 under "Brückner IV"). The IVs turn out to be less relevant in a statistical sense (informed by F-statistics of the first-stage regression). The magnitude of the elasticity is substantially smaller than what was implied in the original studies. For instance, where intuitive direction and statistical significance are achieved, the magnitude of the impact on under-five mortality is −0.224, and that on adult male mortality is −0.144, i.e. a 1% increase in expenditure leads to a reduction of mortality by 0.224 or 0.144%.

4.2.4. Sensitivity checks

Testing a set of different IVs, in an effort to overcome the limitations in the existing instruments with the updated data (see Table A.7), provides the same conclusions as in the "traditional IV" case: we obtain insignificant or counterintuitive results, the relevance of the instruments remains low and the discrepancy to the results in the original studies is large.

4.3. *Specification and robustness checks*

In Appendix B.1, we conduct further specification checks of the analysis based on the hybrid model. Notably, the main models presented above have examined the impact of a change in expenditure on a change in mortality in the same year. Also, in the main model we only address the impact of public health expenditure, ignoring other sources of health care spending. First, we investigated the lagged ($t - 1$, $t - 2$, or $t - 5$) impacts of public health expenditure on current mortality outcomes, with only one lag-specification included at a time. Also, we examined the impact of total health expenditure (public and private expenditures). For more detailed description, see Appendix B.1. The results of the analyses are presented in Table B.1. For the traditional IV approach, again the estimation results are not reliable due to low F-statistics. For the Brückner IV approach, when MI is applied, we again find a small, negative and statistically significant impact for under-five mortality — the size of elasticity is around -0.1 to -0.2 for $t - 1$, $t - 2$ and $t - 5$ models, and the impact diminishes upon increasing the number of lags. For adult female and male mortality, the effect is even smaller and statistically indistinguishable from 0. Similarly, the impacts of total expenditure were not statistically significant or intuitive, except for the case of Brückner's IV approach (see Block D, column (4) of Table B.1), where the elasticity of (current) total health expenditure on under-five mortality is -0.299.

We then allow for lagged structure in the estimation of the impact of expenditure. We include current and lagged health expenditure ($t - 1$, $t - 2$ and $t - 3$) *in the same econometric model* and estimated the conditional impacts of expenditure at each period on current mortality outcomes. The results are summarized in Table B.2. The results from the traditional IV approach show non-significant impacts of contemporaneous as well as any lagged public health expenditure in all models. For the Brückner IV approach, when the MIs are applied, the impact of contemporaneous public health expenditures (column (4)) is negative and statistically significant for under-five mortality and adult male mortality. However, the impacts of lagged public health expenditure (conditional on contemporaneous expenditure) are small and largely statistically insignificant.

The final set of specification checks involves different assumptions for the identification of causal impacts. Although in the main analysis we use instruments that were demonstrated to be statistically relevant in the previous cross-country data studies, we fail to confirm this in the updated data and in the hybrid model. This could suggest that alternative analytic approaches are called for that do not rely on the identification of suitable external instruments. Following this idea, we pursue two approaches: first, we use lagged health expenditure to avoid reverse causality while still using fixed-effect modelling to take into account time-invariant country heterogeneity[25]; second, we incorporate a dynamic structure into the model and construct a set of IVs from observations from previous years — a dynamic panel data approach (Blundell and Bond, 1998; Ssozi and Amlani, 2015). The results of the estimations from the two approaches, with and without the data imputation, are presented in Table B.3. In the table, Blocks A, B and C use only fixed-effect models to estimate the effect of contemporaneous and lagged health expenditure. In Block D, the estimates from Blundell–Bond estimation are presented. The estimates of the impact of health expenditure turn out rather mixed, though overall the magnitudes of the impacts, whether statistically significant or not, are much smaller than expectations based on the results from BGG and MSS.[26]

5. Discussion

In this chapter, we have sought to re-examine the robustness of the empirical relationship between public health care spending and mortality

---

[25] We make a stronger assumption about exogeneity of lagged health expenditure here than the previous models presented in this section. In fact, lagged health expenditure is predetermined but not necessarily exogenous.

[26] The results of the model using the imputed data should be interpreted with caution. As P-values of AR tests indicate, there is no second-order serial correlation. However, the Hansen test indicates that the over-identifying restriction is not valid, meaning that some of the IVs are endogenous.

outcomes using cross-country data, as it was presented in the main approaches used by the previous literature. We have based our analysis on the data and approaches embodied by two key publications in the field — by Bokhari *et al.* (2007) and Moreno-Serra and Smith (2015). We started by quite successfully replicating the published results, using the exact same data used by the studies. Results were more nuanced once we made use of data for the same year(s) as in the original study but available from publicly accessible sources at the time of data retrieval (August 2015). In "updating" the data in this way, while still following the specific estimation strategies from the original papers, we also employed different imputation strategies to fill major data gaps for some variables. On the whole, we found the BGG-based results to still hold qualitatively, though with increased effect size and with weaker performance of the instruments. By contrast, the MSS-based results were substantively affected, and the relevance of the instruments did deteriorate, producing less resemblance to the original results. Across the two studies, in the majority of replication scenarios the effect of public health care expenditure on mortality was found to be negative, although qualitative conclusions based on statistical significance vary and the magnitude of the impact is sensitive to revisions and updates in the data used.[27]

In a further step, we abstracted from the specific estimation strategies in the original papers, among others in order to follow the spirit of the approaches used, without the need for overly strict adherence to their idiosyncratic features, and in order to capture some commonalities with other previous studies in this field. We thus constructed our hybrid versions of the two approaches, complemented by a battery of robustness checks, as well as some changes to the specifications to accommodate certain other empirical approaches used in the literature (e.g. dynamic panel analysis). In sum, the results showed that in the traditional IV model our instrument for public health care expenditure (per capita military expenditure of neighbouring countries) is not statistically relevant and thus the IV estimation coefficients become unreliable. For the Brückner

---

[27] Similar sensitivities of the results to updates in the underlying data have been encountered by Easterly *et al.* (2004), Roodman (2008), Clemens *et al.* (2012) and Roodman (2015) in the context of replicating the results from the literature on the impact of aid on economic growth.

IV streamlined model, at least in some cases the estimated effects were broadly consistent with the previous literature, finding that public spending reduced mortality, although at generally lower effect magnitudes and with mixed degrees of statistical significance.

Our very mixed findings should not be taken to imply that the conclusions from the previous studies are necessarily invalid. Countries covered in the published data and in our updated data do indeed differ and therefore it is to be expected that the analysis leads to different conclusions. Nevertheless, our findings do highlight the potential lack of generalizability of the results to different settings.

Our conclusions need to be seen in the light of the considerable methodological challenges faced by this strand of research, many of which may form the basis of a potential research agenda in this area, as discussed in the following.

5.1. *Data limitations*

The data used for the replication of the two key papers have been obtained directly from the authors of the paper in the case of Bokhari *et al.* (2007) and from data made available via the web appendix for the Moreno-Serra and Smith (2015) paper. With very few exceptions, these data are in principle available from readily and freely accessible data sources, e.g. the WHO's Global Health Observatory and the World Bank's WDI. These (as well as several other publicly accessible databases) are also the data sources we have used when updating and expanding the data employed in our empirical estimates. While the data from these sources represent the most comprehensive ones available and have been (and most certainly will be) used in numerous well-published studies,[28] they are not without quality concerns that may affect the reliability of our impact estimates. This is the case despite the considerable and laudable efforts that international organizations or research institutes have invested to try and establish common standards of how the data should be defined and collected. The

---

[28] The literature in other development areas, e.g. on the role of aid on economic growth, has been shown to suffer from similar data challenges (Easterly *et al.*, 2004; Roodman, 2008).

degree to which quality issues are present will vary by indicator and across countries. For instance, the data collection for one of our key variables — GDP per capita — should be approximately similar across countries, given long-standing efforts to ensure consistent definition of this measure.

Measurement error is likely more severe in the case of our key independent variable (i.e. public health expenditures). As the WHO's methodological background note (World Health Organization, 2012) to their Global Health Expenditure database acknowledges, there are major gaps in the data delivered to WHO from countries (which, if it is delivered, is typically taken on at face value), with the gaps then being filled by various forms of interpolation,[29] extrapolation, imputation and estimation.

Random measurement error in the health expenditure variable would normally bias the estimates of the impact on mortality toward the null, while random measurement error in our dependent variable (mortality) would produce higher standard errors of the impact estimates, reducing the statistical significance of the results (Wooldridge, 2010).[30] As health expenditure enters as a right-hand side variable in our regression model, it is likely that a valid IV strategy could reduce some of the bias resulting from such measurement errors. In our case though, for many of the empirical models the instruments used were weak — and it is this fact that has arguably been a far greater problem in our set of estimates, compared to data quality issues. Moreover, there are at least two sources of measurement error — one embedded in the numbers reported to the data collecting agencies (i.e. WHO), and an additional one as a result of the (not always fully replicable) imputation approaches adopted by such agencies. In this case, it is at least conceivable (though very hard to tell for certain) that measurement error in the health expenditure variable may account for the weakness of the instrumentation in the first-stage estimates.

---

[29] Given that some of the original variables are estimated using previous years' observations, in Table A.8 we present the same analysis based on the streamlined model where we use quinquennial data.

[30] Note also that in case the measurement error is non-random but constant over time, then the fixed-effects approach would resolve this problem.

Arguably, measurement error is far more severe in the case of our dependent variables of interest, i.e. the under-five and gender-specific adult mortality rates — the underlying problem being the often complete absence of functioning vital registration systems in particular in many low-income countries (Alkema and You, 2012). In response, an impressive research "industry" has emerged, developing and applying sophisticated modelling methods to fill the mortality data gaps statistically. The fact that different research teams find considerable differences in, for instance, their under-five mortality estimates for many LMICs, however, underscores the measurement problem at hand.

Short of obtaining the "perfect" data (which will never happen), there are, however, ways in which more purposefully selected, specific data sources would be worthwhile using, if there is reason to believe that they provide better quality data, and even at the cost of reducing the country coverage. Examples on the mortality side might include using data from Demographic and Health Surveys (DHS) only or on the expenditure side to focus on information from detailed IMF Government Finance Statistics, the World Bank's Poverty Assessments and Public Expenditure Reviews (see e.g. Gupta et al., 2003).

5.2. Methodological limitations

There are at least three methodological issues to be borne in mind.

First, following the previous literature that predominantly accounts for country-level heterogeneity and for endogeneity of health expenditure and mortality, we have employed a panel fixed-effect approach, combined with IVs techniques. Incorporating country fixed effect in the model means that we compromise statistical power because the estimation relies only on within-country variations in health care expenditure and mortality. Because there are relatively small variations in these variables over time, and also because the analysis often relies on "weak" IVs, our methods (though being standard in the literature) may be of insufficient power to statistically detect the impact. This potential downside of the fixed-effect approach, however, has to be weighed up against the likely considerable benefits of controlling more adequately for endogeneity through the regression control over unobserved heterogeneity in time-invariant characteristics and also in factors that change slowly over time such as cultural factors or the quality of institution.

Second, our results using the MIs should be interpreted with caution. Although MI has been widely adapted in the applied statistic literature, its applications in health econometric models (in particular as part of IVs approaches) have been rare (Perkins and Neumayer, 2014). We carefully construct our imputation so that it does not violate the exclusion restriction assumption in the IV approach. Yet, detailed statistical properties of the application of the MI approach should be expanded upon in future research. That said, and as we showed, the alternative of not imputing the data would mean that the econometric analysis would have to do without a considerable number of countries with any missing values in the model specifications, producing a highly unrepresentative sample and causing selection bias, the impacts of which in terms of main effects are *a priori* unknown (though likely significant). At the same time, it must be noted that the statistical imputation increases the likelihood of measurement error in the regressions, thereby augmenting the impact estimates as well as the standard errors.

Third, the IV technique has been the standard workhorse for causal analysis in the relevant literature. As in the present study, the validity and relevance of the instruments can generally be questioned — i.e. some instruments occasionally prove to be good in a statistical sense, but that could be sensitive to the choice of data and other variables in the model. Furthermore, it should be noted that the IV approach does not necessarily provide the average treatment effect (ATE), which would be the key quantity of interest, but instead it gives the local average treatment effect (LATE), in which the impact of health expenditure is identified only for the subset of countries for which the expenditure is *actually* affected by the instruments (Angrist and Imbens, 1995; Angrist *et al.*, 1996). In the literature, it is common to assume homogeneity of the IV impact, rather than allowing for heterogeneity of the impacts across countries, so that the estimated IV impacts conveniently represent ATE, despite that in practice it is hard to believe that the impacts of expenditure will be common across countries. For simplicity, the present study, as did the previous studies in the literature, focuses on assumed homogeneous impacts, and abstains from discussing likely differences between the ATE and LATE in this context.[31]

5.3. Policy implications

The primary policy question is whether or not greater public health care expenditures improve population health. The two prominent studies — BGG and MSS — claim that health expenditures do reduce mortality, and that the magnitude of the effect is considerable, hence supporting greater publicly funded health coverage across countries. However, the cross-country-based work presented here (as well as in some of the previous researches, e.g. Filmer and Pritchett (1999) shows that the magnitude and precision of this effect is sensitive to the choice of data and econometric methods. Our results do not necessarily suggest that policies expanding public health expenditure do not save lives at all. Rather, our results confirm the common problems in cross-country data analysis — that the noise in the cross-country data may be so large that the current econometric methods could sometimes fail to robustly detect the health gains at global level. The observation that impact estimates can vary greatly and may also be small in magnitude and/or insignificant is at least partly confirmed by the meta-analysis in Gallet and Doucouliagos (2015), who find a considerable spread in the impact estimates of health expenditures on mortality, as well as a low mean elasticity (i.e. 0.079).[32]

Another important implication of the analysis would be the extent to which our estimates reliably inform the marginal productivity of health care systems across countries — the key variable that would be needed to

---

[31] In this context, it is of note that Gallet and Doucouliagos (2017) report in their meta-regression analysis of the relevant empirical studies (which do include within-country studies) that the magnitudes of the elasticity of life expectancy found by studies using IV approaches are significantly larger than comparable "baseline" non-IV estimates.

[32] Using a meta-regression model of Gallet and Doucouliagos (2017) (using their "Specific" model of conditional mortality rate), the predicted elasticity of the BGG study is −0.283 for under-five mortality and −0.383 for maternal mortality. As MSS did not estimate elasticities, their study is not included in the Gallet and Doucouliagos' meta-analysis.

inform country-specific cost-effectiveness thresholds (Ochalek *et al.*, 2018). In light of the limited robustness to changes in model specification and in data of the empirical findings, coupled with imprecise estimation (due to weak IVs), our results again may not uncover the true (if any) productivity of health care systems across countries, and therefore further improvement in either data, empirical methods or even research design is required.[33]

5.4. *Implications for future research*

Future research should involve the improvement in both the methods for the analysis of cross-country data and in data quality. Global efforts to obtain finer data should improve the data quality over time. Some arguably "better" data already exist, if at the cost of a considerably smaller sample of countries; for example, international household surveys (e.g. the World Bank's Living Standard Measurement Surveys) do provide finer data on health and household health care spending at a more granular level (e.g. observations at household level), which could potentially overcome some of the key limitations in the cross-country data.

Since the impact of public health expenditure on mortality could also be heterogeneous across countries, future research should explore such heterogeneity. The BGG model does allow for differential impacts, conditional on the level of economic development (proxied by the proportion of paved roads) and on the amount of donor funding for health. Using the updated data for the year 2000 in the BGG specification, Figure A.1 summarizes the distribution of the impacts of public health expenditure on mortality. We find that the impacts for under-five mortality are considerably more homogenous than for maternal mortality. Similarly, Wagstaff and Claeson (2004) found that the mortality reducing impact of public expenditure becomes evident only once the quality of

---

[33] An online tool based on Ochalek *et al.* (2018) has been made available at: https://www.york.ac.uk/media/che/documents/Calculating%20cost%20per%20DALY%20averted%20thresholds%20for%20LMICs.xlsm, which enables users to enter new estimates of the elasticity of health outcomes with respect to public health care expenditure, or to carry out sensitivity analysis when using existing published estimates when estimating cost-effectiveness thresholds for LMICs.

governance exceeds a certain threshold level. It may hence be worthwhile to assess possible additional factors that mitigate or promote the impact of public health expenditure, including, for instance, baseline mortality. Quantile treatment effect models could be useful to test and quantify the impacts of public health expenditure across countries (Chernozhukov and Hansen, 2005).

Another possibility would be to use within-country data to investigate the domestic impact of health expenditure on health outcomes. Although there are some research works in high-income countries (for example, Martin *et al.*, 2008; Card *et al.*, 2009; Claxton *et al.*, 2015), the evidence is still limited in LMICs, where policy issues relating to universal health coverage become more relevant and also health care resources are generally scarce, except for some existing studies in major countries such as India (Bhalotra, 2007; Farahani *et al.*, 2010).

At the same time, our findings add further weight to the case for journals to require authors to submit their data along with their papers, so that the data become permanently available to future scholars, thereby allowing for the discrepancies resulting from retrospective corrections to be traced to the changes in the data. The problems we encountered when trying to replicate the exact original MSS results using an updated, revised version of a Stata command (xtivreg2) also suggest that whenever authors use a public-domain user-written program, that the journal should require them to provide the program version information as well as the data and relevant do-files.

Likewise, the agencies producing and publishing the data would benefit research by making available each version of the data, rather than just the latest one that would supersede all previous ones. The producers of such data could also usefully increase the degree of transparency about the exact methods that have been used in imputing gaps in the underlying data, and indeed the extent to which imputation has been undertaken.

Finally, the current literature is largely based on an IV approach in estimating causal impacts of health expenditure, despite the fact that instruments could be sometimes questioned (even if statistically relevant occasionally, they are not always theoretically convincing). An alternative approach would be to use actual policy variations in health care expenditure to inform the impact estimation. Examples of sources of such variations include expansion of public insurance schemes (see Acharya *et al.*, 2012 for a comprehensive review), funding decision rules in health care (Dykstra *et al.*, 2015) and large-scale field or natural experiments that involve the provision of additional health care resources/funding (Wagstaff, 2011; Olken *et al.*, 2014). Carefully evaluating those policy and experimental shocks on expenditure could possibly provide more transparent and robust evidence.

Acknowledgments

This study is financially supported by the International Decision Support Initiative (iDSI), funded by the Bill & Melinda Gates Foundation, the UK Department for International Development and the Rockerfeller Foundation. The authors would like to thank Mead Over, Sebastian Bauhoff, Amanda Glassman, Jessica Ochalek, Mark Sculpher, Peter Smith, Paul Revill, Yot Teerawattananon, Stephen Martin, Alex Rollinger and all participants of the iDSI workshops in York and London for their very helpful support, comments and suggestions. We also thank BGG and MSS for openly sharing their data and codes.

References

Acharya, A., Vellakkal, S., Taylor, F., Masset, E., Satija, A., Burke, M., Ebrahim, S. (2012). The impact of health insurance schemes for the informal sector in low-and middle-income countries: A systematic review. *The World Bank Research Observer*, doi:10.1093/wbro/lks009.

Afridi, M. A., Ventelou, B. (2013). Impact of health aid in developing countries: The public vs. the private channels. *Economic Modelling*, 31: 759–765.

Akinci, F., Hamidi, S., Suvankulov, F., Akhmedjonov, A. (2014). Examining the impact of health care expenditures on health outcomes in the Middle East and N. Africa. *Journal of Health Care Finance*, 41: 1–23.

Alkema, L., You, D. (2012). Child mortality estimation: A comparison of UN IGME and IHME estimates of levels and trends in under-five mortality rates and deaths. *PLoS Medicine*, 9.

Angrist, J. D., Imbens, G. W. (1995). Two-stage least squares estimation of average causal effects in models with variable treatment intensity. *Journal of the American Statistical Association*, 90: 431–442.

Angrist, J. D., Imbens, G. W., Rubin, D. B. (1996). Identification of causal effects using instrumental variables. *Journal of the American Statistical Association*, 91: 444–455.

Angrist, J. D., Pischke, J.-S. (2009). *Mostly Harmless Econometrics: An Empiricist's Companions*. Princeton University Press.

Anyanwu, J. C., Erhijakpor, A. E. O. (2009). Health expenditures and health outcomes in Africa. *African Development Review*, 21: 400–433.

Ariste, R., Di Matteo, L. (2017). Value for money: An evaluation of health spending in Canada. *International Journal of Health Economics and Management*, 17(3), 289–310.

Bhalotra, S. (2007). Spending to save? State health expenditure and infant mortality in India. *Health Economics*, 16: 911–928.

Bidani, B., Ravallion, M. (1997). Decomposing social indicators using distributional data. *Journal of Econometrics*, 77: 125–139.

Blundell, R., Bond, S. (1998). Initial conditions and moment restrictions in dynamic panel data models. *Journal of Econometrics*, 87: 115–143.

Bokhari, F. A. S., Gai, Y., Gottret, P. (2007). Government health expenditures and health outcomes. *Health Economics*, 16: 257–273.

Brückner, M. (2013). On the simultaneity problem in the aid and growth debate. *Journal of Applied Econometrics*, 28: 126–150.

Card, D., Dobkin, C., Maestas, N. (2009). Does Medicare save lives? *The Quarterly Journal of Economics*, 124: 597–636.

Chernozhukov, V., Hansen C. (2005). An IV model of quantile treatment effects. *Econometrica*, 73: 245–261.

Claxton, K., Martin, S., Soares, M., Rice, N., Spackman, E., Hinde, S., Devlin, N., Smith, P., Sculpher, M. (2015). Methods for the estimation of the National Institute for Health and Care Excellence cost-effectiveness threshold. *Health Technology Assessment*, 19: 1.

Clemens, M. A., Radelet, S., Bhavnani, R. R., Bazzi, S. (2012). Counting chickens when they hatch: Timing and the effects of aid on growth. *The Economic Journal*, 122: 590–617.

Dykstra, S., Glassman, A., Kenny, C., Sandefur, J. (2015). Are vaccines fungible? Regression discontinuity evidence from a large aid program. Center for Global Development Working Paper 394.

Easterly, W., Levine, R., Roodman, D. (2004). Aid, policies, and growth: Comment. *The American Economic Review*, 94: 774–780.

Edney, L. C., Afzali, H. H. A., Cheng, T. C., Karnon, J. (2018). Estimating the reference incremental cost-effectiveness ratio for the Australian Health System. *PharmacoEconomics*, 36(2), 239–252.

Farag, M., Nandakumar, A. K., Wallack, S., Hodgkin, D., Gaumer, G., Erbil, C. (2013). Health expenditures, health outcomes and the role of good governance. *International Journal of Health Care Finance and Economics*, 13: 33–52.

Farahani, M., Subramanian, S. V., Canning, D. (2010). Effects of state-level public spending on health on the mortality probability in India. *Health Economics*, 19: 1361–1376.

Filmer, D., Hammer, J. S., Pritchett, L. H. (2000). Weak links in the chain: A diagnosis of health policy in poor countries. *The World Bank Research Observer*, 15: 199–224.

Filmer, D., Pritchett, L. (1999). The impact of public spending on health: Does money matter? *Social Science & Medicine*, 49: 1309–1323.

Gallet, C.A., Doucouliagos, H. (2017). The impact of healthcare spending on health outcomes: A meta-regression analysis. *Social Science & Medicine*, 179: 9–17.

Gani, A. (2009). Health care financing and health outcomes in Pacific Island countries. *Health Policy and Planning*, 24: 72–81.

Gravelle, H. S. E., Backhouse, M. E. (1987). International cross-section analysis of the determination of mortality. *Social Science & Medicine*, 25: 427–441.

Gupta, S., Verhoeven, M., Tiongson, E. R. (2003). Public spending on health care and the poor. *Health Economics*, 12: 685–696.

Hauck, K., Martin, S., Smith, P. (2015). Social determinants of health in low income countries: Do the data support the rhetoric? Mimeo.

Hu, B., Mendoza, R. U. (2013). Public health spending, governance and child health outcomes: Revisiting the links. *Journal of Human Development and Capabilities*, 14: 285–311.

Kizsewski, A., Malaney, P., Mellinger, A., Spielman, A., Sachs, S. E., Sachs, J. D. (2004). A global index of the stability of malaria transmission based on the intrinsic properties of anopheline mosquito vectors. *American Journal of Tropical Medicine and Hygiene*, 70: 486–498.

Kleibergen, F., Paap, R. (2006). Generalized reduced rank tests using the singular value decomposition. *Journal of Econometrics*, 133: 97–126.

Landerman, L. R., Land, K. C., Pieper, C. F. (1997). An empirical evaluation of the predictive mean matching method for imputing missing values. *Sociological Methods & Research*, 26: 3–33.

Lorentzen, P., McMillan, J., Wacziarg, R. (2008). Death and development. *Journal of Economic Growth*, 13: 81–124.

Marseille, E., Larson, B., Kazi, D. S., Kahn, J. G., Rosen, S. (2015). Thresholds for the cost-effectiveness of interventions: Alternative approaches. *Bulletin of the World Health Organization*, 93: 118–124.

Martin, S., Rice, N., Smith, P. C. (2008). Does health care spending improve health outcomes? Evidence from English programme budgeting data. *Journal of Health Economics*, 27: 826–842.

Moreno-Serra, R., Smith, P. C. (2015). Broader health coverage is good for the nation's health: Evidence from country level panel data. *Journal of the Royal Statistical Society: Series A (Statistics in Society)*, 178: 101–124.

Newall, A., Jit, M., Hutubessy, R. (2014). Are current cost-effectiveness thresholds for low-and middle-income countries useful? Examples from the world of vaccines. *Pharmacoeconomics*, 32: 525–531.

Ochalek, J., Lomas, J., Claxton, K. (2018). Estimating health opportunity costs in low-income and middle-income countries: A novel approach and evidence from cross-country data. *BMJ Global Health*, 3(6): e000964.

Olken, B. A., Onishi, J., Wong, S. (2014). Should aid reward performance? Evidence from a field experiment on health and education in Indonesia. *American Economic Journal: Applied Economics*, 6: 1–34.

Perkins, R., Neumayer, E. (2014). Adoption and compliance in second-hand smoking bans: A global econometric analysis. *International Journal of Public Health*, 59: 859–866.

Rajkumar, A. S., Swaroop, V. (2008). Public spending and outcomes: Does governance matter? *Journal of Development Economics*, 86: 96–111.

Revill, P., Walker, S., Madan, J., Ciaranello, A., Mwase, T., Gibb, D. M., Claxton, K., Sculpher, M. J. (2014). Using cost-effectiveness thresholds to determine value for money in low-and middle-income country healthcare systems: Are current international norms fit for purpose? Centre for Health Economics Research Paper No 98. York.

Roodman, D. (2008). Through the looking glass, and what ols found there: On growth, foreign aid, and reverse causality. Center for Global Development Working Paper.

Roodman, D. (2015). A replication of 'counting chickens when they hatch' (Economic Journal 2012). *Public Finance Review*, 43: 256–281, doi:10.1177/1091142114537895.

Sanderson, E., Windmeijer, F. (2013). A weak instrument F-test in linear IV models with multiple endogenous variables. CEMMAP Working Paper. Centre for Microdata Methods and Practice.

Schaffer, M. E. (2010). xtivreg2: Stata module to perform extended IV/2SLS, GMM and AC/HAC, LIML and k-class regression for panel data models. Available at: http://ideas.repec.org/c/boc/bocode/s456501.html.

Ssozi, J., Amlani, S. (2015). The effectiveness of health expenditure on the proximate and ultimate goals of healthcare in sub-Saharan Africa. *World Development*, 76: 165–179.

Stadhouders, N., Koolman, X., van Dijk, C., Jeurissen, P., Adang, E. (2019). The marginal benefits of healthcare spending in the Netherlands: Estimating cost-effectiveness thresholds using a translog production function. *Health Economics*, 28(11), 1331–1344.

StataCorp (2013). *Stata Multiple-Imputation Reference Manual Release 13*. College Station TX: StataCorp LP.

Stock, J. H., Yogo, M. (2005). Testing for weak instruments in linear IV regression. In: Andrews D. W. K., *Identification and Inference for Econometric Models*. New York: Cambridge University Press.

Vallejo-Torres, L., García-Lorenzo, B., Serrano-Aguilar, P. (2018). Estimating a cost-effectiveness threshold for the Spanish NHS. *Health Economics*, 27(4): 746–761.

Wagstaff, A. (2011). Fungibility and the impact of development assistance: Evidence from Vietnam's health sector. *Journal of Development Economics*, 94: 62–73.

Wagstaff, A., Claeson, M. (2004). *Rising to the Challenges: The Millennium Development Goals for Healths*. World Bank.

White, I. R., Royston, P., Wood, A. M. (2011). Multiple imputation using chained equations: Issues and guidance for practice. *Statistics in Medicine*, 30: 377–399.

Wooldridge, J. M. (2010). *Econometric Analysis of Cross Section and Panel Datas*. MIT Press.

World Health Organization (WHO) (2012). *General Statistical Procedures Used to Construct WHO Health Expenditure Database*. Geneva: WHO.

World Health Organization (WHO) (2015a). *General Statistical Procedures Used to Construct WHO Health Expenditure Database*. Geneva: World Health Organization.

World Health Organization (WHO) (2015b). *Cost Effectiveness and Strategic Planning (WHO-CHOICE)*. Available at: http://www.who.int/choice/costs/ CER_levels/en/ [Accessed: December 2015].

World Health Organization Commission on Marcroeconomics and Health (WHO) (2001). *Macroeconomics and Health: Investing in Health for Economic Development*. Geneva: World Health Organization.

Part 2
Economic Evaluation

Chapter 2

Allocating Scarce Resources — Tools for Priority Setting

Jessica Ochalek, Paul Revill and Michael Drummond

Abstract

Given the number of priority setting tools available, which should decision-makers use and when? The choice depends critically on the nature of the decision problem. In particular, the decision-maker needs to be clear on what is to be maximized (e.g. health or welfare more generally), whether there is a budget constraint and whether any other factors (e.g. equity) need to be considered. This chapter summarizes the key strengths and limitations of commonly applied priority setting tools with a particular focus on how they differ in terms of the elements of benefit considered, how these are valued or combined, the extent to which budgetary constraints are recognized and the implicit or explicit criteria used to make a decision on adoption of the programmes being evaluated.

1. Introduction

All health care systems need some means to determine which interventions are purchased and provided for recipient populations. The issue is fundamentally one of economics: resulting from the scarcity of resources, the need to make choices and opportunity costs (benefits forgone) as a result of choices. There is potentially unlimited demand for health care

53

and only finite budgets with which to provide it. As a result of market failures and concern for equity,[1] most health care systems tend not to rely solely on the free market but instead reserve important roles for public authorities. Resource allocation decisions need to be made, for example, about the composition of health benefits packages (HBPs) (the set of interventions made available to the population), which new health technologies will be reimbursed and at what price, and how to develop public health programmes. The academic field concerned with the use of technical tools to inform resource allocation is broadly known as economic evaluation (Drummond et al., 2015).

The normative foundations of economic evaluation were originally set in a neoclassical welfare economics framework, relying on four key tenets: the utility principle (i.e. individuals rank their preferences according to their budget to maximize their welfare); individual sovereignty (individuals themselves are best able to quantify and value their utility); consequentialism (utility is gained only from outcomes and not processes) and welfarism (the value of anything can be judged only by the utility derived from individuals with regard to it) (Culyer, 2012b). As such, improvements in social welfare can be judged only through a Pareto improvement defined where at least one individual is made better off and none are made worse off (Garber and Phelps, 1997; Weinstein and Manning, 1997). Given the paucity of changes that meet this criterion, Kaldor (1939) and Hicks (1939) developed the concept of "potential Pareto improvement", wherein a given change will be a potential Pareto improvement if individuals made better off can compensate those made worse off while still remaining better off (Kaldor, 1939).

Economic evaluation based upon the tenets of welfare economics has a long history and has informed decisions in many sectors of the economy. However, a critique of the Kaldor–Hicks criterion is that it is almost always applied "hypothetically" (i.e. no compensation need actually be

---

[1] Market failures in the market for health care include the relatively high levels of uncertainty around the incidence and duration of disease, asymmetric information between health care professionals and patients inhibiting the ability of individuals to make effective choices around their own health care (e.g. supplier-induced demand) and monopoly power among health care providers (Walker et al., 2011).

paid) and hence some people do inevitably "win" while others "lose". If welfare improvement is valued in monetary terms, as it invariably is in economic analysis (e.g. through measurement of willingness/ability to pay), there is a risk that the better-off make higher expressions of value but do not ever actually have to pay compensation. They would then be more likely to benefit from public programmes, with clear adverse implications for equity.

There have been notable criticisms of the use of welfarism as a normative basis for making resource allocation decisions. Amartya Sen, for instance, was critical of its restrictive assumptions and narrow definition of benefit as a function of individual utilities (Sen, 1980). He instead proposed the use of "capabilities", which determine *how* individuals may live their lives, which have long been seen as the measure of human progress in Artistotelian philosophy (Sen, 1993; Walker *et al.*, 2011). Welfarism is also criticized on the grounds that individuals may not be the best and only judges of their welfare (Drummond *et al.*, 2015).

Similarly, the field of economic evaluation in health care has increasingly embraced an alternative normative paradigm, that of "extra-welfarism" (or "social decision-making"). The extra-welfarist approach differs from the welfarist approach in four general ways: (1) it permits the use of outcomes other than utility; (2) it permits the use of sources of valuation other than the affected individuals; (3) it permits the weighting of outcomes (whether utility or other) according to principles that need not be preference-based and (4) it permits interpersonal comparisons of well-being in a variety of dimensions, thus enabling movements beyond Paretian economics (Culyer, 2012a).

In its applications in health care, the extra-welfarist approach normally assumes the objective to be health gain. Therefore, the approach can be seen to align more closely with the core principles of many health care systems (e.g. the UK National Health Service (NHS), "About the NHS: Principles and values that guide the NHS", 2013) of "equal access for equal need"; whereby, need can be defined as the capacity to improve health and access is in terms of the resources employed.

However, the framework of extra-welfarism also contains implicit value judgements that can be contested. The use of health gain as a sole objective, for instance, does not accord exactly with Sen's capability approach because health is a functioning and not a capability. Similarly, if the tenets of welfare economics are accepted, the maximization of social welfare based on the individuals' subjective assessments of their utilities is unlikely to be realized by adopting an extra-welfarist approach. Furthermore, even if health is accepted as the sole maximand, society may also hold concern for distributional fairness.

The choice of economic evaluation tools can therefore appear as a complex array of approaches laden with assumptions and value judgements. This paper reviews the most common tools, offering examples of applications in low- and middle-income countries (LMICs), and providing guidance to analysts in the choice of tools and policymakers in their interpretation.

2. Understanding Available Priority Setting Tools for Use in LMICs

2.1. *Review of priority setting tools*

In this section, the following tools are reviewed: cost–benefit analysis (CBA), cost-effectiveness analysis (CEA), generalized cost-effectiveness analysis (GCEA), extended cost-effectiveness analysis (ECEA), multicriteria decision analysis (MCDA) and mathematical programming. In each case the key elements of the tool are described and an example of its use given. The main objective is to explore how the tools differ in terms of the elements of benefit considered, how these are valued or combined, the extent to which budgetary constraints are recognized and the implicit or explicit criteria used to make a decision on adoption of the programmes being evaluated.

2.1.1. *Cost–benefit analysis*

Traditional CBA seeks to maximize aggregate social welfare across the sectors of economy, where welfare is estimated based upon the tenets of welfare economics and recommendations adopt the Kaldor–Hicks criterion of compensation. As such, it is grounded in welfare economics. CBA studies generally take a "societal approach" to valuing costs and consequences. In functioning markets, social welfare based on individuals' preferences can be revealed through the market (Sculpher and Claxton, 2012). However, due to market failures in health care, individuals' preferences must be elicited in order to value the consequences of implementing health care interventions. This can be achieved using different approaches to valuing health outcomes, such as the human capital approach, revealed preferences and stated preferences of willingness to pay (WTP) (Drummond *et al.*, 2005). Because all outcomes must be valued in monetary terms, CBA can be used to make allocation decisions across sectors, including the setting of budgets, in addition to that within health care.

The decision of whether or not to implement the intervention under consideration in CBA rests simply on whether the benefits outweigh the costs. Generally, CBAs do not take account of issues such as fixed budget constraints for particular sectors (e.g. health) and therefore fail to accurately reflect the opportunity costs of additional costs being imposed on these budgets. However, it is possible for CBA to reflect fixed budgets by explicitly taking account of the benefits of those activities foregone as a result of the costs imposed on the budget constraint. The challenge lies in knowing what to measure (i.e. what benefits will be forgone) and measuring it (i.e. monetizing the value of health outcomes).

Box 1 illustrates a case where WTP is used to inform health policy decisions. It makes no claims about the efficiency (in terms of improvement

---

Box 1. WTP for ivermectin treatment for river blindness

This study examines the costs and consequences of distributing ivermectin to treat onchocerciasis, also known as river blindness. As the treatment is free from the manufacturer, the only cost included was that of local drug distribution, which ranged from 9 Naira (US$0.11) to 12 Naira (US$0.15) per unit. WTP was measured using contingent valuation, and the resulting community-level median WTP ranged from 20 Naira (US$0.25) to 30 Naira (US$0.38). The authors conclude that WTP for local ivermectin distribution exists in these onchocerciasis-endemic communities (Onwujekwe *et al.*, 1998).

in health outcomes for its cost) of ivermectin treatment, but simply states that people would be willing to pay a certain amount for it. Estimates of WTP can be subject to people's ability to pay, which can lead to inequalities if decisions are based on WTP. However, if not influenced by ability to pay, WTP estimates can be useful in informing decisions around changing the size of the budget for health care. If society's WTP for a given health programme is greater than the cost of providing it, theoretically this is an argument for expanding the budget. However, there are very few examples of CBAs in health care (Drummond *et al.*, 2015). In the literature, the term "CBA" is also often used to describe studies that compare the costs of providing a programme with the cost savings it generates, for example by preventing episodes of illness. Some studies also consider the benefits in terms of the productivity losses averted by preventing or shortening illness episodes. However, these studies do not fall within the welfarist framework as the health benefits are not valued using individuals' preferences.

2.1.2. *Cost-effectiveness analysis*

CEA is also concerned with the costs and consequences of alternative interventions. In contrast to CBA, the use of CEA is restricted to health care programs that produce the same units of outcomes, such as cases of diseases averted or lives saved. Outcomes can be measured in comparable units of health that account for mortality and morbidity, such as quality-adjusted life years (QALYs) or disability-adjusted life years (DALYs), which enable programmes to be compared across disease areas. This approach to CEA is sometimes known as cost utility analysis (CUA) but is more often what is understood as CEA. As outcomes reflect a measure of health, rather than benefit more broadly defined, CEA is consistent with an extra-welfarist approach. This approach allows for interpersonal comparisons of outcomes beyond individuals' expressions of utility and therefore circumvents some of the troublesome equity implications of crude applications of CBA (Culyer, 2012b).

The main components of all CEAs are the cost and effectiveness data. Traditional CEA may use intermediate outcomes (e.g. reduction in blood pressure) or final outcomes (e.g. cases averted), but only final outcomes

---

Box 2. Cost-effectiveness of multiple policy options for HIV treatment

This study examines the cost-effectiveness of potential responses to future high levels of transmitted HIV drug resistance in antiretroviral (ART) drug-naive populations beginning treatment. Costs include all relevant unit costs (e.g. supply chain, transport, human resources, etc.) Outcomes are valued in terms of QALYs. Costs and QALYs are discounted at a rate of 3.5% annually. The incremental cost effectiveness ratios (ICERs) for the different interventions are compared against a threshold of $500 per QALY, which was chosen to represent a realistic maximum level at which many interventions offering similar levels of health gains remain unfunded. The authors find that at a threshold of $500, no policy change is cost-effective, but at a threshold of $1,000 or above and with the prevalence of pretreatment ART resistance greater than 10%, a policy to measure viral load six months after ART initiation is cost-effective (Phillips *et al.*, 2014).

---

can be converted into a broad generic measure of outcomes that comprise effectiveness data in most modern CEAs (i.e. those often defined as CUA) (Drummond *et al.*, 2005).

The study in Box 2 considers the cost-effectiveness of multiple policy options for HIV treatment among treatment-naïve individuals at different levels of resistance to the treatment. The outcomes are valued in terms of QALYs, a generic measure of utility that accounts for the length and quality of life (QoL). However, this is uncommon for CEAs in LMICs: as yet, little QoL research has been conducted in low-income settings on either adults or children with HIV to inform locally relevant health outcomes. Instead, decision rules are more often based on cost per DALY averted (see Section 2.3).

This study uses a decision-making threshold that represents the cost per QALY of other interventions offering similar levels of health gains that remain unfunded. In doing this, the authors have used a maximum acceptable level of cost per QALY based on past funding decisions, which aims to reflect a realistic cost-effectiveness threshold. A good estimate of the cost-effectiveness threshold (Sculpher and Claxton, 2012; Woods *et al.*, 2015), which reflects the opportunity cost (i.e. health forgone elsewhere in the system as a consequence of implementing a given intervention) is critically important in CEA.

This highlights the key difference between CBA and CEA, which is the decision rule that is used. When outcomes are valued in terms of comparable units of health, CEA takes account of the budget for health care explicitly through the comparison of an incremental cost-effectiveness ratio (ICER), which gives the additional cost per additional unit of health outcome (Sculpher and Claxton, 2012). If the ICER falls below the cost-effectiveness threshold, the intervention should be accepted. Alternatively, the decision rule can be framed in terms of either net monetary benefit or net health benefit, where interventions should be accepted if either is greater than 0. Mathematically, the decision rule is identical when using any of the ICER, net health benefit or net monetary benefit for interventions that increase costs and QALYs. Net monetary benefit involves monetizing QALYs where the number of incremental QALYs are multiplied by the value of the cost-effectiveness threshold. This appears similar to CBA where QALYs are also monetized, but in CBA the monetization is typically calculated using the consumption value of a QALY (Sculpher and Claxton, 2012).

2.1.3. Generalized cost-effectiveness analysis

The World Health Organization (WHO), through the CHOosing Interventions that are Cost-Effective (CHOICE) team, has played a central role in the application of CEA in LMICs with the development and use of GCEA (Murray et al., 2000; Hutubessy et al., 2003). GCEA studies typically estimate the cost-effectiveness of interventions at the level of whole WHO regions (e.g. sub-Saharan Africa or Southeast Asia). The approach is also grounded in an extra-welfarist framework, but this is usually not made explicit. The aim is to simultaneously evaluate a wide range of alternatives, often clustered by disease area, and to provide "broad brush" recommendations to inform more specific decision-making within jurisdictions. By providing generalized evidence, it is hoped that cost-effectiveness criteria can inform decisions in settings where more detailed analyses, reflecting localized constraints, are unlikely to be feasible to routinely undertake.

GCEA analyses begin from a "null" position whereby it is assumed that no interventions are provided within a health care system and the task is to build up the set of interventions for provision. This is in part motivated by a concern that use of CEA is often dominated by prospective studies of new interventions compared to current practice, and the potential of larger scale changes in the health sector and identifying appropriate disinvestment opportunities remains unrealized (Murray *et al.*, 2000). However, a problem with assuming a null situation is this does not reflect how existing health care infrastructures need to be adjusted to deliver interventions. Therefore, the real-world costs of implementation are typically underestimated and new interventions may be deemed "cost-effective" whereas the cost of implementing them may be greater than is reflected in the analysis.

A notable, although somewhat cosmetic, difference between generalized and conventional CEA is the choice of outcome measure. Whereas CEA would usually present health outcomes in the form of QALYs, GCEA studies use the DALY measure. Both measures combine morbidity and mortality effects into a single generic unit, but instead of being a measure of health gain, DALYs — which have their origins in burden of disease studies — are a measure of health loss from full and healthy life expectancy. Disability is a more restricted measure of health-related QoL (HRQoL) as represented by QALYs and relates only to functional status. However, DALYs are widely used in studies in LMICs, because of their endorsement by the WHO and because QALYs estimates are not available for many countries (Kularatna *et al.*, 2013).

GCEA assesses whether or not interventions are "cost-effective" based upon the per capita income in a country. Interventions that offer ICERs at less than three times gross domestic product per capita (GDP pc) are deemed "cost-effective" and those at less than one times GDP pc as "cost-effective". Whereas strict application of these decision rules may not be in the spirit of GCEA in providing "broad brush" recommendations to decision-makers, they have been widely used in both GCEA and CEA applications to LMICs. These benchmarks have, however, been criticized as being aspirational and not reflective of what is known about the likelihood of opportunity costs resulting from the use of limited health care budgets (Sculpher and Claxton, 2012; Woods *et al.*, 2015). Their use therefore risks reducing population health and exacerbating health care inequalities. Box 3 provides an example of GCEA.

Box 3. Cost-effectiveness of introducing the RTS,S malaria vaccine

This study examines the cost-effectiveness of the RTS,S malaria vaccine, which reduces the likelihood of contracting malaria from an infected mosquito, compared to non-vaccination. Costs are taken from a societal perspective and include provider costs, including the cost of the vaccine and case management, as well as out-of-pocket (OOP) patient costs. Outcomes are measured as DALYs averted. The authors present ICERs for a range of numbers of infectious bites per year, and compare these to a range of decision thresholds using cost-effectiveness acceptability curves (CEACs). Results are presented for both undiscounted costs and DALYs averted and with both discounting using an annual rate of 3%. They find that the introduction of RTS,S would be most cost-effective in settings with low levels of malaria exposure (Maire *et al.*, 2011).

2.1.4. *Extended cost-effectiveness analysis*

Policymakers and the public are often concerned with maximizing more than just health, and researchers may therefore wish to reflect these other societal preferences explicitly within their decision-making. ECEA aims to incorporate the equity effects of interventions and policies on health as well as financial risk protection outcomes to assist in decisions around extending the coverage of existing interventions/policies. It provides information on the consequences of the programme or intervention disaggregated across different population strata relevant to the decision (by, for example, geography or socio-economic status); first, in terms of health gains and, second, in terms of financial risk protection (as measured by, for example, household expenditure averted). The tool gives policymakers a "dashboard" of information on the joint benefits and tradeoffs in terms of equity in health and financial risk protection associated with different health interventions. Box 4 provides an example.

The study in Box 4 considers deaths averted and private expenditures averted as outcome measures. While these measures are relevant to diarrhoea in this particular context, failing to use a generic measure of utility (e.g. QALY, DALY, etc.) means that these estimates cannot be compared to estimates from other ECEA studies where a different

---

Box 4. An ECEA of treatment and prevention of diarrhoea in Ethiopia

This study assesses the impacts of universal public finance (UPF) of diarrhoeal treatment alone compared to diarrhoeal treatment along with rotavirus vaccination in children under-five in Ethiopia across socio-economic quintiles. The authors first calculate the baseline number of deaths due to diarrhoea and rotavirus by quintile, and then estimate the number of deaths that would occur by quintile following the introduction of UPF of diarrhoeal treatment and the introduction of UPF and rotavirus vaccine combined. For the financial protection measure, the authors calculate private expenditures averted by each intervention as a function of the number of diarrhoeal episodes, the probability of seeking treatment, the associated costs and the proportion of those costs being paid OOP. They find that without factoring in private expenditure averted, the cost per life saved is lower from the intervention with both rotavirus vaccination and diarrhoeal treatment, and thus this intervention dominates (Pecenka *et al.*, 2015).

---

outcome measure is used, and particularly if changes in quality, as opposed to length, of life are the primary outcome. Different ECEAs may use different health outcome measures (e.g. deaths averted and life years (LYs) gained) as well as different measures of financial risk protection (e.g. reduction of private expenditure and reduction in impoverishing health care expenditures). As such, they may not be directly comparable. Common to these and all ECEA studies is that interventions are assumed to be funded by the tax system, and therefore no account is taken of the opportunity costs falling on the budget for health care, when in reality most health interventions are funded through the health care system and displace health gains elsewhere in the system.

Distributional cost-effectiveness analysis (DCEA) offers an alternative framework for incorporating equity concerns into CEA. Unlike ECEA, DCEA allows for the analysis of multiple distributional variables in addition to wealth quintile group. DCEA is set within an extra-welfarist framework that incorporates society's concern for the distribution of health as well as overall health gains. When a setting-specific inequality aversion parameter is specified, DCEA can be used to determine the strategy that results in the best improvement in both average health and reduction in unfair health inequality in the population. As DCEA is relatively new, to date there have been no applications of DCEA in LMICs or HICs. Asaria *et al.* (2015) apply DCEA to compare alternative ways of implementing a Bowel Cancer Screening Programme (BCSP) in the UK.

2.1.5. Multicriteria decision analysis

MCDA is an approach that can be used to assist policymakers in choosing between options where there are two or more relevant criteria. The two main criteria in making choices in health care are efficiency and equity, as discussed before in the context of ECEA and DCEA. However, policymakers may wish to introduce other considerations, such as severity of disease, potential for poverty reduction or the recipients of the health programmes being considered. Of course, many criteria are considered, albeit informally, whenever decisions are made, but MCDA can contribute to the transparency and accountability of the decision-making process by providing an explicit organizing framework.

There are several key steps in conducting an MCDA, including structuring the decision problem, specifying the relevant criteria, measuring the programmes' or alternatives' performance against the criteria, scoring the alternatives on the criteria and weighting the criteria and applying the scores and weights to rank the alternatives. There are several approaches for scoring and weighting, including point allocation and discrete choice experiments. This latter approach, often favoured by economists because of its theoretic foundations in random utility theory, involves asking decision-makers to choose between sets of options that meet the various criteria (attributes) to different degrees (levels).

MCDA has been widely applied in priority setting in LMICs. Jehu-Appiah *et al.* (2008) discuss how MCDA was used to guide the Ministry of Health in Ghana to set priorities between interventions (see Box 5). Mirelman *et al.* (2012) applied a similar methodology to explore the preferences of policymakers for efficiency and equity criteria in Brazil, Cuba, Nepal, Norway and Uganda. Baltussen *et al.* (2013) illustrate how MCDA could be used to improve decision-making in the HIV programme in South Africa.

There is still debate among analysts on how best to conduct MCDAs, although some proposals for good practice have been suggested (Marsh *et al.*,

---

Box 5. Balancing equity and efficiency in health priorities

In this study, MCDA was used to quantify the trade-off between equity, efficiency and other societal concerns in health priority setting in Ghana. Several criteria were defined: number of potential beneficiaries, severity of disease, cost-effectiveness, poverty reduction and vulnerability of the (recipient) population (e.g. not vulnerable, children <5 years, women of reproductive age, old people >65 years). Discrete choice experiments were conducted with policymakers to determine the relative importance of the criteria. Respondents chose their preferred intervention from sets of hypothetical interventions, each consisting of a bundle of criteria that described the intervention in question, with each criterion varying over a range of levels.

The results showed that interventions that target vulnerable populations, (very) severe diseases, many beneficiaries, diseases of the poor and are (very) cost-effective have a higher probability of being selected than interventions without one of those characteristics. The relative contributions showed that the targeting of vulnerable populations was the most important criterion, followed by cost-effectiveness, severity of disease and number of potential beneficiaries. In the rank ordering of interventions, childhood interventions had the highest probability of selection, followed by most interventions targeting communicable diseases, plus two reproductive health interventions (Jehu-Appiah *et al.*, 2008).

2016). One particularly important issue is how to incorporate cost-effectiveness as a criterion. In the study by Jehu-Appiah *et al.* (2008), "costs" and "effects" were combined into a single attribute "cost-effectiveness", which was then traded off against the other attributes. An alternative approach would be to define the utility/attractiveness of an intervention on the basis of all criteria except "costs" and then to link this estimate to costs in a cost–utility analysis/CEA (Jehu-Appiah *et al.*, 2008). The advantage of this approach is that it explicitly reflects the opportunity costs of selecting a given programme in terms of the other alternatives that are forgone, or displaced.

Programme budgeting and marginal analysis (PBMA) is another approach that allows multiple criteria to be applied to the assessment of programmes. Some criteria may directly relate to efficiency and equity, others may relate to organizational and managerial objectives. PBMA can be used to determine how a particular budget can be spent optimally, according to the decision-makers' stated criteria, by investing more in some programmes and disinvesting in others. Our literature review did not find any applications of PBMA in LMICs, but Ball *et al.* (2009) used PBMA to determine the priorities for investment and disinvestment in mental health services in a health authority in the United Kingdom, and Mitton *et al.* (2011) used the approach to determine disinvestment and investment opportunities in a health authority in Canada that was experiencing funding cuts.

2.1.6. *Mathematical programming*

All of the tools presented so far can be viewed as offering "partial" solutions to larger and more complex underlying resource allocation problems. The extent to which and how the tools reflect the larger challenge of constrained optimization of population health benefits from within available resources differs across them. For instance, CEA uses the notion of a cost-effectiveness threshold to reflect the shadow price of the budget constraint whereas traditional CBA would implicitly assume the available budget will adjust to the level required for the funding of the evaluated interventions. A weakness of others, in particular ECEA and MCDA, is that they can be relatively detached from such notions and often do not explicitly consider opportunity costs.

Increasingly, as information improves and computing power increases, analyses are exploring the use of methods — in the form of mathematic programming — to directly inform the full allocation of available resources. In principle, mathematical programming can inform how much to spend on what interventions, for whom, when and where within a country — all while remaining within budget. Box 6, for instance, outlines the use of mathematical programming to allocate the HIV budget in Zambia. The national planner/budget holder's problem is, in effect, solved.

The reason full budget allocation models are not more widely used is that they are difficult to implement and their informational requirements are immense — requiring knowledge of the costs and benefits of all feasible alternatives, for all policy areas. Also, they tend to rely on the

---

Box 6. Prioritizing the allocation of HIV resources in Zambia using mathematical programming

This study uses the Optima mathematical programming model to address the question of "How can HIV funding be optimally allocated to the combination of HIV response interventions that will yield the highest impact?" It both informed the allocation of different given levels of resources and estimated the financial commitments required to meet the national strategic targets.

The model was populated using demographic, epidemiological, sexual behaviour, service use/existing coverage, as well as economic and cost data and was calibrated to the HIV epidemic in Zambia. The relationship between expenditure and outcomes was then established using a mathematical optimization process.

The allocation of resources across HIV programmes depends upon the level of resources available. At 70% of the current budget, funding should be prioritized to HIV treatment and prevention of mother-to-child HIV. If funding were to increase beyond current levels, other interventions such as male circumcision and behavioural change should start to be considered (Masaki *et al.*, 2015).

---

available budget being known, and fixed, so cannot easily inform the allocation of resources between budget areas. Moreover, as everything is estimated at once, the full models need to be re-estimated once a new intervention or piece of information becomes available. Nevertheless, it is likely such approaches will become increasingly prominent as information and computing power further improves in future.

3. Discussion

Given the number of priority setting tools available, which should decision-makers use and when? The key strengths and limitations of each of the tools are summarized in Table 1. It can be seen that no single tool is superior in all respects, so the choice of tool depends on the decision problem being faced and the particular philosophy the decision-maker wishes to apply.

Table 1.	Key features of priority setting tools.

Tool	Strengths	Limitations
Cost–benefit analysis (CBA)	Can inform broad comparisons of programmes having both health and non-health benefits.	In practice, benefit measurement often focuses on productivity gains. Policy choices may lead to inequalities if WTP is constrained by the ability to pay. Assumes that the budget will be increased to accommodate the new programme.
Cost-effectiveness analysis (CEA)	Using a generic measure of health gain (i.e. QALYs or DALYs), comparisons can be made among all health programmes. The opportunity cost of new programmes, in terms of health forgone in displaced programmes, can be identified.	Benefits are restricted to health gains. Normally assumes all QALYs are of equal value.
Generalized CEA (GCEA)	An internationally standardized approach, allowing cross-country comparisons. Can provide "broad brush" recommendations to inform more specific local decision-making.	Assumes a "null alternative", of no current interventions/costs, which may not be realistic. DALYs focus on disability, not HRQoL, more generally. The decision-making threshold often used has been aspirational and does not reflect the budget constraint.
Extended cost-effectiveness analysis (ECEA)	Explicitly considers the impact of programmes on equity, alongside efficiency/cost-effectiveness.	Decision-makers still need to make their own trade-off between efficiency and equity.
Distributional cost-effectiveness analysis (DCEA)	Explicity considers the impact of programmes on defined subgroups of the population.	The relevant subpopulations need to be specified (e.g. socio-economic status, gender, age).

Table 1.　(*Continued*)

Tool	Strengths	Limitations
Multicriteria decision analysis (MCDA)	Enables the consideration of other relevant attributes of programmes in addition to their impact on health.	The opportunity cost of new programmes, in terms of health forgone in displaced programmes, is not identified. The relevant criteria, and the weights to be assigned to them, need to be specified.
Programme budgeting and marginal analysis (PBMA)	Enables the consideration of other relevant attributes of programmes in addition to their impact on health. Disinvestment options can be considered alongside new investments in programmes.	The relevant criteria, and the weights to be assigned to them, need to be specified.
Mathematical programming	Directly answers the overall problem of allocation given resources.	Information- and data-intensive, and must be re-estimated whenever something changes.

For example, if the interest is solely in health gain, perhaps because the decision-maker feels that this is the most legitimate use of the health care budget, then one of the forms of CEA could be the most useful tool. CEA could also be a favoured tool in situations where the decision-makers are conscious that they are operating with a fixed budget and are therefore keen to understand the opportunity cost, in forgone health, of the displacement of existing programmes when new ones are introduced.

On the other hand, if other benefits of programmes, beyond health gain, are considered relevant, a favoured tool could be CBA, if it could be appropriately applied using WTP as the measure of benefit. However, if CBA is used, it should be remembered that this approach implicitly assumes the budget will be increased to accommodate the new programme. If the budget is fixed, it is possible that programmes generating more health could be displaced. Also, if the major additional factor to be considered beyond health gain is equity, decision-makers should be wary of using CBA as it may lead to inequalities. In this situation, a preferred tool would be ECEA or DCEA. In addition, MCDA or PBMA could also be used to consider equity or other attributes of programmes beyond health gain. However, with MCDA it is not easy to identify opportunity costs if operating with a fixed budget and care has to be taken over how "cost" or "cost-effectiveness" is incorporated in the approach.

Nevertheless, MCDA and GCEA are useful "broad brush" approaches for considering a wide range of policy options, whereas the other forms of CEA and CBA usually involve a detailed analysis, meaning that it is only possible to consider a small number of alternative programmes/options in a given study.

Another possibility would be to use two or more of the tools in conjunction with one another. For example, in a project to determine which health programmes and treatments should be included in the health benefit package in Thailand, Youngkong *et al.* (2012) used MCDA to judge the broad acceptability of programmes against several general criteria, but then used CEA to assess the cost-effectiveness of a short list of treatment options in more detail.

Ultimately, however, all approaches are concerned with informing the allocation of the given available resources. If full information on the costs and consequences of all possible alternatives is available, and the budget is known, an approach of mathematical programming could inform the optimal allocation of all resources.

In conclusion, users of these approaches to priority setting should recognize that each approach has its strengths and weaknesses. The choice among them depends critically on the nature of the decision problem. In particular, the decision-maker needs to be clear on what is to be maximized (e.g. health or welfare more generally), whether there is a budget constraint and whether any other factors (e.g. equity) need to be considered.

References

Asaria, M., Griffin, S., Cookson, R. (2015). Distributional cost-effectiveness analysis: A tutorial. *Medical Decision Making: An International Journal of the Society for Medical Decision Making*. Available at: http://www.ncbi. nlm.nih.gov/pubmed/25908564 (Accessed: 6 November 2015).

Ball, H., Kemp, L., Fordham, R. (2009). Road testing programme budgeting and marginal analysis: Norfolk Mental Health pilot project. *Psychiatric Bulletin*, 33(4): 141–144. Available at: http://pb.rcpsych.org/content/33/4/141.short (Accessed: 2 December 2015).

Baltussen, R. *et al.* (2013). Balancing efficiency, equity and feasibility of HIV treatment in South Africa — Development of programmatic guidance. *Cost Effectiveness and Resource Allocation: C/E*, 11(1): 26. Available at: http://resource-allocation.biomedcentral.com/articles/10.1186/1478-7547-11-26 (Accessed: 2 December 2015).

Choices, N. (2013). The principles and values of the NHS in England — NHS choices. Available at: http://www.nhs.uk/NHSEngland/thenhs/about/Pages/nhscoreprinciples.aspx (Accessed: 2 December 2015).

Culyer, A. (2012a). Extra welfarism. In: Cookson, R., Claxton, K., eds., *The Humble Economist*. London: University of York and Office of Health Economics. p. 382.

Culyer, A. (2012b). In Cookson R., Claxton, K., eds., *The Humble Economist: Tony Culyer on Health, Health Care and Social Decision Making*. London: University of York and Office of Health Economics.

Drummond, M. F. *et al.* (2005). *Methods for the Economic Evaluation of Health Care Programmes*, 3rd edn. Oxford: OUP Oxford.

Drummond, M. *et al.* (2015). *Methods for the Economic Evaluation of Health Care Programmes*, 4th edn. Oxford: Oxford Medical Publications. Available at: http://www.amazon.co.uk/Methods-Economic-Evaluation-Health-Programmes/dp/0199665885 (Accessed: 27 November 2015).

Garber, A. M., Phelps, C. E. (1997). Economic foundations of cost-effectiveness analysis. *Journal of Health Economics*, 16(1): 1–31.

Hicks, J. R. (1939). The foundations of welfare economics. *The Economic Journal*, 49(196): 696–712.

Hutubessy, R., Chisholm, D., Edejer, T. T.-T. (2003). Generalized cost-effectiveness analysis for national-level priority-setting in the health sector. *Cost Effectiveness and Resource Allocation: C/E*, 1(1): 8. Available at: http://www.pubmedcentral.nih.gov/articlerender.fcgi?artid=320499&tool=pmcentrez&rendertype=abstract (Accessed: 2 December 2015).

Jehu-Appiah, C. *et al.* (2008). Balancing equity and efficiency in health priorities in Ghana: The use of multicriteria decision analysis. *Value in Health: The Journal of the International Society for Pharmacoeconomics and Outcomes Research*, 11(7): 1081–1087. Available at: http://www.ncbi.nlm.nih.gov/pubmed/19602214 (Accessed: 14 November 2015).

Kaldor, N. (1939). Welfare propositions of economics and interpersonal comparisons of utility. *The Economic Journal*, 49: 549–552.

Kularatna, S. _et al._ (2013). Health state valuation in low- and middle-income countries: A systematic review of the literature. _Value in Health: The Journal of the International Society for Pharmacoeconomics and Outcomes Research_, 16: 1091–1099. Available at: http://www.ispor.org/ValueInHealth/ShowValueIn Health.aspx?issue=97871C03-A964-43FE-88E8-6B1EC5CC0D24 (Accessed: 2 December 2015).

Maire, N. _et al._ (2011). Cost-effectiveness of the introduction of a pre-erythrocytic malaria vaccine into the expanded program on immunization in sub-Saharan Africa: Analysis of uncertainties using a stochastic individual-based simulation model of Plasmodium falciparum malaria. _Value in Health: The Journal of the International Society for Pharmacoeconomics and Outcomes Research_, 14(8): 1028–1038. Available at: http://www.sciencedirect.com/science/article/pii/S1098301511015269 (Accessed: 12 October 2015).

Marsh, K. _et al._ (2015). ISPOR MCDA task force: How best to use it in health care decision making. In _20th Annual International Meeting_, Philadelphia. Available at: http://www.ispor.org/taskforces/multi-criteria-decision-analysis-grp.asp.

Marsh, K., IJzerman M., Thokala P., _et al._ (2016). Multiple criteria decision analysis for health care decision making—emerging good practices: Report 2 of the ISPOR MCDA Emerging Good Practices Task Force. _Value Health_,19(2): 125–137.

Masaki, E. _et al._ (2015). _Zambia's HIV Response: Prioritized and Strategic Allocation of HIV Resources for Impact and Sustainability. Findings from the HIV Allocative Efficiency Study_, Washington D.C. Available at: https://kirby.unsw.edu.au/sites/default/files/hiv/attachment/Zambia HIV Allocative Efficiency Analysis Jan 2015.pdf (Accessed: 2 December 2015).

Mirelman, A. _et al._ (2012). Decision-making criteria among national policymakers in five countries: A discrete choice experiment eliciting relative preferences for equity and efficiency. _Value in Health: The Journal of the International Society for Pharmacoeconomics and Outcomes Research_, 15(3): 534–539. Available at: http://www.sciencedirect.com/science/article/pii/S1098301512014507 (Accessed: 10 August 2015).

Mitton, C. _et al._ (2011). Difficult decisions in times of constraint: Criteria based resource allocation in the Vancouver Coastal Health Authority. _BMC Health Services Research_, 11(1): 169. Available at: http://www.biomedcentral.com/1472-6963/11/169 (Accessed: 2 December 2015).

Murray, C. _et al._ (2000). Development of WHO guidelines on generalized cost-effectiveness analysis. _Health Economics_, 9: 235–251. Available at: http://

www.who.int/choice/publications/p_2000_guidelines_generalisedcea.pdf (Accessed: 2 December 2015).

Onwujekwe, O. E. *et al.* (1998). Willingness to pay for community-based ivermectin distribution: A study of three onchocerciasis-endemic communities in Nigeria. *Tropical Medicine & International Health*, 3(10): 802–808.

Pecenka, C. J. *et al.* (2015). Health gains and financial risk protection: An extended cost-effectiveness analysis of treatment and prevention of diarrhoea in Ethiopia. *BMJ Open*, 5(4): e006402.

Phillips, A. N. *et al.* (2014). Effectiveness and cost-effectiveness of potential responses to future high levels of transmitted HIV drug resistance in antiretroviral drug-naive populations beginning treatment: Modelling study and economic analysis. *The Lancet. HIV*, 1(2): e85–93. Available at: http://www.sciencedirect.com/science/article/pii/S2352301814700219 (Accessed: 18 November 2015).

Sculpher, P. M., Claxton, K. (2012). Real economics needs to reflect real decisions. *PharmacoEconomics*, 30(2): 133–136.

Sen, A. (1980). Equality of what? *The Tanner Lecture on Human Values*, I: 197–220.

Sen, A. K. (1993). Capability and well-being. In: Nussbaum, M. C., Sen, A. K., eds., *The Quality of Life*. Oxford: Clarendon Press. pp. 30–53.

Walker, S., Sculpher, M., Drummond, M. (2011). The methods of cost-effectiveness analysis to inform decisions about the use of health care interventions and programs. In: Glied, S., Smith, P. C., eds., *The Oxford Handbook of Health Economics*. Oxford: Oxford University Press. pp. 733–758.

Weinstein, M. C., Manning, W. G. (1997). Theoretical issues in cost-effectiveness analysis. *Journal of Health Economics*, 16(1): 121–128.

Woods, B. *et al.* (2015). *Country-Level Cost-Effectiveness Thresholds: Initial Estimates and the Need for Further Research*, York: Centre for Health Economics, University of York.

Youngkong, S. *et al.* (2012). Multicriteria decision analysis for including health interventions in the universal health coverage benefit package in Thailand. *Value in Health: The Journal of the International Society for Pharmacoeconomics and Outcomes Research*, 15(6): 961–970. Available at: http://www.sciencedirect.com/science/article/pii/S109830151201618X (Accessed: 2 December 2015).

Chapter 3

Cost-Effectiveness Thresholds: Guiding Health Care Spending for Population Health Improvement

Paul Revill, Jessica Ochalek, James Lomas, Ryota Nakamura,
Beth Woods, Alexandra Rollinger, Marc Suhrcke,
Mark Sculpher and Karl Claxton

Summary

Health care systems need to be designed in ways that support the generation and pooling of health care resources and the allocation of those resources, to deliver health benefits to constituent populations.

Cost-effectiveness analysis (CEA) is a set of tools that offer answers to the question: "How should available resources be allocated to maximize population health benefits?" Health benefits can be defined in various ways, but in most health care systems a principal objective is improvement in population health, as measured using metrics that combine the length and quality of life such as quality-adjusted life years (QALYs) gained or disability-adjusted life years (DALYs) averted.

CEA seeks to identify which drugs, health care technologies, programmes or other interventions offer greater health benefits when funded than health benefits forgone as resources are not then available to fund other priorities. In other words, CEA is about identifying those interventions that offer health benefits greater than their opportunity costs.

Applied CEA studies need to identify (i) the health benefits offered by any intervention being evaluated; (ii) the additional costs imposed on a

75

limited health care budget; and (iii) the opportunity costs (i.e. health benefits forgone) due to a commitment of resources to an intervention's provision. An intervention can only reasonably be deemed "cost-effective" if its benefits outweigh the opportunity costs of health benefits forgone.

The opportunity costs in terms of forgone health benefits are reflected in most CEAs by using a cost-effectiveness threshold (CET). The CET is a measure of the "cost per unit of health benefit (e.g. cost per QALY gained/DALY averted) forgone". Forgone health is the health associated with the interventions that would be displaced were the intervention under evaluation to be funded. For example, if the CET is $1,000 per QALY, then for every $1,000 spent on an intervention, this $1,000 can no longer be spent on other health care priorities resulting in a reduction in population health of 1 QALY.

In most health care systems, the appropriate CET is not readily apparent but depends upon the particular funding arrangements in the system and the health benefits of other interventions with claims on the limited resources available. The opportunity costs incurred in practice depend upon the marginal changes of what is funded when a new intervention is adopted. Hence, a suitable basis for CET measurement is the health gains produced by an additional dollar of health care spending, also called the "marginal productivity" of health care spending — the CET can then be expressed as the reciprocal (costs/unit of health gain) of the marginal productivity.

This approach to determining the CET to guide decisions requires explicit consideration of the "supply-side" ability of the health care system to generate health gains. It is grounded in the realities of the conditions and constraints prevailing in specific health care systems. A focus on the supply-side is required in order to meet the ultimate objective of maximizing population health benefits from within the resources available.

Frequently, in applied CEAs intended to inform resource allocations in low- and middle-income countries, the choice of CETs has not been conceived in this way. Instead, CETs have often represented expressions of value — by some party (individuals, international organizations; though often undefined) — without consideration of the constraints of health care systems.

One such example is the rule of thumb of 1–3 times gross domestic product per capita (GDP pc) in a country, initially set out by the World Health Organization. Another is CETs based upon individuals' statements about willingness to pay to improve their own health. This could be termed the "consumption value of health". It differs notably from the individuals' willingness to contribute to collective health care funding (to improve the health of others) or governments' abilities to generate health care resources. Such CETs are inherently "demand-side" concepts.

The danger of using CETs conceived only from the demand-side is there is no guarantee they will reflect opportunity costs. If they are set too low, CEAs may recommend interventions are not funded when they could generate population health benefits. In this case, there would be lost opportunities for health improvement. Alternatively, and more likely, if they are set too high, interventions could be recommended and funded that displace greater health benefits than they generate. Where evaluations focus on new and higher cost interventions, it is also likely these recommendations will exacerbate existing health inequalities.

The challenge for policymakers, budget holders and analysts alike is to determine and use CETs that reflect supply-side constraints. Unfortunately, however, there are few empirically estimated supply-side CETs. One exception is a study by Claxton *et al.* (2015a, 2015b) and Ochalek *et al.* (2018) that estimated the marginal productivity of the United Kingdom (UK) National Health Service (NHS) and produced a best estimate of the supply-side CET of £12,936, about half of UK GDP pc.

Two papers — Woods *et al.* (2016) and Ochalek *et al.* (2018) — have attempted to estimate supply-side CETs for a wide range of countries. Woods *et al.* (2016) extrapolate from the UK CET to estimate CETs for other countries in the world, based upon data on the relationship between country income and the willingness to pay for health gains. Ochalek *et al.* (2018) estimate CETs using published analyses estimating the causal effects of changes in health care spending on mortality and country-specific data to link this to other health outcomes. In both studies — although uncertainty bounds are wide — the estimated CETs are far lower than those previously posited by WHO: almost all are below 0.6 GDP pc in a country; see Section 4 for full results.

The funding channels for health care delivery in many countries are complex and, where budget silos exist, CETs for particular programmes (e.g. where donor funding is for that programme alone) may differ from CETs estimated based upon the marginal productivity of overall health care spending. However, this is an indication that allocations between disease programmes are unlikely to be optimal and, although at times there may be good reason for vertical funding, resources could be reallocated to where marginal productivity is the highest to improve population health.

It should be highlighted that the estimates of Woods *et al.* (2016) and Ochalek *et al.* (2018) are only one input to understanding true opportunity costs. Notable uncertainties in estimating the correct empirical supply-side CETs in low and middle-income countries persist (see Chapter 1 by Nakamura *et al.*) and further research in this area would be very valuable. The estimates can be used to inform health care spending decisions but estimates from within countries (rather than relying on cross-country estimation) would help to corroborate or provide basis for the revision of these estimates. In all cases, policymakers, budget holders and analysts should carefully consider the other claims on limited resources as well as their likely opportunity costs when informing or making resource allocation decisions.

1. Part 1: Introduction

Countries around the world have to make difficult decisions as to how health care is financed and scarce available resources are allocated to meet the health needs of their populations. The tools of economic evaluation can help to inform resource allocation decisions based upon comparison of the costs and consequences of alternative policy choices. Invariably, whether in Switzerland or Swaziland, the range of interventions that could offer health benefits to patients is beyond what can feasibly be funded from within the available resources. Choices therefore need to be made on the basis of the costs and benefits associated with alternative health care interventions and the *opportunity costs* of committing resources to those interventions — in terms of what benefits those resources could generate if used for alternatives priorities.

Economic evaluation is a set of tools that can be used to inform which interventions should be funded. A common approach to economic evaluation is to use incremental cost-effectiveness analysis (CEA) that compares the incremental costs (Δcosts) and incremental health benefits (Δhealth) of an intervention to other comparators. Results can then be expressed as an incremental cost-effectiveness ratio (ICER) (Δcost/Δhealth), giving the cost-per-unit of health gain provided by the intervention. Health benefits are often represented in the form of quality-adjusted life years (QALYs) gained or disability-adjusted life years (DALYs) averted. To determine whether an ICER offers value for money, and can be justifiably deemed "cost-effective", requires comparison to the opportunity costs of what would have to be given up if the intervention were funded. These are typically represented by a cost-effectiveness threshold (CET).

Notable research efforts have been committed to better understanding and measuring of the health benefits of alternative interventions in low- and middle-income country settings, and similarly although less so their associated costs. In contrast, there have been few studies to inform the choice of CETs — even though this is a critical component of cost-effectiveness assessments. The danger of applying a CET that is too low for any particular context is that an intervention may not be adopted that offers population health gains; whereas, and perhaps more likely, applying a CET that is too high risks interventions being adopted that displace/forgo more health gains than they generate. The choice of CET is therefore critical for efficient allocation of scarce health care resources. The choice ultimately determines which interventions are provided, to whom in the population, and who goes without needed — indeed often lifesaving — health care.

This chapter was initially a report by the Centre for Health Economics, University of York, for the International Decision Support Initiative (iDSI) and informs policymakers (Part 2) and analysts/economic evaluation practitioners (Part 3) on alternative conceptualizations for CETs, and the assumptions underpinning, and implications, of these conceptualizations; and provides estimates of CETs that can be used in applied studies in a wide range of jurisdictions, for different kinds of decisions. Recommendations for policymakers and analysts/practitioners on the interpretation and presentation of findings from CEA studies are then presented (Part 4).

2. Part 2. Deciding When to Invest in Health Care Interventions — A Guide for Policymakers

2.1. Who is this guide for?

This guide (Part 2) is intended to inform budget holders and policymakers in a variety of institutions whose decisions have implications for health care resource allocation in low- and middle-income countries. Such institutions, and the types of decisions with which they are faced, include the following:

- Ministry of Health budget and planning departments — deciding how much of their available budgets to allocate to various departments, disease programmes, providers (e.g. central hospitals, regions, districts).
- Ministry of Health and other partner institutions — deciding upon what interventions to include in basic or essential health care packages.
- Disease programmes (e.g. a HIV programme) — allocating their budgets across various technologies, drugs and interventions within their domain.
- Social health and private insurance schemes — determining the interventions for which enrollees will be covered or reimbursed.
- Health technology assessment (HTA) agencies — assessing which drugs, technologies and interventions should be funded by the public payer.
- International funders (donors) or non-governmental organizations — deciding what types of health care provision to fund; either through domestic institutions or vertically (e.g. through their own or other non-governmental providers).
- International funders and NGOs — deciding how to allocate their resources across countries.

The decisions made therefore relate to investments in different types of drugs, technologies, programmes or activities (herein referred to collectively as "interventions") by a range of institutions for which a central objective can be regarded as improvement in population health.

2.2. What is the challenge facing policymakers and budget holders?

Distinction can be made between revenue generation and pooling for health care provision, and the allocation of prepaid and pooled available resources across competing priorities. Whereas health care systems differ in how these primary roles are carried out, particularly the extent to which collective health care is funded and the role of governments as single payers in the system, ultimately all health care systems exist around a central goal to bring about improvements in population health. The central resource allocation challenge then is to respond to the question "How should available resources be allocated so as to maximize health improvement in the population?". Although individual and collective values may lead some health care systems to also emphasize additional objectives (e.g. financial protection and equity-related concerns, see below), it is a reasonable assertion that health improvement is central to all.

Policymakers and budget holders may sit in different institutions and face different kinds of decisions (as shown above). Insofar, as their primary constituency includes that population of a jurisdiction with entitlement to health care provision — determined through some mandated political process — all decision-makers should have responsibility toward and should be accountable to the population affected by their decisions, including those who benefit from their decisions and those who lose out. Given the primacy of public sector payers in most health care systems, a useful benchmark to assess the value for money of any health care expenditure is therefore the health gains that could be attained with a change in the collective public health care budget (i.e. the marginal productivity of public health care spending).

A useful comparison for institutions that are not the primary organizations involved in the delivery of health care in a country, is to assess whether the interventions they are considering funding would have a greater or lower marginal productivity (i.e. generate more or fewer health gains per dollar spent) than if the funds were channeled into general public sector health care provision. If marginal productivity is higher, there may be a good reason to have or maintain vertical funding. However, if this is not the case, vertical funding is unlikely to be the optimal way to generate health gains and questions may be raised about the sustainability of such funding arrangements. Similarly, when the funding decision facing an organization (e.g. an international donor) is which jurisdiction to commit additional resources to, then the marginal productivities of different jurisdictions can be compared to assess in which locality additional spending would likely generate greatest health improvement.

2.3. What assessments are required when choosing a cost-effectiveness threshold for use within a jurisdiction or by an organization?

Good resource allocation decisions are those that best meet agreed social objectives e.g. using currently available resources. In health care, where the central objective is improvement in "population health", a good decision should involve comparing the additional health benefits of an intervention with the health likely to be lost elsewhere as a consequence of any additional costs. This should also therefore be the aim of cost-effectiveness analysis and other forms of economic evaluation. To be consistent with actions likely to lead to population health improvement, a cost-effectiveness threshold should reflect these health opportunity costs resulting from "supply-side" constraints in the ability of a health care system to generate health improvement.

A variety of methods may be used to determine an appropriate CET that reflects heath opportunity costs resulting from supply-side constraints. In essence, the aim is to have reasonable understanding of the "marginal productivity" of the health care system. This tells us how much health is expected to be generated (additional QALYs gained/DALYs averted) for a given additional expenditure, at the margin, and hence, how much health is expected to be foregone if the resource in question is spent on a new intervention. The possible methods and accompanying available estimates of CETs for use in different jurisdictions are presented in the next section. However, it is first useful to contrast these methods with some other ("demand-side") bases for CETs which have been used and which do not necessarily reflect opportunity costs.

2.4. Contrasting demand-side and supply-side estimates of CETs

Health opportunity costs, which represent the most suitable basis to determine CETs for use in resource allocation decisions related to constrained health care budgets, can be contrasted with opportunity costs that fall on other forms of consumption. These can include private consumption and consumption related to other forms of collective social expenditures (e.g. funded through tax receipts) for which the primary purpose is societal objectives other than health, such as government expenditures in other sectors including education or policing.

Particular confusion has arisen in the appropriate basis for estimating CETs, as CETs applied in practice have typically been based upon individuals' expressions of willingness to pay to improve (or prevent reduction of) their own health — so called "willingness to pay" for health improvement.

It should be noted that individuals' willingness to pay to improve their own health may be different from their willingness to pay into collective health care spending (for which others in the population also benefit). It may also not reflect the available budgets — and the spending opportunities associated with these budgets — that result from the government/public payers' ability to generate and pool collective health care resources. Willingness to pay is a "demand-side" approach to valuing health whereas a "supply-side" concept is required to reflect what the real health care system is producing from the real budget constraint.

However, CETs have not generally been set to reflect health opportunity costs resulting from limited available health care budgets. For instance, values of £20,000–30,000 and US$50,000 per QALY have commonly been applied in the United Kingdom and United States, respectively, without clear rational but with some sense they reflect the consumption value of health (Guide to the methods of technology appraisal 2013, 2013; Neumann et al., 2014). In low and middle income countries, the World Health Organization (WHO) previously recommended thresholds of 1–3 times gross domestic product (GDP) per capita — seemingly on the basis of recommendations from the "Commission on Macroeconomics and Health" report from 2001, although it has since stepped away from this recommendation (Bertram et al., 2016).

It is not very clear what the basis of the 1–3 times GDP CETs really then is and, rather than representing any real notion of value, they may simply be expressions of aspiration. However, the consequence of their use if they are inappropriate measures of the health opportunity cost is, they are likely to reduce, rather than increase, population health. Supply-side measures of CETs are instead required.

2.5. What estimates of suitable thresholds for particular jurisdictions or organizations are available?

There are still worryingly few estimates of supply-side cost-effectiveness thresholds that exist at all across different jurisdictions. Although interest in estimating specific supply-side CETs has increased only very recently, to date few estimates based on within country data are available. One, from the UK, provides an estimated CET based upon thorough analysis of country programmatic spending data and resulting health outcomes. Claxton et al. (2015a) estimated a causal link between changes in expenditure and mortality outcomes using data on different disease areas (programme budget categories). Additional information about the age and gender of the patient population was used to get from mortality to survival effects, and finally, data on health-related quality of life (HRQoL) norms by age, gender and disease were used to obtain morbidity effects. The research resulted in an estimated CET of £12,936 per QALY for 2008/9. It can be noted this is well below 1 times GDP per capita, which was around £26,000 at that time.

A recent study, Woods et al. (2016), uses the Claxton et al. (2015a, 2015b) estimate and extrapolates to other countries using international income elasticities of the value of health. The approach relies upon some core assumptions set out fully in the paper, but it is not clear a priori whether these would likely lead to over- or under-estimates of CETs.

Woods et al. (2016) show opportunity costs are likely to be particularly high, and CETs low as a proportion of GDP per capita, in lower income countries. For instance, the range of CET estimates for Ethiopia, a country with a 2013 GDP pc of US$505, is $10–255 (2–50% GDP pc), and for Indonesia, with a 2013 GDP pc of US$3,457, is $472–1,786 (14–51%

GDP pc). Again, this is in stark contrast to the 1–3 times GDP per capita rule of thumb.

Ochalek *et al.* (2018) employ a different approach, and provide a framework for generating country-level CETs using existing published cross-country estimates of the mortality effect of health expenditure. The estimation strategy is based on a published study (Bokhari *et al.*, 2007), which is expanded upon using measures of mortality, survival and disability outcomes, reflecting the demographic and other characteristics of each LMIC.

The results also suggest that CETs representing likely health opportunity costs tend to be well below national GDP per capita in a large range of countries, although specific estimates of CETs depend upon the particular countries. For instance, using the year 2015 values, CET estimates in Ethiopia are $167–221 (27–36%) of GDP pc = US$619 in 2015, and in Indonesia are $535–778 of 2015 GDP pc = US$3,346).

Supply-side CET estimates from the Woods *et al.* (2016) and Ochalek *et al.* (2018) studies for a full range of countries are provided in Appendix 1.

2.6. What CETs should be used if interventions draw upon resources not generally available for use across the whole health sector?

In many cases, resources committed to particular interventions or to disease programmes (e.g. a country's HIV programme), come from sources other than domestic collectively funded health care budgets (e.g. international donors and non-governmental organizations). This funding is often "vertical" and therefore has to be spent on a specific intervention or programme. This funding does not therefore directly impose health opportunity costs on the country's limited budgets. In these cases, a suitable CET to inform decisions within such a budget silo may differ from the appropriate CET to inform the allocation of overall collective health care funds.

However, it should be noted that external funds could also be used for other purposes — in the same jurisdiction or even in other jurisdictions. In this sense, they do incur health opportunity costs. For international funding decisions, donors can maximize the health gains resulting from their expenditures by committing resources to where the opportunity cost is likely to be highest (i.e. CET's lowest). The way in which external resource commitments are made requires scrutiny in this respect.

2.7. Are there other judgements, in addition to supply-side-based CETs, that are required when deciding whether to invest in particular interventions?

Using supply-side CETs to inform resource allocation decisions assumes that all the benefits of interventions are health benefits and that all the costs fall on health care spending. However, other costs and consequences of interventions may also be relevant in health care decision-making. They include wider impacts on families, communities and other sectors of the economy (e.g. on educational outcomes). They may also include other (direct and indirect) costs (or savings) that are incurred in gaining access to an intervention or that result from associated health outcomes. For instance, these may include direct costs falling on individuals and families in accessing health interventions (e.g. travel, out-of-pocket and care costs), indirect time costs (e.g. loss of wages in individuals and informal carers), as well as costs falling on other sectors of the economy. Finally, how health effects are distributed within a given jurisdiction, e.g. between the rich and the poor, could be of particular concern in many countries.

Non-health effects and costs that fall outside the health budget may be important because alternative interventions may result in different non-health effects that have social value. It is therefore useful, and even in some cases imperative, for policymakers to assess these when making decisions. In principle, non-health and societal impacts could be incorporated in a health economic evaluation. However, there remain methodological challenges in doing so, and it requires two things: firstly, knowledge of trade-offs between non-health and health benefits; and, secondly, knowledge and justification for determining who should make these trade-offs.

Deciding which non-health effects and which costs that fall outside the health budget should be included in primary analyses and who should trade-off health and non-health costs and benefits is therefore troublesome. Since there is no consensus on how to codify societal preferences, conflicts between different elements of social value may result. A particular concern is that health resources, primarily intended to generate "health", may be used to meet other objectives that society may or may not deem to be as valuable as health itself.

Nevertheless, policymakers may wish to consider such non-health effects in the process of making their prioritization decisions.

3. Part 3: Informing Health Care Investment Decisions — A Guide for Analysts

3.1. Who is this guide for?

This guide (Part 3) is intended for researchers and applied analysts working on economic evaluation studies to inform health care resource allocation decisions with implications in low- and middle-income countries. The possible users of such studies are those listed in Part 2.

A large number of economic evaluation studies are produced to guide decisions in low- and middle-income countries. Some of these are well-resourced and produced by analysts familiar with the leading and most technical of available methods. However, others are less well-resourced and need to guide decisions under much tighter time and financial constraints. The capacity for some analysts to keep pace with the changes in methods may also be limited.

It is hoped that this guide will represent a first port of call for analysts looking for information on which cost-effectiveness thresholds they can use to inform decisions in their jurisdiction. It contains useful information for both well-resourced analyses and also studies operating within tighter resource and capacity constraints but nonetheless seeks to usefully inform policymaking.

3.2. What types of decisions does this guide inform?

Cost-effectiveness thresholds (CETs can inform investments in alternative clinical and other health interventions. They can also inform much larger shifts in health care funding, such as in the design of health benefits packages or in changing the balance of funding between programmes (e.g. between hospital-based and primary health care, or by disease programme).

Increasingly, economic evaluation studies are used to inform a wider range of decisions and, as central benchmarks of value in health care systems. CETs also have an important role for informing investments for which impacts on population health are less immediately clear. Examples include, the use of economic evaluation to inform investments in research and efforts to reduce decision uncertainty (e.g. through value of information analysis) or to strengthen health care systems and improve the uptake of clinical interventions (e.g. using value of implementation analysis) (Fenwick *et al.*, 2008).

3.3. The important distinction between "demand-side" and "supply-side" CETs

An important distinction must be made between alternative conceptual bases for CETs. In the past, many CETs used in applied analyses for low- and middle-income countries were detached from appropriate normative and theoretical bases for resource allocation in the context of constraints, and their impacts on population health outcomes were consequentially unclear.

Particular distinction can be made between "demand-side" and "supply-side" notions of CETs.

Various notions have been put forth to motivate the choice of CETs. In general, these have been based upon expressions of the value of health (from various constituents — individuals, international organizations, doctors/experts). These value-based estimates are detached from an assessment of the capacity of health care systems to deliver interventions to a level that would be consistent with these expressions of value (i.e. they are "demand-side" driven, without consideration of supply). In particular, they are detached from constraints on the ability of health care systems to raise money.

In contrast, and more recently, greater attention has been paid to the necessity of grounding CETs in "supply-side" assessments of the health benefits of competing calls on constrained health care budgets. In particular, where the objective is improvement in overall population health, an intervention should only be recommended for funding where a commitment of resources to that intervention will produce health benefits exceeding those displaced or forgone (i.e. opportunity costs) as a result of those resources becoming unavailable for the funding of other priorities (Newall *et al.*, 2014; Revill *et al.*, 2014a, 2014b; Marseille *et al.*, 2015). To do otherwise, and apply demand-side CETs, risks both reducing population health and increasing health inequalities (because interventions only likely to be accessible to a subsection of the population in need are likely to be prioritized).

It is therefore crucial for analysts to be aware of the conceptual/ theoretical bases of alternative possible CETs they may encounter. Some CET estimates are grounded in demand-side notions of the value of health, and are inappropriate to inform allocation of constrained resources; whereas others (although currently, fewer) are based upon supply-side estimates of opportunity costs.

The following sub-sections highlight widely encountered demand- and supply-side estimates, and summarize the current state-of-knowledge on available supply-side estimates for use in a wide range of jurisdictions.

3.4. What "demand-side" CETs exist and have been used?

There are at least four widely encountered bases for CETs that predominantly rely on demand-side notions of value:

- Historical precedents of $50k and £20–30k per QALY thresholds applied in the United States and United Kingdom, respectively, and similar corresponding levels used in other countries (Guide to the methods of technology appraisal 2013, 2013; Neumann *et al.*, 2014).
- 1–3 times gross domestic product (GDP) per capita (pc) thresholds, previously recommended by the World Health Organization (WHO) and used in generalized cost-effectiveness analyses (GCEA) and other studies (Leech *et al.*, 2018).
- Stated preference elicitation studies of individuals' willingness to spend money to improve their own health (or reduce losses in health).

- Revealed preference elicitation studies of individuals' willingness to spend money to improve their own health (or reduce losses in health).

3.4.1. $50k and £30k per QALY CETs

In the United States, a CET of $50,000 per life year gained popularity in the 1990s. The true source of this benchmark is unknown and it was never endorsed by the Panel on Cost-Effectiveness in Health and Medicine who met in 1996 (Grosse, 2008). However, in a meta-analytic review of end-stage renal disease studies from 1968–1998, it was revealed this CET had morphed into one of $50k per QALY gained and was being widely applied in studies (Winkelmayer et al., 2002). Grosse (2008) concluded that the "$50,000 criterion is arbitrary and owes more to being a round number than to a well-formulated justification for a specific dollar value."

Similarly, in the United Kingdom, a CET range of £20,000 to £30,000 per QALY has been used by the National Institute for Health and Care Excellence (NICE) since 2004 (Guide to the methods of technology appraisal 2013, 2013). This range was used in decisions made prior to 2004, but is widely recognized (including by NICE) as a benchmark lacking empirical foundation (Claxton et al., 2015b).

In summary, these values were based on precedent rather than having a clear scientific basis.

3.4.2. CETs 1–3 times GDP per capita in a country

Arguably the most well-known and widely applied "demand-side" CETs in low- and middle-income country are GDP pc-based thresholds adopted by the World Health Organization for use alongside WHO–CHOICE.

Initially published in the Commission on Macroeconomics and Health report from 2001, the true origins of these CETs are unclear, but may have been derived from figures extrapolated using US-based value of a statistical life (VSL) of $6.3 million from 1997 (See below: *Revealed preferences: The value of a statistical life studies.*) However, these estimates were intended to inform decisions regarding overall investments in health care. The use of these thresholds when assessing the value of individual interventions from with constrained budgets is not consistent with population health improvement as they do not reflect the opportunity costs that are imposed on health care systems.

3.4.3. *Stated preferences: Social value of a QALY studies*

The Health Intervention and Technology Assessment Program (HITAP) in Thailand, which was established in 2007, uses a CET based on the estimates of willingness to pay (WTP) for health. This CET is intended to represent the "social valuation" of health versus other consumption and was estimated through stated preferences. This research, published in 2009, estimated the social value of a QALY through the assessment of utilities (through time trade-off (TTO)) and WTP. On the back of this work, the Health Economic Working Group under the Subcommittee for Development of the National List of Essential Drugs and the Subcommittee for Development of the Health Benefit Package and Service Delivery of the NHSO recommended a ceiling CET of 1 times GDP per capita or 120,000 THB per QALY gained (Shiroiwa *et al.*, 2010). The organization has continued to evolve and conduct research, and the threshold was raised to ฿160,000 per QALY in 2013 (Ryen and Svensson, 2014). Although empirically derived, these estimates are aspirational, representing a notion of what ought to be, and should not be mistaken for "supply-side" CETs.

3.4.4. *Revealed preferences: The value of a statistical life studies*

CETs also exist which are based on value of a statistical life studies (VSL). VSL estimates can be derived through both revealed and stated preference studies. The former involves observing decisions relating to mortality risks and peoples' willingness to pay to avoid risk, while the latter asks respondents to choose between hypothetical risk scenarios. Hirth *et al.* (2000) meta-analyzed various VSL estimates and used quality of life weights from the Beaver Dam Health Outcomes study to generate a QALY valuation for the US of $265,000 in 1997. This is thought to be the basis of the estimates from the 2001 WHO Commission on Macroeconomics and Health report that forms the foundation of the 1–3 times GDP per capita CETs.

3.5. What "supply-side" thresholds exist and can be used?

There has been a paucity of supply-side estimates of cost-effectiveness thresholds (i.e. reflecting the marginal productivity of health care systems) in both high- and low-/middle-income countries settings alike. Currently, there are only five known recent sources of supply-side CET estimates that can be used directly in economics evaluations:

- Claxton *et al.* (2015b) — an estimate of the marginal productivity of the UK National Health Service (NHS);
- Woods *et al.* (2015) — which extrapolates this estimate to other countries;
- Ochalek *et al.* (2018) — provides alternative supply-side estimates for a wide range of countries;
- Vallejo-Torres *et al.* (2016) — an estimate of the CET for the Spanish NHS;
- Edney *et al.* (2018) — an estimate of the reference ICER for Australia.

3.5.1. *Claxton* et al. *(2015a)*

Claxton *et al.* (2015a) provided the first example of a supply-side-based CET. The authors make use of the rich data available in the UK on expenditure and mortality outcomes in different disease areas (programme budget categories), as well as health related quality of life (HRQoL) norms by age and gender and HRQoL associated with different diseases. The study estimates the effect of changes in spending on mortality outcomes by exploiting area-level variation in these variables and employing an instrumental variable (IV) approach to control for endogeneity (e.g. the possibility that mortality determines health care expenditures as well as being improved by it). From mortality outcomes, the authors determined deaths averted, and using additional information about the age and gender of the patient population, they determined the survival effects of changes in spending. With additional available information about HRQoL norms by age and gender and HRQoL associated with different diseases, the authors were able to determine the morbidity effects of changes in expenditure. Using the preferred set of assumptions, including using the effect of expenditure on mortality as a surrogate for the effect of expenditure on morbidity, the authors estimated a cost effectiveness threshold for 2008/9 of £12,936 per QALY.

3.5.2. *Woods* et al. *(2015, 2016)*

Woods *et al.* (2015, 2016) use the Claxton *et al.* (2015a, 2015b) estimate and extrapolates this to other countries using information from the literature relating country income to willingness to pay for mortality risk reductions. The validity of this work hinges upon the validity of the UK estimate of a supply-side CET and the validity of previous works looking at the relationship between country income and the value of a statistical life. It also rests upon two assumptions: (i) the ratio of the supply-side CET to the demand-side CET is constant across countries and (ii) the relationship between country income and the value of a statistical life can be translated directly to the relationship between country income and the value of a QALY. They show that CETs based on opportunity costs are likely much lower than those often used in decision-making in LMICs.

3.5.3. *Ochalek* et al. *(2018)*

Ochalek *et al.* (2018) take advantage of econometric methods to control for endogeneity in the estimation of the mortality effects of changes in expenditure when using cross-country data. Using Bokhari *et al.* (2007), the authors show how cross-country econometric models can be used as an input for calculating country-specific CETs through analysis of other health outcomes, use of additional data and explicit modelling assumptions. Bokhari *et al.* (2007), using a cross-section of 127 countries from 2000, model the role of donor funding explicitly and allow for the endogeneity of key inputs into the health production function. Using the framework they have developed, and applying it to results from Bokhari *et al.* (2007), Ochalek *et al.* (2018) estimate a range of CETs for each country. They find that the upper estimate of the range for nearly every country falls below 3 times GDP per capita, and is below 1 times GDP per capita for the vast majority of countries.

Thus, applying these generic "rules of thumb" can do more harm than good: when interventions with ICERs below 1 times GDP per capita but above the true "supply-side" CET are implemented, they will displace more health than they generate, resulting in a net health loss.

More recently, Vallejo-Torres *et al.* (2016) and Edney *et al.* (2018) estimate, and Thokala *et al.* (2018) summarise, supply-side CETs using within-country data for Australia and Spain, respectively. However, to date, no such within country estimates are available in LMICs.

4. Part 4. A Summary of the Evidence on Supply-Side Cost-Effectiveness Thresholds

Table 1 presents estimates of cost-effectiveness thresholds for a selected range of countries from Woods *et al.* (2015; CETs presented in 2013 US\$) and Ochalek *et al.* (2018; CETs 2000 US\$). Results from all countries from both studies are presented in the Appendix 1.

It is clear that in all countries the most likely CETs based upon empirical evidence are well below the 1–3 times GDP pc CETs that have frequently been applied to date in low- and middle-income countries. In fact, with only a few exceptions, the upper-bound estimates are below 60% of GDP pc, particularly in those countries with the lowest levels of per capita income. The implication is that use of CETs to inform resource

Table 1. Supply-side cost-effectiveness threshold estimates for selected countries.

Country	GDP pc, 2013	Woods *et al.* (2015) threshold range, 2013 US\$	Threshold as a % of GDP	GDP pc, 2015	Ochalek *et al.* (2018) threshold range, 2015 US\$	Threshold as a % of GDP
Brazil	\$11208	\$2393–7544	21–67%	\$8,539	\$6048–9318	71–109%
Ethiopia	\$505	\$10–255	2–50%	\$619	\$167–221	27–36%
India	\$1499	\$115–770	8–51%	\$1,598	\$264–363	17–23%
Indonesia	\$3475	\$472–1786	14–51%	\$3,346	\$535–778	16–23%
Kazakhstan	\$13610	\$4485–8018	33–59%	\$10,510	\$3734–5809	36–55%
Malawi	\$226	\$3–116	1–51%	\$372	\$124–164	33–44%
Nepal	\$694	\$22–357	3–51%	\$743	\$206–291	28–39%
Thailand	\$5779	\$1181–3943	20–68%	\$5,815	\$4069–6507	70–112%
Vietnam	\$1911	\$144–982	8–51%	\$2,111	\$1198–1813	57–86%

allocation that are above these levels will likely reduce overall population health and may well exacerbate health inequalities.

This pattern can also be seen graphically. In Figure 1, the estimates from Woods *et al.* (2016) are inflated by countries' GDP pc growth (GDP pc 2015/GDP pc 2013) for comparability with Ochalek *et al.* (2018). In all but a few cases the CET estimates are below the line of 1 times GDP per capita; although uncertainty bounds are nevertheless wide.

These estimates are in no way intended to provide "final answers" to what supply-side CETs are appropriate for different countries. The estimates presented may be considered as plausible values and input to inform resource allocation decisions. More research in this area is urgently needed (as Nakamura *et al.* in Chapter 1 underline), and particularly estimates based on *within* country data which clearly identify the value of competing claims on limited budgets, would be extremely valuable.

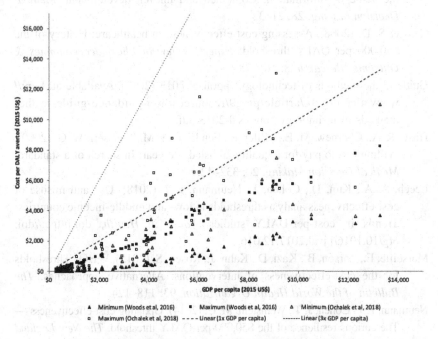

Figure 1. Minimum and maximum costs per DALY averted.

References

Bokhari, F. A. S., Gai, Y., Gottret, P. (2007). Government health expenditures and health outcomes. *Health Econ*, 16: 257–273.

Bertram, M. Y. *et al.* (2016). Policy & practice cost–effectiveness thresholds: Pros and cons thresholds based on gross domestic product. *Bulletin of the World Health Organization*, 94: 925–930.

Claxton, K. *et al.* (2015a). Methods for the estimation of the National Institute for Health and Care Excellence cost-effectiveness threshold. *Health Technology Assessment*, 19: 1–503, v–vi.

Claxton, K., Sculpher, M., Palmer, S., Culyer, A. J. (2015b). Causes for concern: Is NICE failing to uphold its responsibilities to all NHS patients? *Health Econ*, 24: 1–7.

Edney, L. C., Haji Ali Afzali, H., Cheng, T. C., Karnon, J. (2018). Estimating the reference incremental cost-effectiveness ratio for the Australian health system. *Pharmacoeconomics*, doi:10.1007/s40273-017-0585-2.

Fenwick, E., Claxton, K., Sculpher, M. (2008). The value of implementation and the value of information: Combined and uneven development. *Medical Decision Making*, 28: 21–32.

Grosse, S. D. (2008). Assessing cost-effectiveness in healthcare: History of the $50,000 per QALY threshold. *Expert Review of Pharmacoeconomics & Outcomes Research*, 8: 165–78.

Guide to the methods of technology appraisal 2013 (2013). Available at: http://www.nice.org.uk/article/pmg9/resources/non-guidance-guide-to-the-methods-of-technology-appraisal-2013-pdf.

Hirth, R. A., Chernew, M. E., Miller, E., Fendrick, A. M., Weissert, W. G. (2000). Willingness to pay for a quality-adjusted life year: In search of a standard. *Medical Decision Making*, 20: 332–42.

Leech, A. A., Kim, D., Cohen, J., Neumann, P. J. (2018). Use and misuse of cost-effectiveness analysis thresholds in low- and middle-income countries: Trends in cost-per-DALY studies. *Value in Health*, doi:https://doi.org/10.1016/j.jval.2017.12.016.

Marseille, E., Larson, B., Kazi, D., Kahn, J., Rosen, S. (2015). WHO | Thresholds for the cost-effectiveness of interventions: Alternative approaches. *The Bulletin of the World Health Organization*, 93: 118–124.

Neumann, P. J., Cohen, J. T., Weinstein, M. C. (2014). Updating cost-effectiveness — The curious resilience of the $50,000-per-QALY threshold. *The New England Journal of Medicine*, 371: 796–7.

Newall, A. T., Jit, M., Hutubessy, R. (2014). Are current cost-effectiveness thresholds for low- and middle-income countries useful? Examples from the world of vaccines. *Pharmacoeconomics*, 32: 525–31.

Ochalek, J. *et al.* (2018). Estimating health opportunity costs in low-income and middle-income countries: A novel approach and evidence from cross-country data. *BMJ Global Health*, 3(6): pp. e000964, doi:https://doi.org/10.1136/bmjgh-2018-000964.

Revill, P., Asaria, M., Phillips, A., Gibb, D. M., Gilks, C. (2014a). WHO decides what is fair? International HIV treatment guidelines, social value judgements and equitable provision of lifesaving antiretroviral therapy. Discussion Paper. CHE Research Paper. York, UK: Centre for Health Economics, University of York.

Revill, P. *et al.* (2014b). Using cost-effectiveness thresholds to determine value for money in low- and middle-income country healthcare systems: Are current international norms fit for purpose? Available at: https://www.york.ac.uk/media/che/documents/papers/researchpapers/CHERP98_costeffectiveness_thresholds_value_low_middle_income_countries.pdf.

Ryen, L., Svensson, M. (2014). The willingness to pay for a quality adjusted life year: A review of the empirical literature. *Health Econ*, doi:10.1002/hec.3085.

Shiroiwa, T. *et al.* (2010). International survey on willingness-to-pay (WTP) for one additional QALY gained: What is the threshold of cost effectiveness? *Health Econ*, 19: 422–37.

Thokala, P., Ochalek, J., Leech, A. A., Tong, T. (2018). Cost-effectiveness thresholds: The past, the present and the future. *Pharmacoeconomics*, doi:10.1007/s40273-017-0606-1.

Vallejo-Torres, L., García-Lorenzo, B., Serrano-Aguilar, P. (2016). *Estimating a cost-effectiveness threshold for the Spanish NHS*. Available at: http://documentos.fedea.net/pubs/eee/eee2016-22.pdf.

Winkelmayer, W. C., Weinstein, M. C., Mittleman, M. A., Glynn, R. J., Pliskin, J. S. (2002). Health economic evaluations: The special case of end-stage renal disease treatment. *Medical Decision Making*, 22: 417–30.

Woods, B., Revill, P., Sculpher, M., Claxton, K. (2015). *Country-Level Cost-Effectiveness Thresholds: Initial Estimates and the Need for Further Research*. York: Center for Health Economics, University of York.

Woods, B., Revill, P., Sculpher, M., Claxton, K. (2016). Country-level cost-effectiveness thresholds: Initial estimates and the need for further research. *Value in Health*, 19: 929–935.

Chapter 4

Fairer Decisions, Better Health for All: Health Equity and Cost-Effectiveness Analysis

Andrew J. Mirelman, Miqdad Asaria, Bryony Dawkins, Susan Griffin and Richard Cookson

Abstract

This chapter provides an introduction to methods for using cost-effectiveness analysis (CEA) to address health equity concerns, with applications to different country settings. These methods can provide information about the impacts of health investment decisions on inequalities in health and non-health outcomes, and they provide information about the trade-offs that sometimes arise between improving total health and reducing health inequalities. We distinguish two general ways of using CEA to address health equity concerns: (1) equity impact analysis, which quantifies the distribution of costs and effects by equity-relevant variables and (2) equity trade-off analysis, which quantifies the trade-offs between improving total health and other equity objectives. We hope this chapter will raise awareness of the practical tools of CEA that are now available to help give health care and public health policymakers a better understanding of who gains and who loses when making decisions.

1. Introduction

Health equity has risen to prominence on policy agendas, in the wake of the universal health coverage movement (Gwatkin and Ergo, 2011; Asada *et al.*, 2014; Cotlear *et al.*, 2015; Wagstaff *et al.*, 2016) and landmark international reports on inequality in health (Marmot *et al.*, 2008, 2012) and health care (WHO, 2014). However, the cost-effectiveness studies that are routinely used across the globe to inform decision-making in health care and public health rarely provide information about who gains and who loses from alternative decisions (Sassi *et al.*, 2001; Cookson *et al.*, 2009; Culyer, 2012; Johri and Norheim, 2012; Daniels *et al.*, 2016).

Equally, most studies of health equity lack a cost-effectiveness perspective. A cost-effectiveness perspective can enhance health equity research in two important ways. First, as well as understanding the nature and causes of health inequalities, decision-makers need to know how the policy options are likely to impact health inequalities. This requires not only epidemiological analysis of the risk factors that cause health inequalities, but also economic analysis of how policies are likely to modify those risk factors by changing individual and organizational behaviors. Second, when evaluating the health equity impacts of policies, the distribution of opportunity costs matters as well as the distribution of benefits. If costs fall on government budgets for health, education or other public services, for example, this is likely to have a disproportionate impact on disadvantaged populations who rely most heavily on those public services.

This chapter brings together the two different strands of literature on cost-effectiveness analysis (CEA) and health equity, showing how they can be integrated in a practical way. It describes methods for using CEA to provide new information about differences in health-related outcomes that may be considered unfair, or "health inequities".

In recent years, a number of methodological advances in this area have been developed into practical tools (Asaria *et al.*, 2015; Verguet *et al.*, 2015). The technical details of these new methods have been published in scientific journals in a form suitable for health economists, but may require further description to be communicated in a more user-friendly manner suitable for the policymakers and managers who commission and use cost-effectiveness evidence, and for the students and scholars in disciplines outside health economics.

This chapter focuses on methods of analysis, rather than processes of decision-making. Evidence about health inequities generated using the methods described in this chapter is only one input into decision-making, and there are further important issues — not addressed here — about how to design processes of decision-making that appropriately reflect concerns about health inequities (Culyer and Lomas, 2006). Re-aligning the methods of CEA to address equity concerns is only one facet of the much larger question of how to design fair processes of decision-making that appropriately address equity concerns (Culyer, 2012, 2016). Equity-informative CEA can only address a subset of the diverse stakeholder concerns about fairness that may arise in relation to a specific decision, and decision-makers will always need to consider wider issues and wider sources of information. One useful approach to ensuring that decision-makers give due attention to wider equity concerns, for example, is the use of "equity checklists" (Culyer and Bombard 2012; Norheim *et al.*, 2014). More fundamentally, robust institutional structures, processes and incentives are needed to ensure that decision-makers take appropriate steps to reduce inequities in health, as well as new methods of analysis. Analysis of the health equity implications of decisions cannot help to improve decision-making, for example, if it is incompetently conducted or communicated, if it is based upon the idiosyncratic value judgements of a narrow group of experts rather than broader community of stakeholders, if policy advisers lack sufficient training to understand the findings, or if the conclusions are disregarded by decision-makers who merely pay lip-service to health equity concerns.

Implicitly or explicitly, all CEA studies already embody social value judgements in several ways such as: through their scope and methodological decisions, in the relevant policy options and comparators considered, and with their inclusion and analysis of different costs and valuation techniques (Shah *et al.*, 2013). To take just one example, a methodological decision to include productivity costs in the cost denominator will increase the implicit priority given to life-extending treatments for productive citizens, such as high-earning parents of young children, compared with unproductive citizens, such as frail older people. Indeed, the basic ethical underpinning of standard CEA adheres to an equity principle — the principle that health policymakers should seek to increase sum total of population health as much as possible given scarce resources, and hence that each unit of health gain should be valued equally, regardless of who obtains it (Cookson, 2015). These value judgements are rarely mentioned in applied CEA studies or health technology assessment (HTA) reports, but are extensively discussed in textbooks, methods guidance documents and other underpinning literature (Culyer, 2016). This article shows how to go beyond embodying these kinds of pre-specified value judgements about equity within applied CEA studies, and toward using the techniques of CEA to provide new information about the health equity implications of alternative policy options that facilitate deliberation among decision-makers and stakeholders (Culyer, 2012; Culyer, 2016). We thus think it is more useful to talk about getting information out of CEA, rather than incorporating equity within CEA (Cookson *et al.*, 2017).

In Section 2, we introduce key concepts of CEA and health equity. In Section 3, we then describe three general approaches and two specific methods for using CEA to address health equity concerns. These approaches are illustrated with applications to low-, middle- and high-income country settings.

2. Concepts

2.1. *Cost-effectiveness analysis*

CEA compares the incremental costs and effects of one policy option with another policy option — which might be "do nothing" (Drummond *et al.*, 2015). Health effects are often measured using a composite summary index of health, such as the quality-adjusted life years (QALYs) or the disability-adjusted life years (DALYs), to facilitate comparison between policies in different disease areas with diverse and distinct mortality and morbidity impacts. This allows the calculation of a cost per QALY gained, or a cost per DALY averted. A cost-increasing policy option can then be considered cost-effective if its cost per unit of health gain compares favourably with alternative ways of using scarce resources.

The displaced activities will likely be alternative health programmes that produce their own health benefits. Cost-effectiveness can then be interpreted as a test of whether a programme will increase the net total health. A cost-effective policy will have a positive net health impact, because its health gains will outweigh the health losses from shifting expenditure away from other health programmes. By contrast, a cost-ineffective policy will have a negative net health impact, because the health losses from shifting expenditure away from other health programmes will outweigh the health gains. The policy objective underpinning conventional CEA can then be interpreted as the quasi-utilitarian health equity objective of maximizing sum total health in the general population (Culyer, 2006; Cookson, 2015). The interpretation of opportunity costs in terms of foregone health benefits is more problematic when there is no fixed health budget, such as in a single-payer public system; however, in such cases the opportunity costs may instead fall on household consumption (via increased taxes or insurance premiums) or on reductions in public expenditure on programmes not primarily designed to improve health. Whatever the setting in which CEA is used, the recognition of opportunity costs — i.e. that resources used in the provision of a programme would have generated value if used elsewhere — is fundamental to CEA. Every benefit attributed to a programme must be weighed against those displaced when resources are diverted from alternative activities.

Cost-effectiveness studies of specific policy alternatives can help to inform priority setting in at least four decision contexts, each of which involves different, though overlapping, communities of decision-makers, analysts and stakeholders:

1. Pricing and reimbursement of new pharmaceuticals and other health technologies — e.g. whether to fund imatinib for stomach cancer, at what price, and for which patients?
2. Health care benefit package design — e.g. whether to cover diabetes in the national health insurance plan, and if so which diabetes interventions to include in the package?
3. Investments in health care organization and delivery infrastructure — e.g. whether to invest in a community health worker programme, and if so, how many and what kinds of new staff to recruit, located where, and with what pay and conditions?
4. Public health investments and regulations — e.g. whether to implement a sugar tax, and if so how much should it be?

In each case, CEA can provide decision-makers with a standard way of assessing the value for money of specific policy options compared with alternative uses of scarce resources. In (1), for example, the funding for imatinib could be used for other hospital-based cancer treatments — or, with more difficulty, shifted toward primary care. In (2), there may only be enough money to cover diabetes or dementia — but not both. In (3), the investment could instead be used to buy hospital equipment. And in (4), the opportunity costs of a sugar tax will be felt by consumers paying higher food prices — potentially pushing some further into poverty. In each case, equity plays an important but typically unanalyzed role; standard CEA does not tell us who gains most, nor who bears the heaviest opportunity costs.

2.2. *Health equity*

In this chapter, we use the term "health inequities" in a broad sense to refer to differences in health-related outcomes that may be considered unfair, inequitable or unjust (Whitehead, 1992; Norheim *et al.*, 2014). Health equity then refers to the policy goal of seeking to reduce or eliminate health inequities. Under our broad definition, health inequities may include not only inequalities in health *per se* but also inequalities in outcomes related to ill-health and lack of access to affordable health care, such as catastrophic health care expenditure, impoverishment, inability to work and inability to perform domestic tasks such as child care. These outcomes may be unequally distributed — for example, decisions about public funding for a particular medical technology could have differential impacts by social group on health care costs, or on one's ability to work or perform domestic tasks, and the resulting financial risks to households.

Figure 1 shows differences in people's lifetime experience of health in England and Ethiopia in 2011 (Asaria *et al.*, 2015; Dawkins, 2018).

Figure 1 shows healthy life expectancy at birth by health quintile groups. The health quintile groups are based on healthy life expectancy at birth as predicted by just two equity-relevant variables: socio-economic status and sex. We use health quintile groups, rather than socio-economic groups, to emphasize that policymakers may be concerned with many

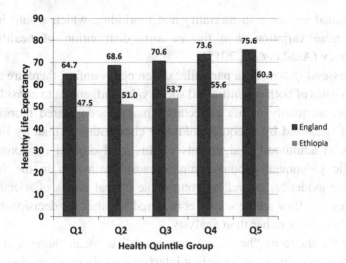

Figure 1. Distribution of healthy life expectancy in England and Ethiopia in 2011.

Note: This figure compares quintile groups of healthy life expectancy at birth as predicted by socio-economic status and sex only.

different sources of inequality in health. In principle, we could also include variation due to further equity-relevant variables such as ethnicity, region and working conditions, among others. The figure shows that there is a gradient in health within each country, but also that there is an inequality between countries since the most advantaged health group in Ethiopia does not achieve as much health as the least advantaged in England. If considered unfair, the differences in Figure 1 represent health inequities.

Differences in health-related outcomes are sometimes considered fair, and equality in health-related outcomes are sometimes considered unfair. For example, providing different health services to people with different needs may be fair, and providing the same services to people with different needs may be unfair. More controversially, if someone's life is cut short by a random accident — a matter of "unexplained" bad luck, not avoidable or remediable by any social action — this might be considered unfortunate or tragic, but not a matter of social injustice (Hausman, 2013). This can make a big difference to inequality analysis. For example, if we consider unexplained variation to be unfair, we would need to include it in Figure 1 and predict the *ex post* distribution of healthy length of life, allowing for unexplained variation in mortality and morbidity, which would include much more variation than the *ex ante* distribution of healthy life expectancy (Asada *et al.*, 2015).

In assessing how far a particular difference is unfair, there are always thorny issues of both scientific and social value judgement to consider. For example, inequality in life expectancy may be considered more unfair when it is caused by unequal childhood circumstances than by lifestyle choices in adulthood. Judgements of this kind depend on contestable scientific judgements about complex causal pathways in the face of imperfect evidence, as well as contestable ethical issues of social value judgement — they are generally considered a matter for decision-makers and stakeholders rather than analysts.

We use the term, "health equity impacts", to mean changes in health inequities brought about by policy interventions. In practice, due to data limitations, modelling of health equity impacts is typically restricted to differences associated with categorical social group variables such as income or wealth, education, ethnicity, gender or region. For example, a social variable commonly used in low- and middle-income country applications is wealth quintile based on a survey of household assets, and a social variable commonly used in high-income country applications is socio-economic quintile group based on small area deprivation. These were the socio-economic variables used to estimate the figures in Figure 1 for Ethiopia and England, respectively. When suitable data are available, health equity impacts can also include impacts between individuals associated with continuous social variables, such as income, or even impacts on the whole-population univariate distribution of health unrelated to any particular social variable, or index of multiple variables.

The tools described in this chapter can be used to provide whatever information about health equity impacts that decision-makers and stakeholders find useful; it is then up to them to draw their own conclusions based on their own value judgements.

2.3. *Accounting for the social distribution of opportunity costs*

The distribution of policy costs matters, as well as the distribution of policy benefits. Understanding health equity impacts requires analyzing not only who gains health benefits but also who bears the opportunity costs — the foregone health benefits that could have been generated through alternative ways of using the same scarce resources may also be unequally distributed. The distribution of opportunity costs will depend crucially on where the funding for the policy or programme comes from. For example, if the money comes from an increase in progressive general taxation, the absolute opportunity costs are likely to be borne disproportionately by the rich, and the opportunity costs in terms of losses in health and well-being may be equally distributed. By contrast, if it is funded by reducing public expenditure on other health, education or welfare services, the opportunity costs in terms of losses in health and well-being may be borne disproportionately by poorer individuals who rely more heavily upon public services. A similar concept could apply to health budget received from foreign aid that would otherwise be used to fund alternative programmes that disproportionately benefit more socially disadvantaged people.

In order to estimate net health equity impact accurately, one needs to compare the health benefits and health opportunity costs using the same metric. To do this, it is usually necessary to measure health outcomes using a generic health measure that can be compared across different diseases, such as QALYs or DALYs, rather than in disease-specific units such as cases of malaria prevented. This is because we typically do not know which patient groups will bear the health opportunity costs, and without a generic measure of health it is hard to compare the value of a case of malaria prevented versus a case of cancer or tuberculosis (TB) or heart disease. The only case in which it might make sense to compute health benefits and opportunity costs in the same disease-specific unit is if there is a fixed budget for a "vertical programme" in a particular disease area, which cannot be used for treating any other disease. In that case, the opportunity costs of alternative uses of the budget will all fall on patients with that specific disease, and so it makes sense to measure both health benefits and opportunity costs in disease-specific units. Where reliable data on morbidity impacts are not available for computing QALYs or DALYs, an alternative can be to measure health benefits in terms of life years or mortality risk reduction. However, this is less comparable with health opportunity costs because some interventions focus primarily on reducing morbidity rather than mortality, and the balance between the two can vary substantially between different disease areas.

Insofar as public and donor expenditures tend disproportionately to benefit socially disadvantaged groups, this provides a tough benchmark for assessing the health equity impacts of specific public or donor-funded programmes compared with other uses of public or donor funding. As Figure 2 shows, interventions that initially seem to have a "pro-poor" health equity impact may in fact be equity-neutral or even "anti-poor",

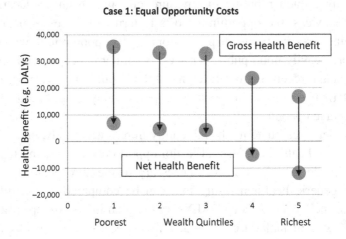

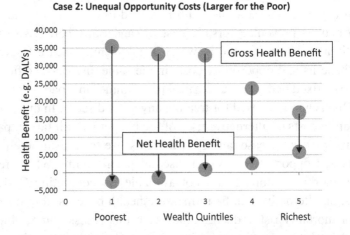

Figure 2. Distribution of net health benefits from a hypothetical programme.

when one considers where the money is coming from and what the alternative uses of that money would be. This is shown with the downward arrows that convert the gross health impacts — considering programme benefits only — to net health impact, after allowing for the health opportunity costs of the alternative uses of money.

Empirically estimating the distribution of opportunity costs is difficult. However, work is under way by researchers at the University of York to estimate the social distribution of the opportunity costs of public health care expenditure in England, and similar studies in future could provide other relevant estimates to be incorporated in future work.

2.4. *Trade-offs between total health and health equity*

Health maximization and health equity are often aligned, but not always. The "health equity impact plane" in Figure 3 helps one to think about the potential trade-offs (McAuley *et al.*, 2016). The vertical axis shows the cost-effectiveness of a health intervention. As explained above, this can be interpreted as its net total health impact — i.e. the total health benefits of the programme minus the forgone health benefits that would have been

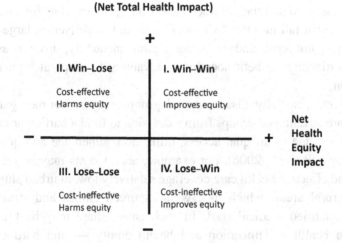

Figure 3. Health equity impact plane.

obtained by spending the money on other health programmes. The horizontal axis shows the net health equity impact, which refers to the impact upon fairness in the distribution of health after allowing for opportunity costs as well as benefits. Health equity impact can be defined and measured in various ways, as discussed in the following.

The plane defines four quadrants. In quadrant I ("win–win"), the policy improves both total health and equity, and in quadrant III ("lose–lose"), the policy harms both. In these two cases, health maximization and equity are aligned. In the other two quadrants, health and equity impacts are opposed and there may be trade-offs. In quadrant II ("win–lose"), the policy is good for total health but bad for equity, and in quadrant IV ("lose–win"), the policy is bad for total health but good for equity.

If all policies fell in the two aligned quadrants (win–win and lose–lose), then there would be no need to analyze health equity impacts. We would then have a guarantee that a policy identified as cost-effective using standard CEA approaches would always improve health equity, and a cost-ineffective policy would always harm health equity.

Many policies do indeed fall into these two quadrants. In low-income countries, for example, investments in high-cost hospital treatments often fall into the "lose–lose" quadrant of being neither cost-effective nor likely to reduce health inequality, insofar as they deliver relatively small health gains per unit of cost and disproportionately benefit wealthy urban elites. By contrast, programmes of vaccination and primary care for infectious diseases often fall into the "win–win" quadrant of delivering large health gains per unit cost and reducing health inequality, insofar as they disproportionately benefit socially disadvantaged groups at high risk of infection.

However, socially disadvantaged groups may sometimes gain less than more advantaged groups from a decision to fund a particular medical technology, due to unequal access, utilization, adherence and quality of care (Tugwell *et al.*, 2006). For example, access costs may be relatively high, and effective health care coverage relatively low, in urban slums and remote rural areas, which lack well-resourced clinics and struggle to recruit qualified medical staff. In such cases, there may be trade-offs between health maximization and health equity — and hard choices between more equal delivery versus larger total health gains.

2.5. Measuring health equity impacts

Health inequities can be measured in different ways depending on the decision problem in hand and the equity concerns of the relevant decision-makers and stakeholders. There are many useful training resources describing how to do so, in general (O'Donnell *et al.*, 2008; Fleurbaey and Schokkaert, 2011; Asada *et al.*, 2014), in the context of health system performance monitoring (WHO, 2013) and in the context of CEA (Asaria *et al.*, 2015). In each case, at least four basic questions must be addressed, such as the following:

1. Equality of what?
2. Equality between whom?
3. Equality indexed how?
4. Equality adjusted how?

In relation to *equality of what?*, for example, the central equity concern might be inequality in health, or inequality in capacity to benefit or inequality in financial risk protection; and there are many different metrics for measuring each of these concepts. In relation to *equality between whom*, for example, the unit of analysis might be individuals or households or geographical areas or social groups, and the inequality breakdowns of interest may relate to socio-economic status, ethnicity, gender or other social variables. In relation to *equality indexed how*, different indices of inequality may contain different normative judgements which can yield quite different patterns of change depending, for example, whether they are defined in terms of relative or absolute differences and in terms of achievement or shortfall (e.g. survival or mortality) (Harper *et al.*, 2010; Arcaya *et al.*, 2015; Kjellsson *et al.*, 2015; Wagstaff, 2015). In relation to *equality adjusted how*, it is rarely enough to measure crude, unadjusted differences in health-related outcomes: one should also consider adjusting for factors that influence the assessment of how far differences are unfair (Asada *et al.*, 2014, 2015). For example, differences in health care utilization may be fair if they are due to difference in needs or preferences; and differences in health outcomes may be fair if they are due to differences in exogenous factors beyond the control of health services, such as a patient's age.

This adjustment process can yield different answers depending on the selection of standardizing variables, the choice of reference values for those variables and different model specifications and methods of adjustment (e.g. direct versus indirect standardization). To measure health inequality that is considered unfair, for example, differences in mortality risk between socio-economic groups may be partly driven by differences in the age structure of the different groups. Insofar as age is not considered to be an unfair determinant of mortality, an adjustment is needed to control for the influence of age on mortality. There are various more or less sophisticated ways of adjusting for fair differences in outcomes, but whatever approach is taken, it is important to be as clear and explicit as possible about the contestable value judgements about fairness that underlie such adjustments.

Health equity concerns can be placed on a spectrum from general to specific. At the broad end of this spectrum is a concern to reduce unfair inequality in lifetime health between all individuals (Norheim, 2010; Robberstad and Norheim, 2011). At the specific end of the spectrum might be concern for equalizing the benefits of a particular policy between urban and rural groups over a particular time period. There are at least four aspects of health equity concern that can vary depending on whether a more general or specific perspective is adopted:

1. Levels versus gains — concern for equality in health levels (more general) rather than concern for the health gains arising from a specific policy (more specific).
2. Outcome specificity — concern for equality in health (more general) rather than concern for equality in the ill-health burden of cancer (more specific).
3. Time horizon — concern for equality over the life course (more general) rather than equality in a particular age group or over a specific time period (more specific).
4. Single versus multiple social variables — concern for inequality by multiple social variables (more general) rather than by one social variable (e.g. urban versus rural).

Figure 4 illustrates a specific equity impact, using a hypothetical example adapted from a 2004 article in the *Lancet* (Gwatkin *et al.*, 2004).

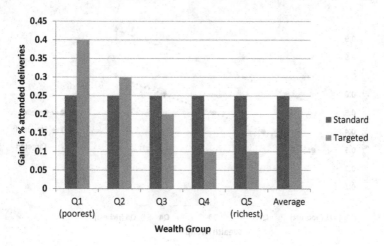

Figure 4. Coverage gains by wealth group, comparing standard and targeted options for improving maternity services in a low-income country — hypothetical example based on Gwatkin *et al.* (2004).

It shows two policies for increasing coverage of skilled birth attendance in a low-income country — a universal policy and a targeted policy that focus on developing maternity service infrastructure in socially disadvantaged areas. The figure shows that the targeted policy is less equal in terms of the distribution of gains: it delivers larger benefits to socially disadvantaged groups, in terms of increases in the proportion of birth deliveries attended by a skilled midwife. From this highly specific perspective, the targeted policy may seem unfair to people in the middle and upper wealth groups who gain less.

However, Figure 5 shows that the targeted policy is more equal in terms of the resulting levels of attended deliveries. If one takes this broader perspective, the targeted policy may seem more fair.

One might also wish to take an even broader perspective, by looking at the impacts on inequalities in lifetime health of the kind illustrated by Figure 1. From this perspective, the targeted policy will seem even fairer, since it will help to reduce the large pre-existing inequality in lifetime health between socio-economic groups. This is easy to show using mathematical indices of inequality. However, an important challenge for communicating lifetime health impacts to decision-makers is that individual policy decisions typically have small impacts on expected lifetime

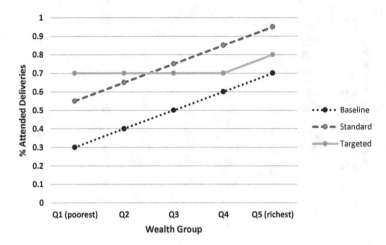

Figure 5. Coverage levels by wealth group, comparing standard and targeted options for improving maternity services in a low-income country — hypothetical example.

outcomes for the average citizen. Health equity impacts still matter, however, even though they seem small from the *ex ante* perspective of expected changes in risk of future mortality and morbidity — since we are still talking about the large and important changes in many people's lives from an ex-post-perspective that looks back at to what degree they experienced a long and healthy life (Eyal *et al.*, 2013). From an *ex ante* population perspective, the cost-effectiveness impacts of most policy decisions also seem small — costing little to the average citizen and adding only a small proportion to average healthy life expectancy. Furthermore, a sustained sequence of small impacts can over time accumulate into a large impact.

2.6. Quantifying health equity trade-offs

When there are trade-offs between health equity and total health — i.e. we know that the policy lies in either the "win–lose" or "lose–win" quadrants of Figure 3 — it can be helpful to provide a more refined quantitative analysis of those trade-offs. As part of a general approach, which we call "equity trade-off analysis", there is a specific method called "equity constraint analysis". This method counts the cost of choosing a fairer but less cost-effective policy, in terms of a reduced total health (QALY equality) benefit. Another specific method, which we call "equity weighting analysis", quantifies how much concern for health inequity is required to recommend a fairer but less cost-effective policy option, using sensitivity analysis. This sensitivity analysis can be done by specifying alternative equity weights for health benefits to different people, or alternative values of an inequality aversion parameter quantifying one's degree of concern for reducing health inequality versus improving total health (Norheim, 2013; Asaria *et al.*, 2016; Wagstaff *et al.*, 2016). Sensitivity analysis can help decision-makers understand the implications of alternative value judgements. The aim of health equity trade-off analysis is thus to help inform a decision-making process, rather than to impose a particular set of value judgements upon decision-makers.

3. Different Approaches to Equity-Informative CEA

This section describes three general ways of using CEA to evaluate policy concerns about health equity, each of which addresses different equity questions (Cookson *et al.*, 2009; Johri and Norheim, 2012). These are: equity evidence review, equity impact analysis and equity trade-off analysis. Table 1 provides a definition of each approach and the questions they help to answer.

We use the umbrella term "equity-informative CEA" to describe any study that uses the methods of CEA to provide information about health equity objectives other than improving total health. We illustrate two specific methods of equity-informative CEA. Extended cost-effectiveness analysis (ECEA), developed by the Disease Control Priorities, 3rd edition project (www.dcp-3.org), examines the social distribution of costs, health effects and financial risk protection effects. Distributional cost-effectiveness analysis (DCEA), developed by the University of York, examines the distribution of health benefits and opportunity costs and then, if health equity trade-offs are identified, conducts equity trade-off analyses to provide further information about the nature of those trade-offs. In practice, ECEA studies have tended to focus on presenting disaggregated information on costs and effects by equity-relevant group,

Table 1. Three general approaches to evaluating health equity concerns.

Approach	Description	Questions answered
1. Equity evidence review	A review of evidence on pre-existing health inequities and the potential distributional impacts of future policies.	What are the relevant health equity issues? What do stakeholders think? What is already known about the size of pre-existing health inequities? What do studies of past policies suggest may be the potential health equity impacts of future policies?
2. Equity impact analysis	Disaggregation of the relevant costs and benefits by equity-relevant subgroups, providing a dashboard of results.	How much do different social groups gain or lose? This may be in terms of money, health services, health outcomes or other outcomes related to ill-health and access to affordable health services, such as financial risk protection.
3. Equity trade-off analysis	*Equity constraint analysis —* Calculation of the health opportunity cost of choosing a fairer option rather than a more cost-effective option. *Equity weighting analysis —* Sensitivity analysis around the value of health equity impacts, based on different concepts of inequality, and the strength of concern for reducing health inequality. Can be done using equity parameters or direct equity weights for specific subgroups.	*Equity constraint analysis —* How much total health benefit is forgone if a more cost-effective option is ruled out on equity grounds? *Equity weighting analysis —* How large is the health equity impact in terms of standard summary metrics of inequality? How much concern for health equity is required to choose a more equitable option compared with a more cost-effective option?

while DCEA studies have, in addition, presented aggregate information about overall net benefits including equity weighting analysis. In theory, however, equity weighting analysis can also be done as part of ECEA and there is no fundamental difference between the two approaches.

We first describe methods of equity evidence review that can be performed alongside or prior to CEA in order to provide information about health equity concerns.

3.1. *Equity evidence review*

Equity evidence review can address a range of health equity questions of interest to decision-makers, for example "What are the relevant health equity issues?", "What do stakeholders think?", "What is already known about the size of pre-existing health inequities?" and "What do studies of past policies suggest may be the potential health equity impacts of the policy options currently under consideration?".

There are published guidelines for using the methods of systematic review of randomized controlled trials to gather information about equity impacts, such as the PROGRESS framework adopted by both the Campbell and Cochrane Collaborations (O'Neill *et al.*, 2014). Box 1 describes a Cochrane systematic review regarding food supplementation for disadvantaged young children; another example is the review by Brown and colleagues (2014) of the equity impact of interventions and policies to reduce smoking in youth and another is the review by Noor and colleagues

---

Box 1. Example of an equity evidence review
Food supplementation for disadvantaged young children —
A systematic review

Kristjansson and colleagues (2015) use the Cochrane systematic review method to examine interventions to address malnutrition in young children. They primarily review the effectiveness of supplementary feeding interventions, but they secondarily look at how such interventions interact with inequalities, implementation and adverse outcomes. We focus in this synopsis on what they find for inequality.

The authors develop a conceptual framework to guide the thinking about how inequalities may factor into childhood nutrition and health. Equity is then evaluated by looking at the outcomes for given subgroups such as age, sex, level of malnourishment (baseline health) and socio-economic status.

Meta-analysis of the studies and differences between subgroups were then conducted. The results of this review and analysis find that supplementary feeding programmes have unequal impacts on certain subgroups, being more effective for children who were poorer and more malnourished, but no difference of impact in other subgroups such as by sex of the child.

---

about reducing inequity in use of insecticide-treated bed nets in Kenya (Noor *et al.*, 2007). Systematic review methods have an important role in helping to avoid the all-too-common trap of falling unknowingly into a selective reading of the evidence, and to avoid duplicating work that has already been done. However, systematic reviews can be resource-intensive, and often require several months of work by large multidisciplinary teams. Furthermore, there are ongoing debates about appropriate review methods for complex interventions where theoretical and observational evidence may play a more central role than randomized controlled trials. So, if the requisite capacity is not available to conduct a systematic review, it may be useful to undertake a rapid review.

It is also possible to conduct a review of philosophical arguments about equity in relation to a particular case, such as the "ethical case review" approach that Miljeteig and colleagues (2010) used to examine end-of-life decisions in a neonatal unit in India. However, in conducting a review of this kind, analysts must be wary of going too far down the road of adjudicating between alternative views of justice in an attempt to answer the question: "what is fair?", rather than clarifying alternative points of view so that decision-makers can make up their own minds.

3.2. *Equity impact analysis*

Equity impact analysis examines who gains and who loses from one policy option compared with another, and by how much. Typically, this approach yields a dashboard of outcomes, showing gains and losses by social groups for various different kinds of costs and effects. This provides the decision-maker with relevant disaggregated information on the equity impacts.

An example of equity impact analysis alongside CEA in a high income context is the study by Holmes and colleagues (2014) of the impacts of minimum alcohol pricing in the UK. This study estimated the social class distribution of effects on alcohol consumption, spending and alcohol-related health harm and found that the benefits are substantially concentrated on heavy drinkers in routine and manual worker households.

The DCP3 project has developed a specific method of CEA that incorporates distributional impact analysis and analysis of financial risk protection effects as well as health effects, called "ECEA" (Verguet *et al.*, 2015b). This method has now been applied to about 20 studies of policy interventions in several different low- and middle-income country settings, producing breakdowns of costs, health benefits and financial risk protection benefits by socio-economic quintile group (Verguet and Jamison, 2017). Box 2 gives an example of ECEA relating to tobacco taxes in China.

Sometimes equity impact analysis only examines the benefits of a policy, not the costs. As explained before, this provides an incomplete picture of health equity impact, since it only looks at one side of the distributional coin: the costs may also be unequally distributed.

Distributional impact analyses can also be performed outside the context of CEA, to look at the impacts of changes in risk factors, health behaviors or the utilization of effective health technologies, rather than the

---

Box 2. Example of an equity impact analysis
Tobacco tax in China — An Extended CEA (ECEA)

This modelling exercise examines a 50% excise tax on cigarettes over a 50-year period. In aggregate, this is estimated to save 231 million life years, add $ 703 billion in tax revenue to government budgets, reduce expenditure on tobacco-related illness and improve financial risk protection.

The ECEA further breaks down model inputs by equity-relevant groups, in this case by five income quintiles. The descriptive tables of the paper show how input variables such as smoking prevalence, cigarette consumption, price elasticity and health utilization are all parametrized according to income quintile.

The results are presented in a dashboard-like format, where the aggregate results are broken down into results for each quintile group. For example, the years of life gained are more concentrated on the poor (79 million in the poorest quintile) than the rich (11 million in the richest quintile), as seen in the following figure. Expenditures on tobacco, which one may worry would be regressive with a new excise tax, also show a progressive distribution in absolute terms, or an inverted-U distribution in relative terms. In either case, the tax is shown not to overly harm the poor.

Lastly, the ECEA also incorporates financial risk protection benefits. In the case of the Chinese tobacco tax, this is measured as a money-metric value of insurance. This is similarly disaggregated by income quintile, showing that there is more financial risk protection for the poorer quintiles.

impacts of specific policy options. For example, Bajekal and colleagues (2012) examined the impacts on coronary heart mortality in England from 2000 to 2007, of changes in risk factors and treatment utilization in different social groups. This kind of study does not directly inform the priority setting task of selecting between specific future policies, as it does not provide information about either the costs of those policies or their effects on risk factors, health behaviors or the utilization of effective health technologies. However, it can provide decision-makers with useful contextual information for policy-making purposes, in raising awareness of the importance of particular factors and their contributions to health inequality.

Finally, a form of distributional impact analysis known as "benefit incidence analysis" looks at the benefits of public health care spending as a whole for different social groups. Traditionally, this kind of analysis has typically assumed that health benefits are proportional to health care consumption, and has only looked at the average benefits of the current overall level of spending rather than the marginal benefits of changes in spending. So, traditional forms of benefit incidence analysis have not been useful for predicting the health benefits of a policy decision to change expenditure from the current baseline level. However, some benefit incidence analyses are now starting to look at marginal benefits, by exploiting data on subnational variation and change in expenditure and outcomes, and so can be more useful for priority setting purposes (Kruse *et al.*, 2012).

3.3. *Equity trade-off analysis*

Equity trade-off analysis examines the trade-offs between improving total health and other equity objectives not usually addressed by CEA. The two main approaches to equity trade-off analysis — equity constraint analysis and equity weighting analysis — are described in the following sub-sections.

3.3.1 *Equity constraint analysis*

From a technical perspective, equity can be analyzed as a constraint on the pursuit of cost-effectiveness, rather than as a goal or outcome to be pursued in its own right (Box 3). The health opportunity cost of imposing this ethical constraint can be calculated as the difference in total health

---

Box 3. Example of an equity constraint analysis
HIV treatment in South Africa — A mathematical programming study

Cleary and colleagues (2010) analyze the equity concern to provide only the most effective treatment as a constraint on improving total health in relation to antiretroviral (ART) HIV treatment in South Africa. They measure cost-effectiveness in terms of QALYs gained per unit of cost, and equity in terms of the percentage of met need for ART.

The study uses mathematical programming to examine different treatment delivery scenarios under different health budgets. As budgets increase, more total health can be provided. However, at given budget levels, there are trade-offs and more cost-effective solutions that deliver larger total health gains by offering some people cheaper but less effective treatments rather than fully meeting their needs by proving the most effective treatment. Hence, particular target levels of met need (the equity constraint) are only achievable by sacrificing total health.

This approach highlights that the opportunity cost of equity can be understood in terms of the amount of health that is foregone by implementing a more equitable solution, as opposed to implementing the most cost-effective solution under a given budget constraint.

---

benefit between the most cost-effective policy option and a more equitable policy option. The health loss associated with choosing a more equitable option thus gives an indication of the value the decision-maker places on equity (Williams and Cookson, 2006). This approach can be implemented by either using a simple cost-effectiveness framework comparing two or more options given a fixed budget, or using more specialized mathematical programming techniques to handle complex choices involving different amounts of expenditure on different programmes (Earnshaw *et al.*, 2002; Epstein *et al.*, 2007).

3.3.2. *Equity weighting analysis*

Another approach that accounts for trade-offs is equity weighting analysis. In contrast to the previous approaches, this approach attempts to quantify the overall health equity impact, using summary indices of inequality, and to analyze trade-offs between the health equity impact and the net health impact (Johansson and Norheim, 2011; Norheim, 2013; Asaria *et al.*, 2015). The basic idea is to conduct sensitivity analysis in order to find out how much you need to care about reducing inequality to recommend a fairer option rather than a health maximizing option. This sensitivity analysis can be done by specifying alternative equity weights for health benefits to different people, or alternative values of an equity parameter, which quantifies one's degree of concern for health equity versus improving total health. Box 4 illustrates this approach using an example

---

Box 4. Example of an equity weighting analysis

Bowel cancer screening in England — A "distributional cost-effectiveness analysis" (DCEA)

This study compares two strategies for increasing uptake of a universal bowel cancer screening programme. The "targeted" strategy focuses on social groups with low uptake, by sending a personalized reminder from their family doctor; the "universal" strategy sends a generic reminder to everyone. Inequality impacts are analyzed by deprivation, ethnicity and gender, and then combined to assess the overall impact. The following illustrations focus on inequality by deprivation. The left-hand panel shows unequal health by deprivation group before the screening programme. The right-hand panel shows unequal uptake of screening from the "standard" programme, and after the "targeted" and "universal" reminder strategies.

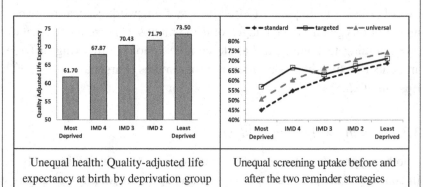

| Unequal health: Quality-adjusted life expectancy at birth by deprivation group | Unequal screening uptake before and after the two reminder strategies |

(Continued)

The left-hand panel shows the resulting changes in health. The targeted strategy is inequality-reducing but produces less total health than the universal strategy, which is inequality-increasing. Which strategy you consider best depends on how much you care about reducing health inequality versus improving total health. The right-hand panel shows how this trade-off can be quantified using the inequality aversion parameter from an Atkinson social welfare function. Which strategy you consider better depends on how much you care about reducing health inequality — in this case, the "targeted" strategy is better if your inequality aversion parameter is greater than 8. Recent survey data suggest the average member of the English general public has an inequality aversion parameter of around 11 (Robson *et al.*, 2017).

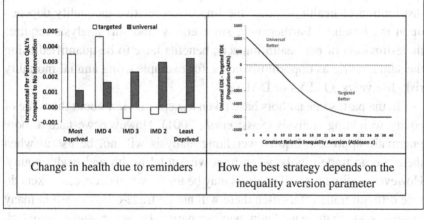

| Change in health due to reminders | How the best strategy depends on the inequality aversion parameter |

comparing more equitable and more cost-effective ways of increasing uptake of colorectal cancer screening in England.

Many different characteristics of health policies and the people affected by them could be used as the basis for setting equity weights, and several different equity weighting systems have been proposed (Wailoo *et al.*, 2009; Cookson *et al.*, 2014). Many of these systems do not pay special attention to the social characteristics of people, but rather focus on their health characteristics — for example, their current severity of illness, or their overall lifetime experience of health including past, present and future health (Nord, 1993; Williams, 1997; Lindemark *et al.*, 2014;

Ottersen *et al.*, 2014, 2016; Rowen *et al.*, 2016). These systems tend to be based upon one or more equity parameters, such as an inequality aversion parameter within a social welfare function, which specifies how much you care about reducing unfair health inequality rather than how much you care about individuals with certain social characteristics (Asaria *et al.*, 2016). An equity parameter then indirectly implies a set of equity weights for people with different characteristics, in conjunction with information about the existing distribution of health between individuals with different characteristics. These implied weights will then change in response to changes in the distribution of health and social variables.

If decision-makers are interested in impacts on relative inequality (e.g. life-expectancy ratios) as well as absolute inequality (e.g. life expectancy gaps), then they will require an estimate of the baseline distribution of health — since the impact on relative inequality depends upon the baseline. Furthermore, since equity trade-off analysis requires the estimation of net health impacts, benefits have to be quantified using the same metric as opportunity costs, for example using annual mortality risk, life years, QALYs or DALYs.

In the past, some authors have taken a sceptical view about the value of equity weighting analysis (Sassi *et al.*, 2001). However, we take a more pragmatic approach. Equity weighting analysis will not be useful when there are no trade-offs between improving total health and health equity. However, equity trade-off analysis may be useful when decision-makers do face difficult trade-offs. Often there will not be trade-offs, as seen in many examples where there are "win–win" scenarios. However, studies may lack information about the additional delivery costs required in disadvantaged communities due to access barriers; or may neglect to analyze the distribution of opportunity costs from public or donor budgets. Due to issues of this kind, there will sometimes be difficult trade-offs that result from social variation in access, adherence and effectiveness, and social variation in opportunity costs, and in such cases there may be a need for equity trade-off analyses (Eyal *et al.*, 2013). Analysis of trade-offs can help decision-makers understand the implications of alternative value judgements; and the use of equity parameters and equity weights can help form useful benchmarks for decision-makers to compare across different decisions. As with the standardly used cost-effectiveness threshold, this kind of benchmark can be useful to decision-makers as a way of justifying their decisions in the face of competing political demands from rival stakeholders, and for facilitating both transparency and consistency between decisions.

4. Conclusion

In response to growing policy concern about health equity, the tools of economic evaluation are being re-fashioned to provide useful evidence about health equity impacts and trade-offs. Our chapter has described the key concepts and methods now available for using CEA to analyze health equity concerns. We have distinguished three general approaches such as (1) equity evidence review, (2) equity impact analysis and (3) equity trade-off analysis. We have also described two specific methods of equity impact analysis that incorporate distributional impact analysis within economic evaluation: ECEA and DCEA. ECEA examines the distribution of costs, health outcomes and financial risk protection outcomes, and DCEA combines distributional impact analysis with equity constraint and trade-off analyses.

Our chapter has the following conclusions for decision-makers who use cost-effectiveness studies:

- Some decisions involve equity trade-offs between total health and health equity.
- Equity trade-offs can occur when delivering services to more disadvantaged communities that require additional investments, due to poor infrastructure, weak governance and barriers to access.
- In the face of equity trade-offs, distributional economic evaluation can be used to provide useful quantitative information to help make fairer decisions and improve health.

Our chapter also has the following conclusions for analysts who produce cost-effectiveness studies:

- Who gains the most depends on the social variation in several factors including health risks, access to care, adherence to care, quality of care, clinical effects and capacity to benefit.

- Providing a full picture of health equity impacts requires analyzing not only who gains but also who bears the opportunity costs of diverting scarce resources from other uses.
- Accurate estimates of health equity impacts require analysis of social inequality in service delivery and the implementation costs of attempting to reduce this inequality, rather than merely assuming that services will be delivered and used in the same way and at the same cost in advantaged and disadvantaged communities.

Health equity findings should include sensitivity analysis that helps decision-makers understand the implications of alternative value judgements about equity. Using CEA to analyze distributional equity impacts and trade-offs requires the same basic analytical skills as standard CEA. However, it is more demanding in terms of data requirements because it requires social distributions of key parameters rather than merely population average values. Data limitations can be particularly severe in low-income countries which lack basic health information systems such as vital statistics on births and deaths, and hospital and primary care administrative data. However, as the DCP3 project has amply demonstrated, distributional economic evaluation studies can successfully be performed in low-income countries using existing datasets. Existing, large-scale survey-based datasets in low-income countries such as UNICEF's Multiple Indicator Cluster Survey (MICS) and ICF International's Demographic and Health Surveys (DHS) include information disaggregated by socio-economic status, which have been useful for obtaining equity-relevant information (ICF-International-USAID, 2016; UNICEF, 2016). Datasets are constantly improving, and in the future it will become increasingly feasible to estimate social distributions of key parameters in economic evaluation studies.

Three important frontiers of research in this field are: (1) research on the distribution of opportunity costs of funding health programmes from different sources (e.g. public health care, donor budgets, taxation), (2) research on the implementation costs of achieving more equal delivery and utilization of services in disadvantaged communities and (3) research on public and stakeholder views about health equity trade-offs to provide benchmark values to help guide decision-makers faced with difficult policy trade-offs. Work on the distribution of opportunity costs issue is ongoing in England, drawing on existing research on variation in health care expenditure and outcomes at subnational level (Claxton *et al.*, 2013). This issue is particularly challenging in low- and middle-income countries where the existence of informal health systems, donor aid and a variety of health financing models creates challenges for identifying where the opportunity costs lie, and is a critical area for further research.

We hope this chapter will help those who produce, commission and use evidence to support priority setting in health care and public health to navigate the practical options for using the techniques of CEA to provide policymakers with more useful information about the health equity implications of their decisions.

Acknowledgments

Richard Cookson and Miqdad Asaria are supported by the National Institute for Health Research (NIHR) (Senior Research Fellowship, Dr Richard Cookson, SRF-2013-06-015). The views expressed in this publication are those of the authors and not necessarily those of the National Health Service (NHS), NIHR or the Department of Health.

For helpful comments, the authors would like to thank Gwyn Bevan, Alan Brennan, Simon Capewell, Kalipso Chalkidou, Brendan Collins, Tony Culyer, Brian Ferguson, Amanda Glassman, John Holmes, Carleigh Krubiner, Ryan Li, Ole Norheim, Martin O'Flaherty, Marc Suhrcke, Aki Tsuchiya, Stephane Verguet and Adam Wagstaff; though our errors and opinions are our own.

References

Arcaya, M. C., Arcaya, A. L., Subramanian, S. V. (2015). Inequalities in health: Definitions, concepts, and theories. *Global Health Action*, 8: 27106.
Asada, Y., Hurley, J., Norheim, O., Johri, M. (2015). Unexplained health inequality — Is it unfair? *International Journal for Equity in Health*, 14(1): 11.

Asada, Y., Hurley, J., Norheim, O. F., Johri, M. (2014). A three-stage approach to measuring health inequalities and inequities. *International Journal for Equity in Health*, 13(1): 98.

Asaria, M., Griffin, S., Cookson, R., Whyte, S., Tappenden, P. (2015). Distributional costeffectiveness analysis of health care programmes — A methodological case study of the UK Bowel Cancer Screening Programme. *Health Economics*, 24(6): 742–754.

Asaria, M., Griffin, S., Cookson, R. (2016). Distributional cost-effectiveness analysis: A tutorial. *Medical Decision Making*, 36(1): 8–19.

Bajekal, M., Scholes, S., Love, H., Hawkins, N., O'Flaherty, M., Raine, R., Capewell, S. (2012). Analysing recent socioeconomic trends in coronary heart disease mortality in England, 2000-2007: A population modelling study. *PLoS Medicine*, 9: 12.

Brown, T., Platt, S., Amos, A. (2014). Equity impact of interventions and policies to reduce smoking in youth: Systematic review. *Tobacco Control*, 23(e2): e98–105.

Claxton, K., *et al.* (2015). Methods for the estimation of the National Institute for Health and Care Excellence cost-effectiveness threshold. *Health Technology Assessment (Winchester, England)*, 19(14): 1.

Cleary, S., Mooney, G., McIntyre, D. (2010). Equity and efficiency in HIV-treatment in South Africa: The contribution of mathematical programming to priority setting. *Health Economics*, 19(10), 1166–1180. doi:10.1002/hec.1542

Cookson, R., Drummond, M., Weatherly, H. (2009). Explicit incorporation of equity considerations into economic evaluation of public health interventions. *Health Economics, Policy and Law*, 4(2): 231–245.

Cookson, R., Griffin, S., Nord, E. (2014). Incorporation of concerns for fairness in economic evaluation of health programs: Overview. In: Culyer, A. J., ed., *Encyclopedia of Health Economics, Volume 2*. San Diego: Elsevier. 27–34.

Cookson, R. (2015). Justice and the NICE approach. *Journal of Medical Ethics*, 41(1): 99–102.

Cotlear, D., *et al.* (2015). Overcoming social segregation in health care in Latin America. *The Lancet*, 385(9974): 1248–1259.

Culyer, A. J. (2006). The bogus conflict between efficiency and vertical equity. *Health Economics*, 15(11): 1155–1158.

Culyer, A. J., Lomas, J. (2006). Deliberative processes and evidence-informed decision making in healthcare: Do they work and how might we know? *Evidence & Policy: A Journal of Research, Debate and Practice*, 2(3): 357–371.

Culyer, A. J. (2012). Hic sunt dracones: The future of health technology assessment — One economist's perspective. *Medical Decision Making*, 32(1): E25–E32.

Culyer, A. J. (2016). HTA — Algorithm or process?; Comment on "Expanded HTA: Enhancing fairness and legitimacy". *International Journal of Health Policy and Management*, 5(8): 501–505.

Culyer, A. J., Bombard, Y. (2012). An equity framework for health technology assessments. *Medical Decision Making*, 32: 428–441.

Daniels, N., Porteny, T., Urritia, J. (2016). Expanded HTA: Enhancing fairness and legitimacy. *International Journal of Health Policy and Management*, 5(1): 1–3.

Dawkins, B. R., Mirelman, A. J., Asaria, M., Johansson, K. A., Cookson, R. A. (2018). Distributional cost-effectiveness analysis in low-and middle-income countries: Illustrative example of rotavirus vaccination in Ethiopia. *Health Policy and Planning*, 33(3): 456–463.

Earnshaw, S. R., Richter, A., Sorensen, S. W., Hoerger, T. J., Hicks, K. A., Engelgau, M., Thompson, T., Narayan, K. M., Williamson, D. F., Gregg, E., Zhang, P. (2002). Optimal allocation of resources across four interventions for type 2 diabetes. *Medical Decision Making*, 22(5 Suppl): S80–91.

Epstein, D. M., Chalabi, Z., Claxton, K., Sculpher, M. (2007). Efficiency, equity, and budgetary policies informing decisions using mathematical programming. *Medical Decision Making*, 27(2): 128–137.

Eyal, N., Hurst, S. A., Norheim, O. F., Wikler, D. (2013). *Inequalities in Health: Concepts, Measures, and Ethics*. Oxford: Oxford University Press.

Fleurbaey, M., Schokkaert, E. (2011). Equity in health and health care. In: Mark, T. G. M., Pauly, V., Pedro, P. B., *Handbook of Health Economics, Volume 2*. Amsterdam: Elsevier. 1003–1092.

Gwatkin, D. R., Bhuiya, A., Victora, C.G. (2004). Making health systems more equitable. *Lancet*, 364(9441): 1273–1280.

Gwatkin, D. R., Ergo, A. (2011). Universal health coverage: Friend or foe of health equity? *The Lancet*, 377(9784): 2160–2161.

Harper, S., King, N. B., Meersman, S. C., Reichman, M. E., Breen, N., Lynch, J. (2010). Implicit value judgments in the measurement of health inequalities. *Milbank Q*, 88(1): 4–29.

Hausman, D. (2013). Egalitarian critiques of health inequalities. In: Eyal, N., Hurst, S. A., Norheim, O. F., Wikler, D., eds., *Inequalities in Health: Concepts, Measures, and Ethics*. Oxford, Oxford Press. 27.

Holmes, J., Meng, Y., Meier, P. S., Brennan, A., Angus, C., Campbell-Burton, A., Guo, Y., Hill-McManus, D., Purshouse, R. C. (2014). Effects of minimum unit pricing for alcohol on different income and socioeconomic groups: A modelling study. *Lancet*, 383(9929): 1655–1664.

ICF-International-USAID (2016). The DHS Program: Demographic and Health Surveys. Retrieved 14 July 2016, from http://www.dhsprogram.com/.

Johansson, K. A., Norheim, O. F. (2011). Problems with prioritization: Exploring ethical solutions to inequalities in HIV care. *American Journal of Bioethics*, 11(12): 32–40

Johri, M., Norheim, O. (2012). Can cost-effectiveness analysis integrate concerns for equity? Systematic review. *International Journal of Technology Assessment in Health Care*, 28(2): 125–132.

Kjellsson, G., Gerdtham, U.-G., Petrie, D. (2015). Lies, damned lies, and health inequality measurements: Understanding the value judgments. *Epidemiology*, 26(5): 673–680.

Kruse, I., Pradhan, M., Sparrow, R. (2012). Marginal benefit incidence of public health spending: Evidence from Indonesian sub-national data. *Journal of Health Economics*, 31(1): 147–157.

Kristjansson, E., Francis, D. K., Liberato, S., Jandu, B. M., Welch, V., Batal, M., Greenhalgh, T., Rader, T., Noonan, E., Shea, B., Janzen, L., Wells, G. A., Petticrew, M. (2015). Food supplementation for improving the physical and psychosocial health of socio-economically disadvantaged children aged three months to five years. *Cochrane Database of Systematic Reviews* (3). doi: 10.1002/14651858.CD009924.pub2.

Lindemark, F., Norheim, O. F., Johansson, K. A. (2014). Making use of equity sensitive QALYs: A case study on identifying the worse off across diseases. *Cost Effectiveness and Resource Allocation*, 12(1): 1.

Marmot, M., Bell, R. (2012). Fair society, healthy lives. *Public Health*, 126: S4–S10.

Marmot, M., Friel, S., Bell, R., Houweling, T. A., Taylor, S., Commission on Social Determinants of Health (2008). Closing the gap in a generation: health equity through action on the social determinants of health. *The Lancet*, 372(9650): 1661–1669.

McAuley, A., Denny, C., Taulbut, M., Mitchell, R., Fischbacher, C., Graham, B., Grant, I., O'Hagan, P., McAllister, D., McCartney, G. (2016). Informing Investment to Reduce Inequalities: A Modelling Approach. *PLoS One*, 11(8): e0159256.

Miljeteig, I., Johansson, K. A., Sayeed, S. A., Norheim, O. F. (2010). End-of-life decisions as bedside rationing. An ethical analysis of life support restrictions in an Indian neonatal unit. *Journal of Medical Ethics*, 36(8): 473–478.

Noor, A. M., Amin, A. A., Akhwale, W. S., Snow, R. W. (2007). Increasing coverage and decreasing inequity in insecticide-treated bed net use among rural Kenyan children. *PLoS Med*, 4(8): e255.

Nord, E. (1993). The trade-off between severity of illness and treatment effect in cost-value analysis of health care. *Health Policy*, 24(3): 227–238.

Norheim, O., Baltussen, R., Johri, M., Chisholm, D., Nord, E., Brock, D., Carlsson, P., Cookson, R., Daniels, N., Danis, M., Fleurbaey, M., Johansson, K., Kapiriri, L., Littlejohns, P., Mbeeli, T., Rao, K., Edejer, T. T.-T., Wikler, D. (2014). Guidance on priority setting in health care (GPS-Health): The inclusion of equity criteria not captured by cost-effectiveness analysis. *Cost Effectiveness and Resource Allocation*, 12(1): 18.

Norheim, O. F. (2010). Priority to the young or to those with least lifetime health? *The American Journal of Bioethics*, 10(4): 60–61.

Norheim, O. F. (2013). Atkinsons Index applied to health. In: Eyal, N., Hurst, S. A., Norheim, O. F., Wikler, D., eds., *Inequalities in Health: Concepts, Measures, and Ethics*. Oxford: Oxford Scholarship Online. 30.

O'Donnell, O., van Doorslaer, E., Wagstaff, A., Lindelow, M. (2008). Analyzing health equity using household survey data: A guide to techniques and their implementation. Washington, D.C., World Bank.

O'Neill, J., Tabish, H., Welch, V., Petticrew, M., Pottie, K., Clarke, M., Evans, T., Pardo, J., Waters, E., White, H., Tugwell, P. (2014). Applying an equity lens to interventions: Using PROGRESS ensures consideration of socially stratifying factors to illuminate inequities in health. *Journal of Clinical Epidemiology*, 67(1): 56–64.

Ottersen, T., Mæstad, O., Norheim, O. F. (2014). Lifetime QALY prioritarianism in priority setting: Quantification of the inherent trade-off. *Cost Effectiveness and Resource Allocation*, 12(1): 1.

Robberstad, B., Norheim, O. F. (2011). Incorporating concerns for equal lifetime health in evaluations of public health programs. *Social Science Medicine*, 72(10): 1711–1716.

Robson, M., Asaria, M., Cookson, R., Tsuchiya, A., & Ali, S. (2017). Eliciting the level of health inequality aversion in England. *Health Economics*, 26(10), 1328–1334.

Rowen, D., Brazier, J., Mukuria, C., Keetharuth, A., Hole, A. R., Tsuchiya, A., Whyte, S., Shackley, P. (2016). Eliciting societal preferences for weighting QALYs for burden of illness and end of life. *Medical Decision Making*, 36(2): 210–222.

Sassi, F., Archard, L., Le Grand, J. (2001). Equity and the economic evaluation of healthcare. *Health Technology Assessment (Winchester, England)*, 5(3): 1.

Thokaka, P., Devlin, N., Marsh, K. et al. (2016). Multiple criteria decision analysis for health care decision making — An introduction: Report 1 of the ISPOR MCDA Emerging Good Practices Task Force. Value in Health, 19: 1–13.

Tugwell, P., de Savigny, D., Hawker, G., Robinson, V. (2006). Applying clinical epidemiological methods to health equity: The equity effectiveness loop. *BMJ*, 332(7537): 358–361.

UNICEF (2016). Multiple Indicator Cluster Surveys (MICS). Retrieved 14 July 2016, from http://mics.unicef.org/.

Verguet, S., Jamison, D. T. (2017). Applications of extended cost-effectiveness analysis (ECEA) methodology in DCP3. In: Jamison, D. T., Nugent, R. A., Gelband, H., *et al.*, eds., *Disease Control Priorities, Volume 9*. Washington, D.C.: World Bank.

Verguet, S., Laxminarayan, R., Jamison, D. T. (2015). Universal public finance of tuberculosis treatment in India: An extended cost-effectiveness analysis. *Health Economics*, 24(3): 318–332.

Wagstaff, A. (2015). Commentary: Value Judgments in Health Inequality Measurement. *Epidemiology (Cambridge, Mass.)*, 26(5): 670.

Wagstaff, A., Cotlear, D., Eozenou, P. H. V., Buisman, L. R. (2016). Measuring progress towards universal health coverage: With an application to 24 developing countries. *Oxford Review of Economic Policy*, 32(1): 147–189.

Wailoo, A., Tsuchiya, A., McCabe, C. (2009). Weighting must wait. *Pharmacoeconomics*, 27(12): 983–989.

Whitehead, M. (1992). The concepts and principles of equity and health. *International Journal of Health Services: Planning, Administration, Evaluation*, 22(3): 429–445.

Williams, A. (1997). Intergenerational equity: An exploration of the fair innings argument. *Health Economics*, 6(2): 117–132.

Williams, A. H., Cookson, R. A. (2006). Equity-efficiency trade-offs in health technology assessment. *International Journal of Technology Assessment in Health Care*, 22(1): 1–9.

World Health Organization (2013). Handbook on health inequality monitoring with a special focus on low-and middle-income countries, World Health Organization.

World Health Organisation (2014). WHO methods for life expectancy and healthy life expectancy. Global Helath Estimates Technical Paper WHO/HIS/HSI/GHE/2014.5. Geneva, Department of Health Statistics and Information Systems, WHO.

Chapter 5

Economic Evaluation of Social Care and Informal Care Interventions in Low- and Middle-Income Countries

Helen Weatherly, Rita Faria, Alexandra Rollinger,
Bernard van den Berg, Levison Chiwaula, Pritaporn Kingkaew,
Aurelio Mejia, Janet Seeley, Stella Settumba and
Sax Sandanam

1. Introduction

Low- and middle-income countries (LMICs) are increasingly using economic evaluation to inform decisions about which health care interventions might be funded publicly, given public sector finance and resource constraints (Shillcutt *et al.*, 2009). Typically, economic evaluation has been used to evaluate health care interventions under the driving force of health technology assessment (HTA) programmes (Oortwijn *et al.*, 2010). This is similar to the pattern in high-income countries (HICs), where the use of economic evaluation for HTA is almost the norm (http://www.hinnovic.org/health-technology-assessment-across-the-world/).

In parallel with increasing interest in the economic evaluation of health care interventions, interest in the economic evaluation of social care interventions is increasing. In the UK, for example, the National Institute for Health and Care Excellence (NICE, 2015) recently extended economic evaluation methods guidance to interventions with a social care focus. In contrast to health care interventions, where the perspective on costs comprises health care and personal social services, in social care interventions, a wider perspective is supported. This includes consideration of the costs falling on the public sector and the societal costs where appropriate, hence informal care costs which fall on the private sphere might be included (NICE, 2015). In terms of outcomes, the guideline recommends that for social care interventions, effects on people for whom services are delivered (users, carers) might be included when relevant. In summary, the guideline acknowledges the potential contribution of informal carers without prescribing methods for the measurement and valuation of informal care.

In LMICs, social care is almost completely the responsibility of the family and there are few publicly funded social care services. In dementia, for example, in LMICs direct social care costs are small, and informal care provision, that is care provided by social networks like the family, extended family and other social structures predominate. By contrast, in high income countries (HICs), informal care and formal social care account for the majority of costs (45% and 40%, respectively), and a much lower proportion of the costs are direct medical costs (15%) (WHO, 2012). Given the scale of informal care input in LMICs that comes with this type of health care need, the interface between health care interventions and informal care is, it can be argued, much more important in LMICs than in HICs. The very use of health care interventions can promote the need for social care and informal care. Whilst in HICs, the links with, and even integration of health and social care systems is becoming more prominent, the interface between health care interventions and informal care is potentially much more significant in LMICs.

With the family playing a very important role in providing social care in LMICs and with little public spending on social care, it might be expected that LMICs are unlikely to evaluate social care interventions. On the other hand, the unmet demand for health and social care, together with the role of family in providing care in LMICs, makes the evaluation of social care alongside health care interventions as potentially informative and useful in decision-making. When choosing between different services to fund, governments and donors make difficult decisions about which benefits to value most and which benefits to forgo. More investment in HIV/AIDS treatment, for example, may come at the expense of less investment in end-of-life care. Furthermore, the contribution of family networks to the care of ill and vulnerable individuals could be recognized and accounted for. Relevant examples of social care interventions linked to health care interventions include those forms of health care with community outreach, such as maternity services, HIV care and care of senior citizens. The evaluation of such health care interventions could therefore consider how much informal input is required from the family to make them effective. It is noteworthy whether such health care interventions are designed in a way that mobilizes more informal care than otherwise might be the case. The suggestion therefore is that guidelines for evaluating such interventions might pay more attention to the contribution of social care and informal carers in LMICs, compared to HICs.

This chapter explores the use of economic evaluation to evaluate social care interventions, particularly those linked to health care interventions in LMICs. Furthermore, it aims to explore and describe the availability of methods guideline to facilitate undertaking evaluations generally within LMICs, and the availability of social care-specific methodological guideline. Additionally, it explores if and how informal care is incorporated in the economic evaluation of interventions.

To explore the use of economic evaluation methods guideline in LMICs across all health and social care interventions, an online survey was undertaken. To illustrate the LMIC experience in more detail, five within-country case studies were produced. Section 2 describes the methods used to undertake the online survey and the case studies. Section 3 presents the main results from the survey and the case studies, and Section 4 discusses the case studies. Section 5 discusses the implications of these findings for the economic evaluation of social care interventions and informal care in LMICs, including recommendations for future research.

2. Methods

2.1. *Study sample*

All countries were categorized as low-income countries (LICs), lower middle-income countries (l-MICs) and upper middle-income countries (u-MICs) according to the World Bank national income definitions (http://data. worldbank.org/about/countries-and-lending-groups). There are 135 LMICs in total. The aim was that the online survey be completed by all LMICs that had official HTA or Pharmacoeconomic studies (PES) guideline; however, it is not known how many LMICs offer this guidance.

To obtain contacts for the online survey, LMIC HTA networks were accessed based on the HTAi registry. HTA networks comprised HTAsiaLink; INAHTA and RedETSA. Key individuals in the LMIC HTA networks were identified from network-member directories (www. inahta.org/our-members/members/; www.vortal.htai.org; www.ispor.org/ htadirectory, viewed in June 2015). This search revealed that among LMICS there were 31 registrations with a HTA network, representing 19 countries. Some countries, such as South Africa, had more than one HTA organization registered on the International Society for Pharmaco-economics and Outcomes Research (ISPOR) list. Over time, registrations with the HTA network are increasing and recently Egypt has been added to the list (January 2016), taking the total to 20 LMICSs. Added to this, it is not known how many LMICs have some form of HTA which is not registered with an HTA network, therefore informal links with LMICs were also utilized.

2.2. Survey design

A survey was designed (RF, AM, HW) to collect information (see Appendix 2 for the survey) on whether cost-effectiveness studies of social care interventions were undertaken to inform public sector decision-making and if so, the availability of methods guidance specific to social care. Additionally, information was obtained on whether and how informal care was incorporated in economic evaluation studies.

The survey had three components. First, participants were asked for their contact details, the name of the organization and country they worked in, the availability of official within-country guidelines for conducting HTA or PES and further details as available (perspective for costs, type of costs included, preferred measure of outcomes), the type of interventions evaluated by the organization (drugs, medical devices, diagnostic tests, surgical procedures, public health interventions and social care interventions) and whether social services were available and publicly funded. The second part of the survey focused on social care interventions and was to be completed only if social care interventions were evaluated by the organization. It asked whether the organization had ever evaluated a social care intervention, details of the evaluation if so and whether the official guidelines provided specific methods guidance for the economic evaluation of the interventions. The third part focused on informal care to explore whether the official guidelines provided guidance on the inclusion of informal care in HTA and, if so, details on the recommended methodology.

2.3. Survey implementation

An introductory text was sent to key individuals in the LMIC HTA networks and our informal network, inviting them to participate in the research and to circulate to other network members, specifying the aims and objectives of the survey, as well as providing a link to the survey. Using this strategy, the aim was to ensure that all regions were represented. The survey was administered using Qualtrics survey software www.qualtrics.com/. Through the online survey (see Appendix 2), individuals from HTA agencies in LMICs summarized their country's or agency's general economic evaluation methods guideline and the available health and social care interventions methods guidance, including informal care.

None of the survey questions were set as mandatory and therefore participants were not required to provide an answer to all prior questions in order to progress. Survey routing was used whereby participants' answers determined the appropriate follow-up questions, thus avoiding irrelevant questions. By displaying only relevant questions, it was hoped that participants would be more likely to answer all of the questions presented to them. Two reminder emails were sent to all contacts while the survey was live. These methods were selected to enhance the number of fully completed survey responses. Participants were asked to provide their name and contact details in case there were any follow-up questions.

2.4. *Case studies*

To obtain a more detailed picture of the economic evaluation methods guideline for health and social care interventions, six individuals working for five HTA organizations were identified from the contacts held by Centre for Health Economics (CHE) and the co-authors, comprising Colombia, Malawi, Thailand, Uganda and Zambia. These individuals were invited to produce short case studies of approximately 500 words describing their agency's or country's economic evaluation methods guidelines and practices in social care and informal care. In contributing case studies, all authors were given co-author status in the final report as recognition of their contribution. No financial reimbursement was offered for producing the case studies.

The case studies aimed to provide a detailed context and an LMIC perspective on the use of economic evaluation within health and social care and informal care. Contributors were asked to describe their country's experience of the funding, evaluation and decision-making for social care interventions and whether and how informal care was considered in HTA. Contributors were asked whether social care interventions were publicly funded, whether social care interventions were formally evaluated in terms of costs and benefits and how such evaluation was conducted. They were also asked to consider describing evaluation of informal care.

2.5. *Definition of social care interventions and informal care*

In the online survey and for the case studies, social care interventions were defined as services which help people with their daily activities and meet their non-medical, personal needs. These interventions assist people to live independently and safely when they cannot do so on their own. Such interventions, and often health care interventions too, can impact on the use of informal care.

Informal care refers to the help provided to people from family and friends (van den Berg *et al.*, 2004). Tasks might include personal care, as well as organizing personal affairs. Such care might also be provided by formal, paid carers too. Examples of social care interventions are provided in Box 1. For the purposes of this research, the terms social care and long term care were used interchangeably.

Box 1. Examples of social care and formal and informal carer interventions

Interventions	Definition and examples
Personal care	In which people receive assistance from carers with activities of daily living, such as washing, using the toilet, eating, dressing and moving around.
Organizing personal affairs	Assistance from carers with managing transport for medical appointments, medicines management, managing finances and keeping the house clean.
Provision of special equipment	Specialist equipment includes personal alarms, stair rails, stair lifts, walking frames. Also includes e.g. telehealth to help monitor users' health in their own homes, and telecare such as personal alarms to alert others when something is wrong.
Befriending services	Where people with loneliness issues are assigned to a befriender who provides friendly conversation and companionship on a regular basis over a long period of time.

---

3. Results

The main survey ran from 5 June 2015 to 28 August 2015. Twelve out of the 19 LMICS registered with an HTA network were contacted, including Armenia, Brazil, China, Colombia, Costa Rica, Ecuador, Malaysia, Mexico, Peru, Philippines, South Africa and Thailand. The remaining seven countries, comprising Belarus, Bosnia and Herzegovnia, Bulgaria, Cuba, Georgia, Nicaragua and Turkey were not contacted owing to a lack of access to accurate contact details. Responses were obtained from 11 out of the 12 LMICs contacted. Responses from a further nine LMICs were obtained as part of our informal LMIC network, taking the total to 20 responses (see Table 1). Completed contributions were obtained from individuals working in 20 out of the 135 LMICs (15%) including 11 responses from the 53 u-MICs (21%), six from the 51 l-MICs (12%) and three from the 31 LICs (10%). It is not known how many LMICs in total have HTA- or PES-type guidance, therefore the level of survey coverage

Table 1. Participating countries (*n* = 20).

Country	Region	GNI per capita (Atlas method)*	Income band	Participating organization	Registered with HTA network[a]	Operate official HTA/PES guidelines
1. Armenia	Europe	$3,930	l-MIC	Yerevan State Medical University	✓	
2. Bhutan	Asia	$2,340	l-MIC	Essential Medicines and Technology Division	✓	✓
3. Brazil	Latin America	$12,310	u-MIC	DECIT SCTIE Ministry of Health (Brazil)	✓	✓
4. China	Asia	$6,710	u-MIC	China National Health Development Research Center	✓	✓
5. Colombia	Latin America	$7,770	u-MIC	Instituto de Evaluación Tecnológica en Salud	✓	✓
6. Costa Rica	Latin America	$9,780	u-MIC	Caja Costarricense de Seguro Social	✓	
7. Ecuador	Latin America	$5,810	u-MIC	Ministry of Health (Ecuador)	✓	
8. Guyana	Africa	$3,940	l-MIC	Ministry of Public Health (Guyana)		
9. India	Asia	$1,530	l-MIC	National Health Systems Research Centre		
10. Indonesia	Asia	$3,740	l-MIC	Center for Health Economics & Policy Studies		✓
11. Kazakhstan	Europe	$11,560	u-MIC	Republican Center for Health Development		✓
12. Malawi	Africa	$280	LIC	University of Malawi		
13. Malaysia	Asia	$10,850	u-MIC	Malaysian HTA Section Ministry of Health (Malaysia)	✓	✓

14. Mexico	Latin America	$9,720	u-MIC	CENETEC-Salud		✓	✓
15. Nepal	Asia	$730	LIC	Details not provided			
16. Peru	Latin America	$6,230	u-MIC	Ministry of Health (Peru)		✓	
17. Philippines	Asia	$3,340	l-MIC	Department of Health (Philippines)		✓	
18. South Africa	Africa	$7,410	u-MIC	PRICELESS, University of the Witwatersrand		✓	
19. Thailand	Asia	$5,840	u-MIC	Health Intervention & Technology Assessment Program		✓	
20. Uganda	Africa	$630	LIC	Medical Research Council/ Uganda Virus Research Institute			

Notes: *2013 data (Information sourced from the World Bank: www.data.worldbank.org/indicator/NY.GNP.PCAP.CD).
a ISPOR HTA directory, INAHTA, HTAsiaLink.

is not clear. Organizations undertaking economic evaluations comprised ministries of health, university-based institutions and HTA agencies. Organizations in the following regions of the world were represented; Africa, Asia, Europe and Latin America.

3.1. *Availability of official HTA and PES guidelines by national income category (n = 20)*

Based on the survey findings, 11 out of the 20 participating LMICs produced official HTAs or PES guidelines. Of those, the majority (8) were u-MIC. None of the participating LICs and three of the l-MIC countries reported that there are official HTA and PES guidelines available.

Of the 11 countries which produced official guidelines, nine were reported to offer economic evaluation methods guidelines. The stated perspective for the type of costs that were included in economic evaluations were health care costs only (4), health and social care costs (4), a societal perspective on costs (1). In the remaining countries, no methods guideline was provided for recommending a specific cost perspective. The country which recommended a societal perspective on costs (Thailand) stated that the costs comprised health care, private out-of-pocket (OOP) costs and informal care costs.

3.2. *Health outcome measures preferred by countries with official HTA and PES guidelines (n = 8)*

In LMICs which had official guidelines for conducting HTA or PES, the preferred measure of outcomes were health related. Eight out of the 11 countries offering official guidelines focused on health outcomes, and all stated that they recommended the quality-adjusted life years (QALYs) approach to quantify health care outcomes. Other health outcomes that were also recommended included: life years (5), the disability-adjusted life years (DALYs) (4) and other unstated measures of health (4). The remaining three countries stated that their official guidelines did not specify a preferred measure of outcome.

3.3. *Use of informal care in official guidelines*

Of the 11 countries that reported having official guidelines, seven reported that no recommendation was made on methods for evaluating informal care. Of the three countries with recommendations, one participant reported that in their country, although the official guideline referred to informal care (Brazil), it did not specify how to measure and value this care. Two participants stated that their official guidelines included informal care and provided specific advice on how to evaluate it (India and Thailand) (Figure 1). In both cases, the participants reported that researchers were advised to quantify informal care either by monetizing informal care by measuring the time spent on informal care and assigning a unit cost, or by including the informal care burden within the health outcome, for example as a QALYs decrement or an increased DALYs burden.

3.4. *Interventions evaluated using economic evaluation*

When asked about the types of interventions evaluated by their organizations, the most commonly selected types were drugs (19), diagnostic tests or techniques (15), medical devices such as hearing aids (13) and health promotion activities e.g. stop smoking interventions (11)

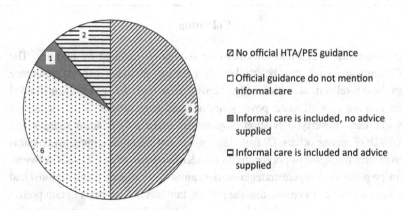

Figure 1.   Use of informal care in official guideline (*n* = 18).

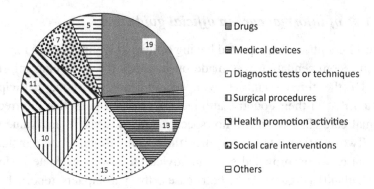

Figure 2. Interventions evaluated using economic evaluation (*n* = 20).

(Figure 2). These figures are consistent with the most commonly quantified costs reported above. Health care costs were identified as the most common cost to quantify within economic evaluations. Representatives from the seven participating countries reported that their organizations had undertaken economic evaluations of social care interventions which help people with their daily activities. Thirteen out of 20 participants stated that social care services were funded by the public sector.

4. Case Studies

Colombia

In Colombia, social and informal care is mainly provided by families. The Colombian mandatory health benefit package includes explicit reference to health-related activities only. However, within the government-funded programmes to alleviate poverty, individuals may receive some degree of social care. Poverty-alleviation programmes include *De ciero a siempre* and *UNIDOS*, among others. *De cero a siempre* (www.deceroasiempre.gov.co) aims to protect the rights of poorer children under five years of age. *UNIDOS* (www. anspe.gov.co/es/anspe/estrategia-unidos) aims to coordinate local, regional and national policies to ensure that the poorest families in Colombia obtain preferential access services offered by the government. These programmes identify individuals at need and signpost them to existing services. The publicly funded

(Continued)

services are mainly related with health care, public health and nutrition support, although some local charities may provide social care.

HTA in Colombia is to inform decisions about the inclusion of drugs, procedures and devices in the health benefit package include assessment of effectiveness, safety, budget impact and in a few cases by cost-effectiveness analysis. Formal assessment of social and informal care interventions has not been undertaken. The perspective for costs is health. Social and informal care costs are generally not included, as these costs usually fall outside the remit of the Ministry of Health.

Malawi

Formal provision of social care in Malawi hardly exists and this gap is filled by family, friends and sometimes volunteers that are organized as support groups and community-based organizations (CBOs). Most of the individuals who are in need of long-term care such as people with disabilities and people living with HIV and AIDS (PLHIV) depend on family and friends in the form of informal care.

Malawi does not have formal guidelines for conducting economic evaluations, although decision-making on new programmes and interventions are guided by results of economic evaluations. To that effect, economic evaluation studies have been conducted to inform different decisions in general as well as in HIV/AIDS (for example, Orlando *et al.*, 2010; Fasawe *et al.*, 2013; Rutstein *et al.*, 2014).

The existing economic evaluations are not on informal care and they do not include the costs of informal care. In the past few years, there have been attempts to measure and value informal care and include them in economic evaluations of treatments for HIV. One such study is the Lablite Project (lablite.org), which aims to establish the cost-effectiveness of decentralization of treatment. The work recognizes the information and methodological gaps, and makes attempts to provide options for measuring and valuing informal care. A related study and more relevant to economic evaluation of social care, is a study that is assessing the effectiveness of

(Continued)

(*Continued*)

facility-based peer support and community-based peer support in providing prevention of mother to child transmission (PMTCT) under Option B plus (Rosenberg *et al.*, 2014). A secondary analysis in this research is to assess the cost-effectiveness of facility-based peer support to women that are on PMTCT under option B plus and using community-based support to mothers on PMTCT under option B plus. The work will establish the cost-effectiveness of the different types of carers (facility-based peer support and community-based peer support) to retain women in care. The utilization of the results from this cost-effectiveness study will depend on the findings of the clinical trial in parallel with this study. If the clinical trial results show that the interventions improve health outcomes, the Ministry of Health will use the findings from the cost-effectiveness study to inform decision-making.

Thailand

In Thailand, social care for people with disabilities and the elderly is typically provided by their families and relatives as this fits with the cultural norms and the traditional mindset (Jongudomsuk *et al.*, 2015). However, around 9% of the elderly live alone (National Statistical Office, 2014). Social care interventions such as temporary or long-term personal assistants, and home repairs or improvements for the elderly who face difficulties are available through the public sector. Informal care tends to be provided through community-based volunteer workers and peer groups through the Senior Citizen Centres in the communities (Jitapunkul and Wivatvanit, 2009, Jongudomsuk *et al.*, 2015). The Thai government has issued a monthly allowance for the elderly (฿600–1,000) and people with disabilities (฿500) through a universal tax-financed scheme. The amount of money that is offered through these schemes is insufficient to fully meet needs, based on the current prices (2014–2015).

With the increased demand for social care due to an aging population, private for-profit paid caregivers and nursing homes have become popular to supplement the supply provided by the public and voluntary sectors. Therefore, some families need to pay OOP to cover these services. Only 0.75%

(Continued)

---

of the Thai elderly have paid caregivers as their main caregivers (National Statistical Office, 2014), as the cost is prohibitive to poorer families.

Economic evaluation can play a major role in assisting decision-makers when tackling the issue of social care interventions. However, having searched the Thai HTA database,[1] of the 177 economic evaluation studies undertaken, there has been no economic evaluation of social care interventions (the search covered the entire database up until 30 July 2015). This may be due to the fact that what counts as social care interventions are often burden provided by families rather than the public sector.

From the Thai HTA guideline, informal care cost is recommended for inclusion as a form of direct non-medical costs when conducting cost-effectiveness analysis using a societal perspective (Riewpaiboon, 2014). The informal care cost used the time conversion derived from the Gross National Income (GNI) per capita per hour. This HTA guideline set the standard for all economic evaluation studies aimed at policy-decision-making in Thailand, especially for the development of the Universal Coverage Benefit Package (Mohara *et al.*, 2012) and the National List of Essential Medicines (Teerawattananon *et al.*, 2014). It is noteworthy that there is no explicit system to utilize cost-effectiveness analysis for the development of social care benefit packages under the responsible agency, the Ministry of Social Development and Human Security.

Uganda

In Uganda, social care is mainly provided by families, friends and community members. Some private organizations like Hospice and the AIDS Support Organization (TASO) provide social care in selected communities.

The Ministry of Health in Uganda, through the national minimum health care package, has focused its health care service provision on preventive, curative and maternal and child health services (www.health.go.ug/National_Health.pdf). This may include, but on a very limited scale, some plans for social care including household follow-up of HIV infected persons,

---

(Continued)

[1] A database that contains economic evaluation studies related to the Thai context published in either Thai or English through http://db.hitap.net/.

(Continued)

---

pregnant mothers and new borns, and is mainly carried out by volunteer community health workers in Uganda, called village health teams (VHTs).

There is a lack of a comprehensive social security system in Uganda. The national social security fund (www.nssfug.org) works as a saving scheme and is only available to people in private formal employment. The Ministry of Gender, Labour and Social Development, is piloting the Expanding Social Protection Program (ESPP) (www.socialprotection.go.ug/) in a few districts. This initiative was approved by the parliament in 2010 to provide social protection and improve social care and support services for the elderly, orphans and other vulnerable groups. Through direct cash transfers, approximately US$8 a month is given to individuals over 65 years of age under the senior citizens grants and to families with old people, people with disabilities and orphans. It is expected that this amount would cover both direct costs of health care-seeking and indirect costs such as transport and would be used as compensation for those out of a job. Currently, there are ongoing discussions about a national roll out of these grants. There are plans to do a cost-effectiveness study by ESPP: www.opml. co.uk/sites/default/files/OPM_Uganda%20Report_web_FINAL.pdf.

Health care in Uganda is "free for all" at the government facilities. Free services include consultation and treatment for selected services as specified in the minimum health care package, but do not include re-imbursement for laboratory supplies and drugs purchased by patients due to stock-outs, income loss due to illness, home care support, transport to and from facilities and catering and laundry services for in-patients.

The key health policy document is the Health Sector Strategic and Investment Plan (HSSIP). A costing of the HSSIP 2010/11–2014/15 was done (Chapter 9 of the HSSIP). The costing only considered direct costs in the production, and delivery of health care and was done from the provider perspective, which means the costs to the user and any other indirect costs were not included.

There is a proposed national health insurance scheme that has not yet been approved by the parliament: www.parliament.go.ug/new/index. php/about-parliament/parliamentary-news/477-national-health-insurance-scheme-bill-in-the-offing. A costing of the proposed scheme estimates that an 8% salary contribution from all employees in the formal sector will avail adequate funding for the scheme. However, this proposed scheme only covers direct provider costs of health care and not indirect costs.

Zambia

Zambia is a land-locked country located in the Southern Africa. Its population is around 14 million. Health care is provided by the government, church organizations, private sector and alternative providers, funded through a mix of public, donor and private contributions. There is little formal provision of social care.

The Central Province is one of the 10 Zambian provinces and can illustrate the experience of health and social care in Zambia. The Central Province has 1.3 million people. Life expectancy at birth is 53 years, similar to the average in the country. Approximately two-thirds of the population lives in poverty. Access to health care is poor, particularly in rural hard-to-reach areas.

The Kabwe diocese covers the Central Province of Zambia. It runs five rural health centres, 30 home-based care centres, and five orphanages, where it cares for the health and education of over 3,000 children who are either orphan or vulnerable. Until recently, funding for the education of orphans and vulnerable children was donor-funded. Although education is officially free, in reality children are required to pay fees to be allowed to attend school. Fees are between £5 and £70 per year, depending on the education level, which is unaffordable for many orphans and vulnerable children. There has since been a change in priorities toward HIV/AIDS medication in detriment to other care services. As a result, more than 3,000 children have now limited access to education. This is an example of how prioritizing health may have adverse consequences in other important areas, such as education.

---

5. Discussion

A growing number of LMICs use economic evaluation alongside HTA to inform decisions on public funding of health care interventions. This trend reflects the idea that decisions on which interventions to publicly fund should be made on the basis of transparent evidence, informed by rigorous analysis (Glassman and Chalkidou, 2012; Chalkidou *et al.*, 2014). Most countries that responded to the online survey have methods guidelines for economic evaluation. These are generally health-focused: the perspective on costs is health or health and social care, the outcomes include the impact of the intervention on health, and two countries offer guidance on methods for evaluating informal care. In taking this approach, cross-sector impacts beyond health are typically omitted. The exceptions are Thailand, which accepts a societal perspective and whose methods guidelines, along with those for India, recommend that informal care is measured and valued, and guidance is provided as to how to undertake this analysis.

In LMICs, economic evaluation is seldom used in social care. For at least some of the LMICs, the lack of evaluation of social care interventions reflects that it is largely provided by family and friends in the private sphere and that social care is typically not publicly funded. Across the five countries covered in the case studies, there is little public provision of social care and clarity is required on what constitutes social care. Social care may be a small component of poverty reduction programmes (e.g. Colombia) or take the form of direct cash transfers (e.g. Uganda, Thailand), and such programmes might stimulate use of social care. If cash transfers were seen as an essential component of a programme, this could perhaps be subjected to economic evaluation.

It is relevant to consider the social context of LMICs. Whereas in Europe the number of individuals living alone is around 21–58%, the percentage is much lower in LMICs, e.g. 9% in Thailand. Some cultures, such as the Asian culture, are more likely to see as the norm that people's offspring should care for relatives (whether parents, grandparents or the broader family network). Given that public finances do not typically fund social care, economic evaluation research tends to focus on health care interventions. In the future, however, if the demand for social care increases, state-level solutions may become more relevant. As LMICs become richer, there may be more public resources to devote to health as well as social care.

Given the significant contribution of informal care in LMICs, at a minimum, it would be useful to measure the physical quantities of informal care required by some health care interventions. The quantification of informal carer input could be used to highlight this contribution and, where it occurs, to examine the impact of implementing those health care interventions with cross-sector impact, including possible cost-shifting consequences. Consideration of the value of informal carer input is a step further and is likely to be a lot more difficult, particularly in subsistence economies. The opportunity cost of some family member's time would be very small (e.g. the grandmother who probably has to stay in the house anyway), whereas that of others (e.g. someone who has to give up working in the fields) could be quite high. These valuation issues are also faced in HICs too when, for examples, people retire.

Economic evaluation across health and social care raises methodological challenges, which are common to HICs and LMICs. In economic evaluation, the benefits of interventions are compared to their opportunity costs, which are the benefits forgone or activities displaced in order to invest in the chosen intervention/s. In the Zambia case study, for example, education for vulnerable or orphan children may not have been funded in order to increase the resources available to fund HIV/AIDS interventions. Therefore, the benefits of educating these children may have been forgone in order to achieve the benefits of treating more people, or fewer people with more (costly) intervention in the HIV/AIDS community. If funding decisions are made across sectors, including health, social care and other sectors, use of a common measure of benefit is helpful to compare across different interventions. The challenge is to develop a measure that is both sensitive and reliable to quantify the impact of a wide range of interventions across sectors.

The use of economic evaluation requires the availability of trained professionals to conduct the analyses and country-specific data, as well as funding and political recognition that investment in economic evaluation to inform decision-making is good value for money. Oortwijn *et al.* (2010) have suggested that HTA might be developed further in MICs by promoting understanding of the concept of HTA through sharing expertise and experiences in MICs among professionals, policymakers, academia, industry, health insurance sector, patients, consumer organizations and people in general. In addition, they suggest that another priority is capacity-building since most countries lack the capacity of trained and experienced personnel to carry out, interpret and use the results of HTA. These capacity issues have also been discussed in Tantivess *et al.* (2009). A recent review of HTA tools in sub-Saharan Africa showed a gap in HTA methodology used in poor resource countries. There is a need to develop appropriate methods and approaches further (Kriza *et al.*, 2014). In those LMICs which offer methods guidelines for the economic evaluation of social care interventions, it would be useful to explore the incentives for undertaking such evaluations locally, to undertake locally relevant evaluations to examine the experience of conducting such evaluations and to follow through to explore findings in terms of the impact on practice.

To our knowledge, this is the first study on the methods and practice of economic evaluation of social care interventions in LMICs. It emphasizes the link between health, social care and informal care and the different implications in LMICs as compared to HICs. It adds to the knowledge base on the conduct of economic evaluation for decision-making in LMICs and notes some challenges faced. The survey provides a snapshot of the methods and practice of economic evaluation in health and social care in LMICs. Over half (12/19) of the LMICs registered within the ISPOR HTA network responded. Feedback on the survey and case studies suggests that there are differences in interpretation of what constitutes social care. The distinction between health and social care and poverty-reducing cash transfers may sometimes be unhelpful. Arguably, if all these interventions share a common public budget, decisions on their funding could be informed by economic evaluations comparing their costs and benefits. To achieve this, however, more research and guidance is needed on the appropriate costs and outcomes for inclusion in the analysis, as well as methods for measuring and valuing informal care and the appropriate threshold value.

Acknowledgments

Many thanks are due to Mike Drummond for his excellent comments, to Paul Revill for organizing this venture and to Yot Teerawattananon who liaised with HTAsiaLink secretariat to survey their members.

References

Chalkidou, K., Culyer, T., Faden, R. *et al.* (2014). Methods for economic evaluation project. Bill and Melinda Gates Foundation, NICE International, the Health Intervention and Technology Assessment Program (Thailand) and Centre for Health Economics, University of York.

Fasawe, O., Avila, C., Shaffer, N., et al. (2013). Cost-effectiveness analysis of option B+ for HIV prevention and treatment of mothers and children in Malawi. *PLOS One*, 8(3): e57778.

Glassman, A., Chalkidou, K. (2012). Priority-setting in health: Building institutions for smarter public spending. Center for Global Development Brief.

Jitapunkul, S., Wivatvanit, S. (2009). National policies and programs for the aging population in Thailand. *Ageing International*, 33: 62–74.

Jongudomsuk, P., Srithamrongsawat, S., Patcharanarumol, W., Limwattananon, S., Pannarunothai, S., Vapatanavong, P., Sawaengdee, K., Fahamnuaypol, P. (2015). *The Kingdom of Thailand Health System Review*, Health Systems in Transition. World Health Organization, Asia Pacific Observatory on Health Systems and Policies.

Kriza *et al.* (2014). A systematic review of Health Technology Assessment tools in sub-Saharan Africa: Methodological issues and implications. *Health Research Policy and Systems*, 12: 66.

Mohara, A., Youngkong, S., Velasco, R. P., Werayingyong, P., Pachanee, K., Prakongsai, P., Tantivess, S., Tangcharoensathien, V., Lertiendumrong, J., Jongudomsuk, P., Teerawattananon, Y. (2012). Using health technology assessment for informing coverage decisions in Thailand. *Journal of Comparative Effectiveness Research*, 1: 137–46.

National Institute for Health and Care Excellence (NICE) (2015). Process and methods guides. Developing NICE guidelines: The manual.

National Statistical Office (2014). The 2014 Survey of the older persons in Thailand. Ministry of Information and Communication Technology.

Oortwijn, W., Mathijssen, J., Banta, D. (2010). The role of health technology assessment on pharmaceutical reimbursement in selected middle-income countries. *Health Policy*, 95: 174–184.

Orlando, S., *et al.* (2010). Cost-effectiveness of using HAART in prevention of mother-to-child transmission in the DREAM-Project Malawi. *JAIDS Journal of Acquired Immune Deficiency Syndromes*, 55(5): 631–634.

Riewpaiboon, A. (2014). Measurement of costs for health economic evaluation. *Journal of the Medical Association of Thailand*, 97 (Suppl 5): S17–26.

Rosenberg, E. N., van Lettow, M., Tweya H., *et al.* (2014). Improving PMTCT uptake and retention services through novel approaches in peer-based family-supported care in the clinic and community: A three-arm cluster randomized trial (PURE Malawi). *Journal of Acquired Immune Deficiency Syndrome*, 67: S114.

Rutstein, S.E., Kamwendo, D., Lugali, L., *et al.* (2014). Measures of viral load using Abbott RealTime HIV-1 Assay on venous and fingerstick dried blood spots from provider-collected specimens in Malawian District Hospitals. *Journal of Clinical Virology*, 60: 392–398.

Shillcutt, S. D., Walker, D. G., Goodman, C. A., Mills, A. J. (2009). Cost effectiveness in low- and middle-income countries. *Pharmacoeconomics*, 27(11): 903–917.

Tantivess, S., Teerawattananon, Y., Mills, A. (2009). Strengthening cost-effectiveness analysis in Thailand through the establishment of the health intervention and technology assessment program. *Pharmacoeconomics*, 27(11): 931–945.

Teerawattananon, Y., Tritasavit, N., Suchonwanich, N., Kingkwaew, P. (2014). The use of economic evaluation for guiding the pharmaceutical reimbursement list in Thailand. *Zeitschrift für Evidenz, Fortbildung und Qualität im Gesundheitswesen*, 108: 397–404.

van den Berg, B., Brouwer, W. B. F., Koopmanschap, M. A. (2004). Economic valuation of informal care. An overview of methods and applications. *European Journal of Health Economics*, 5: 36–45.

World Health Organisation (WHO) (2012). Dementia. A public health priority.

Part 3

Health System Issues

Chapter 6

Paying for Performance for Health Care in Low- and Middle-Income Countries: An Economic Perspective

Martin Chalkley, Andrew J. Mirelman, Luigi Siciliani and Marc Suhrcke

Abstract

Pay-for-performance (P4P) arrangements, which are fixtures of health systems in high-income countries (HIC), have been deployed across many low- and middle-income country (LMIC) settings as well. P4P programmes in HICs have typically addressed the challenge of over-delivery, controlling costs while maintaining adequate services and getting the best clinical practice, or quality of care. In LMICs, health systems are similarly concerned with issues of quality, but they may also grapple with problems of low demand, lack of resources and poor governance. By revisiting the overall framework for understanding P4P arrangements and their benefits and risks in the context of health care delivery, this chapter draws on experiences with P4P in HIC to assess how the insights from economic theory apply in practice in LMICs. Issues of programme design and unintended consequences are summarized, and LMIC case examples of where these concepts apply and are missing from the evidence of P4P programmes in LMIC settings are also reviewed. The evidence on P4P in LMICs is still in its infancy, both in terms of evidence of impact (especially as far as health outcomes are concerned), and in terms of the attention to potential unintended consequences. However, it is critical to return to the basic economic understanding of how the contractual arrangements and incentives of P4P inform programme design and ultimately impact health outcomes and service delivery.

1. Introduction

The idea that a payment should be linked to observing and verifying some tangible outcome delivered has an obvious intuitive appeal. The funder can influence what gets done and receives evidence to ensure that what was intended was done. In the jargon of economics, the verification arrangements of the funder generate *incentives* to *perform* appropriately. For convenience, we refer to these arrangements as pay-for-performance (P4P).

P4P is a ubiquitous part of the landscape of health care in high-income countries (HIC) and increasingly discussed and implemented in low- and middle-income country (LMIC) health systems (Miller and Babiarz, 2014). There are potentially important insights to be gained from the economics of incentives in terms of when their use may be appropriate, what the unintended consequences might be and how those unintended consequences might be mitigated or avoided altogether.

HICs have typically relied on P4P programmes as part of their efforts to address the challenge of over-delivery, i.e. to control costs while maintaining adequate services and getting the best clinical practice, or quality of care. In LMICs, health systems are similarly concerned with issues of quality, but they may also grapple with problems of low demand, lack of resources and poor governance. Despite obvious differences in terms of focus between HIC and LMIC settings, the insights gained from experience with P4P in HICs are potentially valuable for LMIC health systems.

The purpose of this chapter is to draw on the development of P4P in HICs and to assess how the insights from economic theory apply in practice in LMICs. We begin by revisiting the overall framework for understanding P4P arrangements, their benefits and their risks in the context of health care delivery. We next discuss the issues of programme design and unintended consequences and summarize the evidence regarding the impact of P4P programmes in LMIC settings.

2. P4P from an Economic Perspective

2.1. *Delegation and conditionality*

At a very general level, there is a problem that those wanting to ensure the delivery of things have to delegate the actual delivery. In health care as in the delivery of many services, the actual delivery process needs to be undertaken by experts, professionals or health care workers. In the language of economics, the delegator is termed the *principal* and the delegate is termed the *agent*. While there are a diversity of principals and agents in many health care settings, for convenience in our exposition we use the terms *funder* and *delivery organization*, respectively. Between the funder and the delivery organization, there is an agreement often referred to as the *contract*.

One approach to the problem of delegation is for the funder to simply articulate what it would like to be done and to pay the delivery organization a reasonable sum to achieve that. We would call this an *unconditional payment* in the sense that the delivery organization will be paid irrespective of any evidence of its performance. In a health care setting, this corresponds to the funder simply making a payment to the delivery organization and essentially letting it "get on with the job". Such completely unconditional payments for health care delivery are increasingly rare.

If the funder could simply instruct the delivery organization and verify that what it has required has actually been done, then there would not be any problem. The whole matter of incentives would be handled simply by an agreement of the form "do what I want, and I will pay for your effort in doing it". We could call this a *fully specified payment* — the delivery organization will receive a financial transfer only if they satisfy all of the precise requirements that the funder stipulates.

But in reality, there are limitations to this approach. First, the funder may not be able to establish exactly what was done, or even if they can establish it, they may need to convince a separate agency that is charged with enforcing the agreement. Second, the funder may not be sure what they actually want done — i.e. it may depend on what the delivery organization is going to learn or observe. Third, there may be costs to the funder and the delivery organization for monitoring, documenting and validating that the services were delivered.

P4P can be viewed as specifying a *conditional* payment. The funder may want to, for instance, have a particular target population vaccinated, with the target defined in terms of the most vulnerable or those individuals who would realize the largest health benefit in a locality. A conditional payment might take some items which are simple to observe, verify characteristics of individuals and pay a price-per-service use for those individuals who could be verified as having received the service. A key observation is that, in LMICs, as in HICs, there is a growing reliance on these conditional payments — a movement toward more P4P in the provision of health care (Eijkenaar *et al.*, 2013).

2.2. The design of P4P schemes

2.2.1. Linear versus nonlinear incentive schemes

P4P schemes can be designed in a number of different ways in terms of the strength and nature of the provider incentive. A common distinction is between a *linear* payment with a fixed amount paid for each additional unit of performance observed (for example, each person vaccinated) and a *nonlinear* payment where payment is conditioned on thresholds and where per-unit payment can vary when the volume is below, above or between different thresholds.

Linear payment systems, with a fixed per-unit price have the advantage of being simple to implement but do not perform well in the presence of large variations in the characteristics of those who have to be treated. Delivery organizations are likely to differ in aspects such as: costs, altruism and population served. This heterogeneity calls for the payment to be nonlinear and gradually adjusted for different degrees of performance (Baron and Myerson, 1982). The payment received increases with performance but not necessarily at a linear rate. Figure 1 provides an example and compares a nonlinear scheme where the unit price increases with the degree of performance with a one with a constant price. For example, when some providers have a much lower marginal cost than

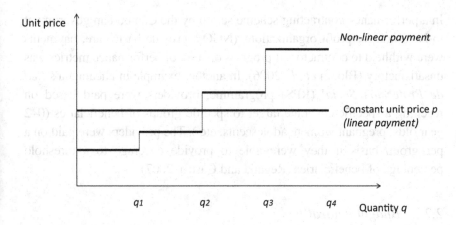

Figure 1. Linear versus nonlinear payments.

others, a linear incentive scheme would either leave large profits to the efficient providers or drive the less-efficient providers out of the market, which might then impact on delivery for individuals who can only be served by inefficient providers. A nonlinear incentive scheme can mitigate (but not eliminate) this tension by paying higher unit prices for some levels of production, but this entails additional contractual complexity (Laffont and Martimort, 2002).

The central message here is that nonlinear schemes can generate more sophisticated incentives but they are more difficult (or costly) to design and implement. As might be expected, emerging P4P schemes in LMICs may start with linear arrangements. For example, in the health P4P scheme set up by the Rwandan government, a linear payment was made based on a scaled score from 0 to 1, with a quality score of 1 meaning a facility received 100% of the payment. Scores of 0.5 and 0.8 would receive 50% and 80% of the payment, respectively (Basinga *et al.*, 2011). In another P4P programme in the Philippines, the Philippines Child Health Experiment, physician bonuses were paid linearly based on the number of patients seen after the physician met a quality threshold based on clinical performance vignettes (CPVs) (Peabody *et al.*, 2014).

There are very few complex, nonlinear contract designs in LMIC P4P schemes. However, a withholding design, where payment is not made unless a given performance threshold is met, is an example of a simplified nonlinear contract. Withholding type schemes are seen in several LMIC programmes.

In a performance contracting scheme set up by the Cambodian government to have non-for-profit organizations (NGOs) provide basic care, payments were withheld to contractors if progress on a set of performance metrics was unsatisfactory (Bloom *et al.*, 2006). In another example in Nicaragua's *Red de Protección Social* (RPS) programme, providers were paid based on reaching a specific coverage target to specific groups of beneficiaries (0–2 year olds, pregnant women, adolescents, etc.). The providers were paid on a per group basis if they were able to provide coverage to a threshold percentage of beneficiaries (Regalia and Castro, 2007).

2.2.2. Budget neutrality

A critical aspect in the design of any P4P scheme is whether it replaces a current payment scheme or if it is introduced on top of a current payment scheme. In the former case, this can be referred to as budget neutral. An example of a budget-neutral scheme would be when the delivery organization replaces a fixed budget with a linear payment (fixed price) system with no fixed budget element. An example of the second is where a top-up price is added to a fixed budget and there is an additional cost to the funder.

In theory, there is no reason why a funder cannot introduce P4P and finance it by withholding resources from other revenues of the delivery organization. For example, a P4P scheme combined with a smaller fixed budget component can replace a system fully based on a fixed budget. In practice, this may be difficult in certain institutional contexts, and introducing a P4P scheme while also providing additional resources, at least in the first year, may help convince delivery organizations to adopt the scheme.

In practice, the issue of budget neutrality is important for evaluating the impact of a scheme, as well as its cost-effectiveness. An increase in performance may come from the conditioning on performance, or it may come from the increase generosity in overall resources. Additionally, some P4P schemes may be introduced as payment in a specific project budget or as a modest percentage of the overall budget.

An example of this issue is highlighted in a recent evaluation of a P4P programme in two counties in Shandong, China to curb irrational drug use. In one treatment group, a move was made from fee for service (FFS) to capitation with 20% of the capitated budget being withheld based on performance. Since none of the health centres received the full 20% back, the authors rightly note that P4P scheme is actually providing a lower budget overall than a group that receives 100% of the capitation (Sun *et al.*, 2016). An opposite example can be seen in a national performance-based contracting programme in Cambodia, where a bonus-based incentive led to providers with performance contracts receiving more resources overall than those providers without performance contracts (Van de Poel *et al.*, 2016).

Examples of programmes where the P4P component comprises a fraction of the overall budget come from programmes by the NGO, Cordaid, in Tanzania and Zambia. In Tanzania, the P4P programme comprised 8–10% of the total health budget for the region where it was implemented, while in the Zambia programme, the contribution was 17%. The remainder of the budgets were not performance-based and came from sources such as the ministry of health, cost recovery and insurance. In each of these P4P programmes, 50% of this portion of the overall budget was provided upfront and the other 50% was paid based on performance (Canavan and Swai, 2008; Vergeer and Chansa, 2008).

2.2.3. *Sticks or carrots?*

A P4P scheme can be designed in such a way that it gives extra resources for the additional, or improved, care provided (a carrot or bonus) or can give an amount of payment and then withhold resources in case of underperformance (a stick or punishment). Withholding may be a more natural option if the initial resources are provided to set up the services, i.e. to build capacity and cover the key costs to make the provision of services viable. In theory, the two schemes should be equivalent. In practice, they may lead to different outcomes. Delivery organizations may receive a grant to build capacity so that most of the money is provided even if the performance target is below the necessary threshold.

In sub-section 2.2.2, we pointed out that two programmes, one in China and one in Cambodia, have different contract designs with respect to withholding payment or paying with bonuses. A literature review of LMIC P4P programmes also found that there is a split, and in some cases programmes can have a blend of withholding and bonuses (Grittner, 2013). The lack of consensus on which design is preferred means that this needs to be carefully considered during the programme design stage with respect to the context, political acceptability and desired goals.

2.3. Unintended consequences

Some fundamental issues in conditioning payment arise when the delivery organization knows, or is able to observe things, that are hidden from the funder. This is generically referred to as *imperfect information* in the economics literature. In this sub-section, we discuss the underlying concepts of five important types of unintended consequences that may arise in P4P programmes. Four of these are related to the conditionality (multitasking, gaming, selection and equity) while the remaining one — crowding-out — is a cross-cutting theme relevant to incentivizing health care more generally. These potential unintended consequences have emerged as topics of interest due to experiences with P4P in HICs and LMICs, and each one is discussed here in more detail (Witter *et al.*, 2012; Roland and Dudley, 2015).

2.3.1. Multitasking

One of the most common potential problems with P4P is what is known as *multitasking*. Although some dimensions of performance are quantifiable and contractible, others are not. In health care, it is often assumed that *quality* broadly falls into the latter category, i.e. it is non-quantifiable and non-contractible. The concern is that P4P schemes could generate improvements in the quantifiable dimensions of care at the expense of reductions elsewhere (Eggleston, 2005). So, by paying for *volume* we might sacrifice *quality* or *appropriateness* of treatment.

Multitasking happens when different aspects of performance are substitutes — that is, increasing one reduces the other. In such cases the P4P scheme has to be designed with care. There has been a lot of theoretical interest in how P4P schemes might be adapted to account for multitasking. Responses to multitasking that have been explored include introducing other regulatory or monitoring mechanisms or reducing the power (the level of reward relative to the marginal benefit) of the incentive scheme to balance the benefits from improved performance with reductions from other care (Kaarboe and Siciliani, 2011). The general message from multitasking is that you get what you pay for, but you might not want what you get.

The evidence for multitasking in LMIC P4P schemes is very weak, in the sense that it has rarely been a focus of the research to date. A 2012 Cochrane review of P4P schemes in LMICs found that only two out of nine identified studies looked at multitasking and whether incentivized activities were traded off with non-incentivized ones (Witter *et al.*, 2012). In an evaluation of the P4P programme in Tanzania run by the NGO, Cordaid, the evaluators found that the incentivized focus on curative interventions may distract from preventive services (Canavan and Swai, 2008). In a separate Cordaid P4P programme in Zambia, a focus on inpatient turnover rates in health centres was thought to distract from the focus of these centres to deliver primary health care services (Vergeer and Chansa, 2008). However, in both studies, no significant multitasking was found.

Further evidence of the distortions that a P4P programme can cause is mentioned in a qualitative review of the P4P scheme in the health sector in Rwanda where providers felt they had to focus on remunerated activities over non-remunerated ones (Kalk *et al.*, 2010). In addition to substitution among health services, providers also felt they were neglecting health-producing activities in favour of fulfilling bureaucratic conditions for the reward, such as doing required paperwork (Kalk *et al.*, 2010).

2.3.2. *Gaming*

A second concern with P4P is the potential for gaming: the data used to measure performance might be manipulated by the delivery organization to inflate reported performance. For a P4P scheme to work as intended, information on contractible dimensions of care needs to be reliable. This is not always the case because health information systems tend to be complex and often the information upon which payment is conditioned is self-reported by the delivery organization. For example, for child immunization it could be difficult for the funder to verify that the immunization took place. The ideal response to gaming is for the funder to base the P4P scheme on information which is outside of the control of the delivery organization and which is easily measurable, so that there is little scope for misclassifying patients in more remunerative groups.

If some gaming is unavoidable, the funder will either have to introduce some effective monitoring systems (for example, a system of random audit) although these tend to be costly, or there may again be a case for reducing the power of the incentive scheme (Kuhn and Siciliani, 2009).

An example of gaming is seen again in the qualitative evaluation of the Rwanda health sector scheme. Providers mentioned that they had retrospectively filled in reporting forms inaccurately (Kalk *et al.*, 2010). This behavior was justified by the providers in interviews as being due to that fact that the P4P programme was externally imposed and the performance indicators were counterproductive to producing health.

2.3.3. *Selection or cherry-picking*

A related but distinct concern to gaming is what is known as *cherry-picking*. If the cost of providing an incentivized service differs across patients, and the differences in costs are not reflected in the P4P payment, the delivery organization may have a financial incentive to select patients with low costs and avoid patients whose costs are above the payment (Ellis, 1998). The problem is exacerbated if patients with lower costs have the lowest capacity to benefit from the treatment. It may be a smaller concern if it is precisely those patients with lower costs that stand to gain most from the scheme.

One potential response for the funder is to design P4P schemes which differentiate payment according to the expected costs. But this may be problematic in at least two ways. First, the funder may have little reliable information to condition the payment on; and second, differentiating payments for different types of patients opens up the door to gaming. The delivery organization has a financial incentive to assign patients to the most remunerative category for payment, a practice which is sometimes referred to as *upcoding* (Dafny, 2005).

There have not been any studies in the LMIC P4P schemes that have found evidence of a selection effect, or cherry-picking. Examples, however, do exist from the HIC contexts. For instance, one study of a substance abuse treatment programme in the United States found that a performance-based system led to the selection of less severe cases for treatment (Shen, 2003).

2.3.4. *Equity concerns*

Somewhat related to the above selection problem, another key concern with the introduction of P4P is that improvement in performance may come at the cost of reduced equity, understood as a widening of the gap in health or health care utilization between lower and higher socio-economic groups. For example, if there were cherry-picking or selection-occurring, then it is likely that the most socio-economically advantaged patients (with better health) would benefit most from the scheme, further exacerbating the health gap between the rich and the poor.

Similarly, if multitasking is an issue and the incentivized dimensions of care benefit mostly the patients in better health, then the introduction of P4P will further increase disparities between groups based on health, which may have implications for socio-economic disparities as well.

The funder can in some instances address this issue by identifying the groups of patients who are more vulnerable and introduce an additional incentive (e.g. a top-up payment) for those groups. Such an incentive, while possibly beneficial, is likely to be imperfect. Although the vulnerable group has on average worse health than the non-vulnerable group, there may be some patients in the non-vulnerable group with worse health than the healthiest in the vulnerable group.

An example is in relation to income. Poor individuals are likely to be in worse health and more costly to treat. A general incentive scheme is likely to benefit richer individuals (who are cheaper to treat) more than poorer individuals who are more costly to treat. An incentive scheme targeted at the poor (as opposed to the general population) may be helpful to reduce socio-economic inequalities in health and address the highest needs, but needs to account for the differences in patient cost as well as the cost of targeting.

In a re-analysis after the primary impact evaluation of the health sector P4P scheme in Rwanda, it was found that there are important inequities in the effect of the scheme (Lannes et al., 2016). Improvements in utilization were found to be highest for more affluent groups, and in some cases, to even decrease service use for the poor. The Rwanda P4P did not include differential payment, or top-up payments to incentivize providing services to worse-off groups. On the other hand, P4P schemes such as the World Bank-supported performance-based financing (PBF) programmes in Burundi did provide higher capitation rates to the services delivered in remote areas (Witter, 2013; Bonfrer et al., 2014a, 2014b).

2.3.5. Crowding out

Acknowledging all issues identified so far, some analysts have argued that even if care is perfectly conditioned on payment, P4P may have adverse consequences on the intrinsic motivation of delivery organizations. For example, Le Grand (2003) argues that the introduction of prices may turn health care delivery organizations from *knights* to *knaves*. It is easily argued that health care delivery organizations are intrinsically motivated. Doctors have to endure long years of training and nursing, and midwifery and community health work are vocational jobs often associated with low pay. The key concern is that although the delivery organization may respond to the financial incentive introduced by P4P, this could be offset by a reduction of intrinsic motivation. In turn, this makes the introduction of P4P less effective. In practice, it is hard to reliably attribute low response of P4P schemes to intrinsic motivation as opposed to other contextual factors given that intrinsic motivation is difficult to define or observe.

Finding any evidence of crowding out in LMIC P4P schemes is also difficult. In health activities of the sectoral Public Sector Reform Programme in Tanzania, it was identified that if the financial incentives from the P4P scheme did not adequately account for context, there would be potential for crowding out (Leonard and Masatu, 2010; Songstad et al., 2012). The effect of a P4P programme may also have the opposite effect. For example, in the health sector scheme in Rwanda, there is qualitative evidence that a P4P scheme increased motivation through providing better working conditions for providers (Kalk et al., 2010).

3. P4P Programme Evidence in LMIC

In this section, we summarize the characteristics and effectiveness of several P4P schemes across LMIC settings. To do so, we conducted a purposive review of the P4P literature in relevant databases (e.g. PubMed, EconLit, and Google Scholar) and from previous systematic reviews.[1] To narrow the list of selected programmes, we only included those that had contracts between funders and health-care delivery organizations and where a quantitative evaluation was conducted. Ultimately, we selected 14 P4P programmes using a single case example per country and covering as disparate a set of countries as possible, to examine in depth. We have listed each of these programmes and their characteristics in Tables 2–4.[2] Of the 14 programmes, six were performance-based finance (PBF) schemes, six were contracting-out models, one had characteristics of both over the scheme's life course and one final scheme was a purely public sector scheme. Geographically, the schemes took place across Latin America, Asia and Africa. Most of the schemes were implemented either in the late 1990s or early 2000s and several had pilot programmes before proceeding to scaling-up. A programme in Costa Rica was introduced as early as in 1988, and the most recent year of introduction in our sample is 2007 for the programme in Zambia, though in terms of programme scale-up, Burundi's programme was most recently scaled-up from a pilot in 2011.

3.1. *Programme characteristics*

P4P programmes for health in LMICs may have funders that include country governments, bilateral donor agencies, multinational development banks and international NGOs. Delivery organizations typically include public sector providers, private sector providers, NGO providers or faith-based organizations. There are different models for contractual arrangements, which have been summarized in previous reviews (Eldridge

---

[1] A list of these reviews and associated programme countries are in Table 1.
[2] The Senegal and Madagascar programmes are presented as one since they are based on the same model and have been evaluated jointly.

Table 1. Programmes covered in literature reviews of P4P programmes.

Source	Grittner 2013	Morgan 2011	Eichler 2013	Witter 2012 (Cochrane)	Witter 2013 (agent)	Loevinsohn 2005 (contracting)	LaGarde 2009 (Cochrane)	Liu 2008
Number	PBF programmes	PBI programmes	PBI programmes	P4P of health svcs	P4P with some MNCH component	Contracting programmes	Contracting out	Contracting out
1	Afghanistan	Afghanistan	Afghanistan	Burundi	Afghanistan (ngo, gov)	Cambodia	Bolivia	Bangladesh
2	Bangladesh (urban)	Belize	Bangladesh	China	Argentina (province)	Bangladesh (rural)	Cambodia	Bangladesh
3	Bolivia	Benin	Cambodia	DRC	Brazil (local gov)	Bangladesh (urban)	Pakistan	Bolivia
4	Burundi	Burundi	DRC	Egypt (pending results)	Burundi (facility)	Bolivia		Cambodia
5	Cambodia	DRC (Cordaid)	Egypt (social)	nsi Phillipines	Cambodia (district)	Guatemala		Costa Rica
6	Costa Rica	DRC (EC)	Haiti	Rwanda	Cambodia (midwife)	Haiti		Croatia
7	DRC	DRC (Wbank)	Nepal	Rwanda (Basinga)	DRC (facility)	India (urban TB)		Guatemala
8	Haiti	Egypt	Phillipines	Rwanda (Soeters)	DRC (ngo)	India (private practitioners)		Haiti
9	Nicaragua	Honduras	Rwanda	Tanzania	Egypt (facility)	Madagascar and Senegal		India

10	Rwanda	Rwanda	Uganda (pending results)	Haiti (ngo)	Pakistan	Madagascar
11	Senegal and Madagascar	Senegal	Vietnam	India (gov agency)		Senegal
12	Tanzania	Tanzania	Zambia	India (maternal hcw)		South Africa
13				Liberia (ngo)		
14				Nepal (hcw)		
15				Nicaragua (facility)		
16				Pakistan (hcw)		
17				Phillipines (facility)		
18				Phillipines (maternal hcw)		
19				Rwanda (facility)		
20				South Sudan (intl ngo)		
21				Tanzania (facility)		
22				Tanzania(hcw)		
23				Uganda (facility)		
24				Zambia (facility)		

Others

Miller 2014 — lists 26 P4P programmes that have not been formally evaluated

Table 2. Extracted P4P programmes — Characteristics (characteristics of selected P4P programmes in LMIC).

Characteristics	Afghanistan	Bangladesh	Bolivia	Burundi	Cambodia	Costa Rica	DRC
Programme name	Unnamed (contract out)	Bangladesh urban primary health care (contract out)	Bolivia urban primary health care (PHC) (El Alto health service — contract out)	Burundi nationwide PHC P4P	Cambodia Rural PHC and district hospital svcs (contract out)	PHC worker cooperatives	PBF in Southern Kivu
Time frame	2003–2005	1998 pilot, 2005 scale-up	1999	2006 pilot with national scale-up in 2011	1998 pilot	1988, scale up in 2000	2005
Principal	World Bank/USAID/EC	Gov. and ADB	Gov. and MOH	NGO and donors	MOH and ADB	Gov.	Gov. and NGOs
Agent	NGO's and MOPH	Four local NGOs	Local NGO	Health facilities	NGOs	Primary care cooperatives	Health facilities
Services	Essential PHC services	Immunization, prenatal and obstetric care, family planning (FP), disease management	PHC services	PHC services	Rural PHC, district hospital services	PHC services	Preventive care, TB, HIV/AIDS testing
Targeting	General population	Poor households	General population	Not identified	Poor households	General population	General population

		Haiti	Nicaragua	Philippines	Rwanda	Senegal & Madagascar	Tanzania	Zambia
Characteristics	Programme name	Bonus for NGOs delivering PHC in Rural areas	Social protection network (RPS)	Philippine Child Health Experiment/Quality Improvement Demonstration Study (QIDS)	Rwanda PBF	Senegal: Community Nutrition Project (CNP); Madagascar: Secaline project (contracting out)	Tanzania Mission PBF	Zambia Mission PBF
	Time frame	FFS 1995, switch to P4P in 1999	2000–2002 pilot, extended for five years	2003–2007	Three districts, Butare in 2001 and Cyangugu in 2002, Kigali in 2005. P4P component introduced in 2005	Senegal: 1996 pilot, 1998 scale-up. Madagascar: 1994 start and scale-up	2006–2008	2007–2008
	Principal	Donor and iNGO	Gov. and IADB	Gov. (Philippine Health Insurance Corp.)	Donor Gov and iNGO	WBank/WFP/German Dev. Bank/Japan/ UNICEF and Gov.	iNGO	iNGO
	Agent	NGOs	NGOs and private for profit providers	Physicians in district community hospitals	Public and private not-for-profit facilities	Local NGOs	Faith-based facilities	Faith-based facilities
	Services	Basic health care services	Child health, reproductive health, maternal health	Hospitals services	Maternal and child health, curative services, HIV/AIDS (immunization, prenatal care, deliveries)	Nutrition services	Essential health services package	HIV, maternal health, hospital svcs (PHC in one facility)
	Targeting	General population	Poor households. Geographic combined with hh-level assessment of assets	Hospitals were primarily from poor districts	General population	Poor households. 1st stage geographic, 2nd stage based on nutrition/health status	General population	General population

Table 3. Extracted P4P programmes — Programme design.

	Afghanistan	Bangladesh	Bolivia	Burundi	Cambodia	Costa Rica	DRC
Scheme design	Payment of fixed amount plus performance bonus	Specific coverage targets	Contract based on achieving process and outcome indicators	Fixed amount plus quality bonus	Mix of contracting-in and contracting-out	Payment based on service production and coverage	Fixed amount plus quality bonus
Indicators	Outputs, nationally defined management indicators, based on MICS 2003 (World Bank). Inputs (EC/USAID)	Output only (e.g. # of centres providing immunization, FP, or lab tests)	Output only (eg. # of instit. Deliveries and output visits)	Menu of utilization indicators	Incidence of sickness, incidence of diarrhoea in children, infant mortality, service utilization	Service utilization, general mortality, child mortality	Coverage indicators of basic services (e.g. FIC, women protected from tetanus, assisted deliveries, HIV+ on antiretroviral therapy (ARV))
Quality indicators	(Unsure)	% clients reporting waiting times are acceptable, % prescriptions with specific diagnosis		Composite quality index (153 indicators, later reduced)	Perceived quality of care used as indicator		

Payment Scheme Design

Payment type	Payment size and schedule	Who received $$$
Bonus (World Bank). Withholding (USAID)	10% of contract value, paid in stages. Final 5% at end of contract (World Bank)	NGO
Bonus	NA	NGO
Withholding	NA	NGO
Payment based on service utilization and reward withheld if quality target not met	Quantitative-based payments paid monthly (FFS), quality-related payments given as quarterly bonuses (15% of quantitative payment, increased to 25% later)	Facilities, then have autonomy over how it is used. No more than 50% can go to staff incentives, rest must go to improve service quality
Penalties to NGOs for not achieving targets. Bonuses to health workers	HCW salaries: 55% basic, 15% bonus for punctuality, 30% bonus for performance if monthly financial targets were met	NGO
Withholding	NA	Cooperatives received and had autonomy over funds
Fixed amount per targeted action per month plus bonus (as withheld bonus?)	Reward is 15% of fixed amount if quality score was 100% and proportionally less for lower scores	Health facilities

(Continued)

Table 3. (*Continued*)

	Haiti	Nicaragua	Philippines	Rwanda	Senegal & Madagascar	Tanzania	Zambia
Scheme design	Fixed amount plus quality bonus	Payment based on achieving pre-defined targets	Payment if certain CPV quality score is met	Pay for incremental svcs (pilot). Pay according to quality-adjusted quantity of svcs (scale-up)	Payment of fixed amount plus performance WFP/German Dev. performance/ Japan/UNICEF coverage country payment based on service production and coverage	Fixed payment plus performance bonus	Fixed payment plus performance bonus
Indicators	Output: % of clinics with four methods of FP. Outcome: Use of oral rehydration therapy (ORT) for diarrhoea, immunization coverage, coverage of three antenatal visits. High-level: Coordination with MOH	Group-specific performance targets	Health status of children under six. Indicators of weight, height and blood test related to pneumonia and diarrhoea	Assisted deliveries, FIC, tetanus immunization of Preg Women, acceptance of FP and HIV testing	(Outcome and impact level) % malnourished children, child anthropometry, % children weighed monthly, % women attending education sessions	(Multiple levels). Availability of essential drugs, % of supervised deliveries, # new voluntary counseling and testing (VCT), utilization of output and input	(Multiple levels). Availability of essential drugs, % of supervised deliveries, # new VCT, utilization of output and input

Payment Scheme Design

Quality indicators	Bonus		Clinical performance vignettes (CPV)	Quantity-adjusted quality (post scale-up). Quality indicators include inputs (staffing, drugs, etc.) and processes			
Payment type	Withholding		Bonus	Withholding	NA	Upfront payment and retrospective payment (withholding)	Upfront payment and retrospective payment (withholding)
Payment size and schedule	95% of budget as fixed and up to 10% bonus for achieving targets	3% of annual budget paid upfront. Payments were made quarterly or biannually for reaching coverage of groups enrolled in RPS programme as "all or nothing". FFS for services for up to 10% of households not in RPS	Amount of bonus = no. of patients' times 100 Philippine pesos	Bonus paid for incremental service provision during pilot. Quality-adjusted quantity during scale-up	Monthly payment per indicator multiplied by quality index (range: 0–1). Varying % of performance bonus (40%–95%) forwarded to staff, by district	Withholding. Guaranteed 50% and performance based 50% reward paid every six mos. P4P programme is only 8–10% of total budget overall so reward was around 4%	Withholding. Guaranteed 50% and performance based 50% reward paid every six mos. P4P programme is 17% of total budget overall
Who received $$$	NGO	Contracted health care provider	Physician	NGO	Health facilities, have discretion over usage	Health facilities (though donor determined max % of allocation on staff, infrastructure, running costs, etc.)	Health facilities (though donor determined max % of allocation on staff, infrastructure, running costs, etc.)

178 · M. Chalkley et al.

Table 4. Extracted P4P programmes — Evaluation evidence.

	Afghanistan	Bangladesh	Bolivia	Burundi	Cambodia	Costa Rica	DRC
Evidence of improved non-monetary incentives	Yes		External evaluation found, provider motivation improved when they had autonomy over where incentives are allocated				
Evidence of perverse incentives					Yes (Bloom et al., 2006)		
Quantitative evaluation design	Broad comparisons	Controlled before and after study (Mahmud et al., 2002)	Before and after comparison with a control group/district (double differences)	Controlled cohort study (Rudasingwa et al., 2015)	Randomized assignment of districts + double differences	Interrupted time series (single difference) over 10 years compared to publicly managed facilities (Gauri et al., 2004; Loevinsohn, 2008)	Before and after comparison with a control group/district (double differences)
Evaluation results	Rapid increase in services that appear better in programmes with P4P. Better performance on quality scorecards for P4P programmes	11% improvement in quality score, 3.4% improvement on household survey indicators	21% difference in difference (DiD) for deliveries and 1% DiD for bed occupancy (management contract (MC) versus control)	38–66% increase in quality indicators. Bonfrer et al. (2014a) find increase in quality and utilization of maternal and child health (MCH) (but not equitably and not for all services)	Service delivery contract (SDC) and management contract (MC) better than control on seven indicators (21.3% SDC versus control; 9.3% MC versus control). Van de Poel et al. (2015) find more	22% more general visits and 42% more dental in cooperatives and decrease in medical expenditures	Patients in P4P pay less for similar or better quality

Evaluation Evidence

Other	Basic package costed at $0.65 per capita per year. Contract length is four years. Reported problems: on-time payment to NGO and adequate monitoring and evaluation (M&E)			Based loosely on Rwanda programme. Quantitative targets provided to facilities for planning but quantitative-based payment is only on services provided. Cost per capita $4.30. Bonfrer et al. (2014b) find differential effects among poor	User fees introduced at same time. Had control group. Van de Poel et al. (2015) find complement with voucher scheme. VdP also finds differences by contracting out or not		Evidence of pro-poor impact found. $2.40 per capita per year compared to $9–12 for control districts. Allowed for autonomy and community engagement on user fees too
Contract type (service delivery SDC, management MC, control CC from Loevinsohn (2005))	SDC	Limited MC in phase II, expanded MC in phase III			SDC, MC and CC		
References	Sondorp et al. (2009), Canavan et al. (2008)	Liu et al. (2008), Loevinsohn (2008), Mahmud et al. (2002), Project website: http://uphcp.gov.bd/	Loevinsohn and Harding (2005), Lavadenz et al. (2001)	Witter et al. (2012), Busogoro and Beith (2010), Rudasingwa et al. (2015), Bonfrer et al. (2014a, b)	Loevinsohn and Harding (2005), Soeters and Griffiths (2003), Bushan et al. (2002), Bloom et al. (2006), Van de Poel et al. (2015)	Loevinsohn (2008), Cercerone et al. (2005), Gauri et al. (2004)	Soeters et al. (2011), Witter et al. (2012), Bertone et al. (2011)

(Continued)

Table 4. (*Continued*)

		Haiti	Nicaragua	Phillipines	Rwanda	Senegal and Madagascar	Tanzania	Zambia
Evaluation Evidence	**Evidence of improved non-monetary incentives**	Yes		Yes	Yes		Yes	Yes
	Evidence of perverse incentives				Suggestive (Kalk et al., 2010), also some evidence of gaming		Suggestive (Canavan et al. 2008)	Yes (Vergeer and Chansa, 2008)
	Quantitative evaluation design	Before and after (without control group)	Before and after comparison with a control group/district (double differences)	Randomized assignment to district hospitals + DiD	Randomized assignment of districts + double differences	Before and after in Senegal	Controlled before and after	Controlled before and after
	Evaluation results	Single diff: −3% prenatal care, +32% vaccination coverage	5% increase in children <3 accessing preventive health checks (18.1% intervention, 13.1% control)	Improvements in self-reported health (improved 7% in treated) and wasting (incr. 9% in control)	23% increase in instit. Deliveries. Increase in child preventive visits. Improvements in prenatal quality scores	Severe and moderate malnutrition declined 6% and 4%	Nothing significant	Nothing significant

Other	Had mechanism to determine if a contracted NGO was "ready". Had quality indicator in pilot but dropped in scale up (waiting times seen as indicator of good quality)	Combined with CCT too. Pro-poor impact found		Gov fund 5%, community fund 4%, remaining by donors. Cost per capita $15 in Senegal, $48 in Madagascar	Control group: Gov. health facilities with no P4P; districts received help covering management costs	Initial goal to incentivize workers to provide set of services. Quality came later in 2005. Concurrent demand-side programmes that targeted the poor. Lannes et al. (2016) find efficiency gains but lack of gains in poor. Skiles et al. (2015) find it improved quality conditional on seeking care but not on seeking care	Control group: Gov. health facilities with no P4P; districts received help covering management costs
Contract type (service delivery SDC, management MC, control CC from Loevinsohn (2005)	SDC			SDC			
References	Eichler et al. (2007), Loevinsohn and Harding (2005)	Regalia and Castro (2007)	Peabody et al. (2014), Witter et al. (2012)	Marek et al. (1999), Loevinsohn and Harding (2005)	Canavan et al. (2008), Witter et al. (2012)	Basinga et al. (2010), Rusa et al. (2009), Soeters et al. (2005), Canavan et al. (2008), Meesen et al. (2007), Kalk et al. (2010), Lannes et al. (2016), Skiles et al. (2015), Basinga et al. (2011)	Vergeer and Chansa (2008), Witter et al. (2012)

and Palmer, 2009). Examples of common contracting models include the "contracting out" model and the PBF model (Liu *et al.*, 2008; Lagarde and Palmer, 2009). In each contracting model, the government may serve as either a funder or delivery organization, and external groups such as NGOs and multinationals may serve as either service providers (in the case of contracting out) or as sources of financing (in the case of PBF), or as both.

What is conditioned on — and used for — payment in LMIC P4P programmes also varies by programme. P4P programmes are a move away from paying for inputs, or just providing resources. There are three primary items that may be conditioned on: health service activities, process measures of quality and health outcomes. The first two may be considered as outputs while the third is a measure of outcome. Output-based performance is typically based on service utilization, which makes sense if it is controllable by the service provider. Frequently, these outputs can include elements of quality as well such as completing a full course of vaccination or receiving the total number of recommended antenatal care (ANC) visits.

Complex quality-based metrics have been used in several programmes. One example is the Burundi PBF's 220 item checklist to assess quality (Bonfrer *et al.*, 2014a, 2014b). Other programmes have employed sophisticated methods such as Clinical Performance Vignettes (CPV), which was done in the Philippines' Quality Improvement Demonstration Study (QIDS), a P4P programme rolled out to 30 district hospitals in the country (Peabody *et al.*, 2014). Other quality metrics may consist of patient-reported outcomes or even waiting times. Performance that was based on health outcomes has also been utilized in programmes — examples can be seen in the performance-based contracting programme in Cambodia and in donor-funded child nutrition programmes in Senegal and Madagascar (Marek *et al.*, 1999; Van de Poel *et al.*, 2016).

3.2. *Have they worked? Evidence from evaluated P4P programmes*

In Section 2.3, we have highlighted examples of unintended consequences in LMIC P4P programmes, although this evidence is limited. Here, we describe some findings from quantitative impact evaluations of the selected 14 programmes. As reported in previous systematic reviews, this is intended to give a sense of the relative success or failure of these programmes. For brevity, each of the programmes from Tables 2–4 is named by the country where it was implemented.

Impact evaluation methods: Most evaluation designs adopted before and after design, and looked at differences between a treatment and a control group. This allows for difference-in-difference analyses, though typically there is little discussion of the validity of the underlying assumption of the treatment and control groups moving in parallel prior to the treatment (i.e. the parallel trends assumption). Four of the programmes (Afghanistan, Cambodia, the Philippines and Rwanda) employed randomization in their roll-out which allowed for an arguably more rigorous evaluation.

Improvements in process measures: In many of the selected P4P evaluations, positive findings for process improvement were found; however, the schemes in Tanzania and Zambia did not find any process improvement at all. Common process measures included immunization rate, ANC visits completed, tetanus vaccine delivered during ANC visit and facility delivery. While the effect sizes differed across programmes, they may potentially be quite large. This may partly be explained by the differences in baseline levels of various process measures. For example, in the Rwanda programme, there was a 23% increase in institutional deliveries, which had a baseline of 35%, but there is a negligible effect on ANC visits, which have a baseline of 95% (Basinga *et al.*, 2011). In some cases, this could be due to the difference in a pilot versus a scale-up programme. This was seen in the case of the Burundi PBF programme where impacts on institutional delivery and ANC visit were found in the pilot, but not in the scaled version of the programme (Bonfrer *et al.*, 2014a, 2014b).

Improvements in quality measures: Several of the selected programmes found improvements in quality measures. One example was in Afghanistan where the programme included a "balanced scorecard" with five domains and a total of 20 quality indicators. Of these, significant impacts were only seen for three indicators in the domain of service provision. These three were: time spent with patients, completeness of medical histories and the amount of counselling provided (Engineer *et al.*, 2016). The percentage point differences in intervention and comparison groups for these three indicators were 5.9%, 6.2% and 4.1%, respectively.

Improvements in health outcomes: Two examples of programmes that reported impacts on health outcomes were in the Philippines and in Senegal/Madagascar. The former found an improvement in self-reported health and the latter found a reduction in severe and moderate malnutrition. Neonatal mortality rate (NMR) has been another health outcome of interest, and is potentially sensitive to the incentivized maternal and child health efforts that are a focus of several P4P schemes. However, results from the schemes in Cambodia and Rwanda failed to find any impact on NMR (Chari and Okeke, 2014; Van de Poel *et al.*, 2016). This also highlights the point that health outcomes are produced by a complex array of factors, including quality of services, and that incentive programmes do not always lead to the desired effects — simply incentivizing service delivery is not enough to improve outcomes.

Complementarities with demand-side programmes: Several of the selected P4P schemes were also introduced with demand-side incentive programmes such as vouchers and cash transfers. An evaluation of a combined P4P scheme and cash transfer scheme in Nicaragua found that there were positive impacts from such a combined approach. Additionally, in the short-term the removal of the demand-side cash transfer did not diminish the positive impact (Regalia and Castro, 2007). The programme in Cambodia combined a voucher for delivery with a P4P scheme and found that there was a significant impact in terms or improved institutional delivery (Van de Poel *et al.*, 2016). However, this complementary impact was not seen for the poorest women, leaving the question of how to ensure more equitable outcomes from these combined approaches.

Across a diverse set of programmes, country contexts and evaluation approaches, we show predictably that there are mixed results. In part, this may be due to the variable methods applied for evaluating impact, but this may also be due to differences in the scheme design and context (i.e. demand and supply factors) where they are conducted. Overall, there is more evidence of effects on process, or output measures than there is for health outcomes, and there have been several examples where quality measures have been examined.

4. Conclusion

P4P can be understood as a response to being imperfectly able to condition payment to match all aspects of the delivery of health care that a funder could potentially be concerned with. The imperfection is important because in practice all schemes encounter trade-offs — by paying for each person treated, one might get more treatment but increase the risk of missing the most vulnerable, or costly individuals. Schemes are limited by the information that can be observed to condition payment on and the ability of the funder to ensure that the delivery organization does not manipulate data. There is no guarantee that P4P will actually improve outcomes. If unintended consequences, such as multitasking, gaming and selection are important enough then it may be better to make an unconditional payment. In any event the detail is crucial — what is being contracted over, who is doing the contracting, what they can observe, how they choose to structure the payment (linear or nonlinear, with sticks or carrots) will all play a role in determining the success of a P4P scheme. Schemes that appropriately condition payment might be highly complex, and understanding the practical constraints that can operate may lead to relatively simple schemes, with a smaller number of choices that need to be made in terms of design.

These issues have been extensively discussed and analyzed in relation to health care in HICs, most especially with regard to hospital services where there has been a substantial take-up of fixed price (linear) prospective payment systems for hospital services (Roland and Dudley, 2015). This has led to the establishment of incentives for improving quality of health care and controlling costs (Roland and Dudley, 2015; Markovitz and Ryan, 2016). However, since these issues are specific to the concerns and priorities of HIC health care systems, it remains to be seen how they will play out in LMICs that tend to face not only shortages in the quality but also in the quantity of health care provided. As this chapter has shown, the evidence on P4P in LMICs is still in its infancy, both in terms of evidence of impact (especially as far as health outcomes are concerned), and in particular in terms of the attention to potential unintended consequences, and how they may be contained.

Acknowledgments

This report is financially supported by the International Decision Support Initiative (iDSI) — funded by the Bill & Melinda Gates Foundation, the UK Department for International Development and the Rockerfeller Foundation.

References

Baron, D. P., Myerson, R. B. (1982). Regulating a monopolist with unknown costs. *Econometrica*, 50(4): 911–930.

Basinga, P., Gertler, P. J., Binagwaho, A., Soucat, A. L., Sturdy, J. R., Vermeersch, C. (2010). Paying primary health care centers for performance in Rwanda. *World Bank Policy Research Working Paper Series*, Vol.

Basinga, P., Gertler, P. J., Binagwaho, A., Soucat, A. L., Sturdy, J., Vermeersch, C. M. (2011). Effect on maternal and child health services in Rwanda of payment to primary health-care providers for performance: An impact evaluation. *The Lancet*, 377(9775): 1421–1428.

Bertone, M. P., Mangala, A., Kwété, D., Derriennic, Y. (2011). Review of the results-based financing experiences in the Democratic Republic of the Congo. *Bethesda, Md.: Health Systems*, 20: 20.

Bhushan, I., Keller, S., Schwartz, B. (2002). Achieving the twin objectives of efficiency and equity: Contracting health services in Cambodia.

Bloom, E., Bhushan, I., Clingingsmith, D., Hong, R., King, E., Kremer, M., Loevinsohn, B., Schwartz, J. B. (2006). Contracting for health: Evidence from Cambodia. http://faculty.weatherhead.case.edu/clingingsmith/cambodia 13jun07.pdf (Accessed: 25 November 2012).

Bonfrer, I., Soeters, R., Van de Poel, E., Basenya, O., Longin, G., van de Looij, F., van Doorslaer, E. (2014a). Introduction of performance-based financing in Burundi was associated with improvements in care and quality. *Health Affairs*, 33(12): 2179–2187.

Bonfrer, I., Van de Poel, E., Van Doorslaer, E. (2014b). The effects of performance incentives on the utilization and quality of maternal and child care in Burundi. *Social Science & Medicine*, 123: 96–104.

Busogoro, J.-F., Beith, A. (2010). Pay-for-performance for improved health in Burundi. *Bethesda, MD: Health Systems*, 202: 20.

Canavan, A., Swai, G. (2008). *Payment for Peformance (P4P) Evaluation: 2008 Tanzania Country Report for Cordaid*. Amsterdam: KIT Development Policy & Practice, Royal Tropical Institute, KIT.

Canavan, A., Toonen, J., Elovainio, R. (2008). Performance based financing: An international review of the literature.

Cercerone, J., Briceno, R., Gauri, V. (2005). Contracting PHC services: The case of Costa Rica. In: Laforgia, G.,ed., *Health Systems Innovations in Central America: Lessons and Impact of New Approaches*. Washington, D.C.: World Bank.

Chari, A. V., Okeke, E. N. (2014). Can institutional deliveries reduce newborn mortality? RAND Labor and Population Working Paper. RAND: 47.

Dafny, L. (2005). How do hospitals respond to price changes? *American Economic Review*, 95(5): 1525–1547.

Eggleston, K. (2005). Multitasking and mixed systems for provider payment. *Journal of Health Economics*, 24(1): 211–223.

Eichler, R., Agarwal, K., Askew, I., Iriarte, E., Morgan, L., Watson, J. (2013). Performance-based incentives to improve health status of mothers and newborns: What does the evidence show? *Journal of health, population, and nutrition*, 31(4 Suppl 2): S36.

Eichler, R., Auxila, P., Antoine, U., Desmangles, B. (2007). Performance-based incentives for health: Six years of results from supply-side programs in Haiti. *Center for Global Development working paper*.

Eijkenaar, F., Emmert, M., Scheppach, M., Schoffski, O. (2013). Effects of pay for performance in health care: A systematic review of systematic reviews. *Health Policy*, 110(2–3): 115–130.

Eldridge, C., Palmer, N. (2009). Performance-based payment: Some reflections on the discourse, evidence and unanswered questions. *Health Policy and Planning*, 24(3): 160–166.

Ellis, R. P. (1998). Creaming, skimping and dumping: Provider competition on the intensive and extensive margins. *Journal of Health Economics*, 17(5): 537–555.

Engineer, C. Y., Dale, E., Agarwal, A., Agarwal, A., Alonge, O., Edward, A., Gupta, S., Schuh, H. B., Burnham, G., Peters, D. H. (2016). Effectiveness of a pay-for-performance intervention to improve maternal and child health services in Afghanistan: A cluster-randomized trial. *International Journal of Epidemiology*, 45(2): 451–459.

Gauri, V., Cercone, J., Briceno, R. (2004). Separating financing from provision: Evidence from 10 years of partnership with health cooperatives in Costa Rica. *Health Policy and Planning*, 19, 292–301.

Grittner, A. M. (2013). *Results-Based Financing: Evidence from Performance-Based Financing in the Health Sector*. Bonn, Germany: German Development Institute.

Kaarboe, O., Siciliani, L. (2011). Multi-tasking, quality and pay for performance. *Health Economics*, 20(2): 225–238.

Kalk, A., Paul, F. A., Grabosch, E. (2010). 'Paying for performance' in Rwanda: Does it pay off? *Tropical Medicine & International Health*, 15(2): 182–190.

Kuhn, M., Siciliani, L. (2009). Performance indicators for quality with costly falsification. *Journal of Economics & Management Strategy*, 18(4): 1137–1154.

Laffont, J.-J., Martimort, D. (2002). *The Theory of Incentives: The Principal-Agent Model*. Princeton, NJ: Princeton University Press.

Lagarde, M., Palmer, N. (2009). The impact of contracting out on health outcomes and use of health services in low and middle-income countries. *The Cochrane Database of Systematic Reviews* (4): CD008133.

Lannes, L., Meessen, B., Soucat, A., Basinga, P. (2016). Can performance-based financing help reaching the poor with maternal and child health services? The experience of rural Rwanda. *The International Journal of Health Planning and Management*, 31(3): 309–348.

Lavadenz, F., Schwab, N., Straatman, H. (2001). Redes públicas, descentralizadas y comunitarias de salud en Bolivia.

Le Grand, J. (2003). *Motivation, Agency, and Public Policy: Of Knights and Knaves, Pawns and Queens*. Oxford Scholarship Online.

Leonard, K. L., Masatu, M. C. (2010). Professionalism and the know-do gap: Exploring intrinsic motivation among health workers in Tanzania. *Health Economics*, 19(12): 1461–1477.

Liu, X., Hotchkiss, D. R., Bose, S. (2008). The effectiveness of contracting-out primary health care services in developing countries: A review of the evidence. *Health Policy and Planning*, 23(1): 1–13.

Loevinsohn, B. (2008). *Performance-Based Contracting for Health Services in Developing Countries: A Toolkit*, World Bank Publications.

Loevinsohn, B., Harding, A. (2005). Buying results? Contracting for health service delivery in developing countries. *The Lancet*, 366: 676–681.

Mahmud, H., Ullah Khan, A., Ahmed, S. (2002). Mid-term health facility survey — Urban primary health care project. *Dhaka: Mitra and Associates*.

Marek, T., Diallo, I., Ndiaye, B., Rakotosalama, J. (1999). Successful contracting of prevention services: Fighting malnutrition in Senegal and Madagascar. *Health Policy and Planning*, 14(4): 382–389.

Markovitz, A. A., Ryan, A. M. (2016). Pay-for-performance: Disappointing results or masked heterogeneity? *Medical Care Research and Review*. https://doi.org/10.1177/1077558715619282.

Meessen, B., Kashala, J.-P. I., Musango, L. (2007). Output-based payment to boost staff productivity in public health centres: Contracting in Kabutare district, Rwanda. *Bulletin of the World Health Organization*, 85, 108–115.

Miller, G., Babiarz, K. S. (2014). Pay-for-performance incentives in low- and middle-income country health programs. In: Culyer A. J., ed., *Encyclopedia of Health Economics*. Elsevier. pp. 457–466.

Morgan, L., Beith, A., Eichler, R. (2011). Performance-based incentives for maternal health: Taking stock of current programs and future potentials. Bethesda, MD: Health Systems, 20, 20.

Peabody, J. W., Shimkhada, R., Quimbo, S., Solon, O., Javier, X., McCulloch, C. (2014). The impact of performance incentives on child health outcomes: Results from a cluster randomized controlled trial in the Philippines. *Health Policy and Planning*, 29(5): 615–621.

Regalia, F., Castro, L. (2007). Performance-based incentives for health: Demand- and supply-side incentives in the Nicaraguan Red de Proteccion Social. CGD Working Paper. Washington, DC: Center for Global Development.

Roland, M., Dudley, R. A. (2015). How financial and reputational incentives can be used to improve medical care. *Health Services Research*, 50(Suppl 2): 2090–2115.

Rudasingwa, M., Soeters, R., Bossuyt, M. (2015). The effect of performance-based financial incentives on improving health care provision in Burundi: A controlled cohort study. *Global Journal of Health Science*, 7: 15.

Rusa, L., Schneidman, M., Fritsche, G., Musango, L. (2009). Rwanda: Performance-based financing in the public sector. In: Eichler, R., Levine, R., eds., *Performance Incentives for Global Health: Potential and Pitfalls*. Washington, D.C.: Center for Global Development.

Shen, Y. (2003). Selection incentives in a performance-based contracting system. *Health Services Research*, 38(2): 535–552.

Skiles, M. P., Curtis, S. L., Basinga, P., Angeles, G., Thirumurthy, H. (2015). The effect of performance-based financing on illness, care-seeking and treatment among children: An impact evaluation in Rwanda. *BMC Health Services Research*, 15: 1.

Soeters, R., Griffiths, F. 2003. Improving government health services through contract management: A case from Cambodia. *Health Policy and Planning*, 18: 74–83.

Soeters, R., Musango, L., Meessen, B. (2005). Comparison of two output based schemes in Butare and Cyangugu provinces with two control provinces in Rwanda. *Global Partnership on Output Based Aid (GPOBA)*.

Soeters, R., Peerenboom, P. B., Mushagalusa, P., Kimanuka, C. (2011). Performance-based financing experiment improved health care in the Democratic Republic of Congo. *Health Affairs*, 30: 1518–1527.

Sondorp, E., Palmer, N., Strong, L., Wali, A. (2009). Afghanistan: Paying NGOs for performance in a postconflict setting. In: Eichler, R., Levine, R., eds., *The Performance-Based Incentives Working Group. Performance Incentives for Global Health: Potential and Pitfalls.* Washington, D.C.: Center for Global Development. 139–164.

Songstad, N. G., Lindkvist, I., Moland, K. M., Chimhutu, V., Blystad, A. (2012). Assessing performance enhancing tools: Experiences with the open performance review and appraisal system (OPRAS) and expectations towards payment for performance (P4P) in the public health sector in Tanzania. *Global Health*, 8: 33.

Sun, X., Liu, X., Sun, Q., Yip, W., Wagstaff, A., Meng, Q. (2016). The impact of a pay-for-performance scheme on prescription quality in rural China. *Health Economics*, 25(6): 706–722.

Van de Poel, E., Flores, G., Ir, P., O'Donnell, O. (2015). Impact of performance based financing in a low-resource setting: A decade of experience in Cambodia. *Health Economics*, 25(6): 688–705.

Van de Poel, E., Flores, G., Ir, P., O'Donnell, O. (2016). Impact of performance-based financing in a low-resource setting: A decade of experience in Cambodia. *Health Economics*, 25(6): 688–705.

Vergeer, P., Chansa, C. (2008). *Payment for Performance (P4P) Evaluation: 2008 Zambia Country Report for Cordaid.* Amsterdam: KIT Development Policy & Practice, KIT: 94.

Vergeer, P., Chansa, C. (2008). Payment for Performance (P4P) evaluation: 2008 Zambia country report for Cordaid.

Witter, S. (2013). Pay for performance for strengthening delivery of sexual and reproductive health services in low- and middle-income countries: Evidence synthesis paper. Washington, DC, The World Bank: 72.

Witter, S., Fretheim, A., Kessy, F. L., Lindahl, A. K. (2012). Paying for performance to improve the delivery of health interventions in low- and middle-income countries. *Cochrane Database of Systematic Reviews*, CD007899.

Chapter 7

Public Financial Management and Health Service Delivery: A Literature Review*

Yevgeny Goryakin, Paul Revill, Andrew J. Mirelman, Rohan Sweeney, Jessica Ochalek and Marc Suhrcke

Abstract

This chapter provides a summary review of the existing academic literature, both theoretical and empirical, on the contributions of public financial management (PFM) systems and reforms to improving the effectiveness of health service delivery based on a literature review conducted by Goryakin *et al.* (2017). We consider both population health indicators as well as more proximate process indicators related to health system performance. The existing literature is limited and only 53 articles are reviewed, divided across three subthemes: first, "system quality" studies, on the impact of PFM quality and good governance generally; second, "health system strengthening" studies, including articles on medium-term expenditure frameworks (MTEFs), reforms related to budget transparency and participatory budgeting and decentralization; third, studies on the impact of donor-related reforms such as the introduction of sector-wide approaches (SWAps). The theoretical literature predicts that high-quality PFM systems will have a positive impact on various dimensions of performance; whereas evidence from empirical studies is more limited,

---

*The opinions expressed and arguments employed herein are solely those of the authors and do not necessarily reflect the official views of the OECD or its member countries.

though generally positive. Overall, evidence shows good governance has an important role in health service delivery. Increased public funding of health programmes is likely to be more effective in countries with better governance, but what this means in practice is highly context-specific.

1. Introduction

Public financial management (PFM) reforms are widely seen as having an important part to play in the efforts of low- and middle-income countries (LMICs) to improve the welfare of their populations. Many countries have expressed a commitment to strengthening their PFM systems in several high-level international initiatives and declarations,[1] and development partners are paying increasing attention to countries' PFM performance when making decisions about committing development assistance (de Renzio, 2006; de Renzio *et al.*, 2010, 2011).

PFM describes the ways that governments manage public resources, including systems for budget preparation, approval, execution and evaluation (Cabezon and Prakash, 2008; Andrews *et al.*, 2014). This chapter focuses primarily on the quality dimensions of PFM including: the credibility, reliability and efficiency of the budget process; the transparency of the budget process; the extent of appropriate institutionalized accountability and the appropriate use of earmarked and extra-budgetary funds. We review, synthesize and critically discuss the existing literature on the contributions of PFM systems and PFM reforms to improving the effectiveness of health service delivery. To proxy the quality of health services, we use more proximate "process indicators" of the performance of health services delivery, such as the extent of the utilization of different health services, patient satisfaction levels and waiting times.

This chapter first summarizes the theoretical foundations of the hypotheses that have been identified and addressed in the literature around the link between PFM quality and effective health service delivery. It then provides a broad summary of the evidence to support (or contradict) these

---

[1] Examples include the 2005 Paris Declaration, the 2008 Accra Agenda for Action and the 2011 Busan Partnership for Effective Development Cooperation.

hypotheses. A more detailed summary of the evidence is available from Goryakin *et al*. (2017), where judgements on the strength of the evidence are also discussed.

2. Methods

The hypotheses around the link between PFM quality and effective health service delivery were identified from a review of the literature which included studies that provide theoretical and/or empirical evidence for the presence or absence of associations — ideally causal associations — between higher or lower quality PFM systems, and the presence of PFM reforms and indicators suggesting "better" or "worse" health service delivery. For a detailed explanation of the search strategy including inclusion and exclusion criteria used in this review see Goryakin *et al*. (2017). In brief, the search terms aimed to account for a broad range of *potentially* relevant quality measures. These included, for example, aggregate scores such as the Public Expenditure and Financial Accountability (PEFA) score (as used in Fritz *et al*., 2014), proxies for PFM quality, quality of governance-specific PFM-related reforms and initiatives designed to improve the accountability, transparency and responsiveness of those tasked with managing health systems (e.g. the introduction of community scorecards, sector-wide Approaches (SWAps) and participatory budgeting).

The outcome measure used was the quality of health services, which is difficult to measure. Health system performance can be assessed with the help of standard population health indicators such as life expectancy at birth and child mortality rates; however, the quality of a country's health system is not the only driver of population health outcomes, so we relied on indicators more closely related to the performance of health services.[2] The Organisation for Economic Co-operation and Development

---

[2] Any articles that proposed links between population health outcomes and PFM quality were also considered as given the overarching goal of health services is to improve health, population health indicators such as life expectancy at birth and mortality and morbidity indicators as the relevant outcome variables may be used as outcomes in some cases. This was not the primary outcome, however, as in practice, it is difficult to establish a credible direct link between PFM and population health outcomes because such outcomes are at least co-determined by a range of factors beyond the control of health systems.

(OECD) suggests a range of indicators for evaluating health system performance, which are presented with the objective of gaining "a broader view of public health" (OECD, 2015). Bearing in mind these limitations, we considered a long list of possible outcome indicators, including both population health outcomes and process indicators. For the purpose of the review, the following indicators were considered most relevant:

Input/process indicators:

- the availability of medicines in the public sector;
- the number of avoidable hospital admissions;
- waiting times in the public sector;
- immunization coverage;
- health service utilization.

Health outcome indicators:

- infant mortality rate/maternal mortality rate;
- life expectancy at birth;
- avoidable hospitalizations/mortality;
- surgical complication rates;
- mortality from cardiovascular diseases;
- general satisfaction with health.

Efficiency:

- measured by technical/allocative efficiency scores derived from stochastic frontier analysis models of public health service delivery or from data envelopment analysis.

We also reviewed studies that treated the allocation of funding towards health in the total budget as an outcome variable. Despite not being a perfect measure of health service delivery, we considered the impact of decentralization and participatory budgeting on budgetary allocations to health, for example, to be of interest in this review because health expenditures are an important determinant of the quality of health service delivery. In addition, we included studies which considered the combined impact of spending on health and the quality of governance as an additional measure of PFM quality (as discussed in the following). The theory underlying the identified hypotheses is discussed below, followed by a summary of the evidence.

In Section 3, we first lay out the theoretical predictions outlined in the literature about the relationship between PFM quality and PFM-related reforms with various dimensions of effective health service delivery. We then scrutinize each of these theoretical predictions in light of the existing empirical evidence. We group the evidence into the following three broad categories:

- The first group is made up of "system quality" studies, including studies on the impact of PFM quality itself as well as the impact of good governance.
- The second group comprises studies on the impact of "PFM-related reforms", which include medium-term expenditure frameworks (MTEFs), reforms related to budget transparency and participatory budgeting, decentralization reforms and several other types of reforms, as well as good governance practices such as transparency, accountability and lack of corruption. The studies in this group can also be considered part of the so-called "health system strengthening" literature. These studies, while not explicitly measuring PFM systems, are concerned with dimensions of health systems that are potentially important for well-functioning PFM systems.
- The third group contains studies on the impact on health service delivery of donor-related reforms such as the introduction of SWAps.

3. Results

We first lay out the theoretical predictions outlined in the literature about the relationship between PFM quality and PFM-related reforms. The implicit/explicit hypotheses regarding the relationship between PFM and health service delivery were drawn out from the selected studies and are summarized in Table 1 alongside a concluding set of remarks identifying the degree to which the hypotheses have been supported by the reviewed empirical evidence.

In the following, we lay out the theoretical predictions outlined in the literature about the relationship between PFM quality and PFM-related reforms with various dimensions of effective health service delivery that underlie each of the hypotheses presented in Table 1. Then the empirical evidence for each is summarized.

Table 1.   Summary of hypotheses and evidence reviewed.

	Hypothesis	Summary of evidence	Number of studies reviewed
PFM system quality	1. Better PFM quality is positively related to health service delivery.	The evidence on the impact of PFM quality (as measured by broad generic indicators) on health service delivery is uncertain. One study found that the CPIA rating of the quality of budgetary and financial management had a positive and significant association with public sector efficiency in the health sector. Another found that a narrower range of PEFA scores and the broader Country Policy and Institutional Assessment (CPIA) index were unrelated to efficiency in service delivery.	2
Quality of governance	2. The quality of general governance is positively related to health care delivery.	A range of indicators of the quality of governance were found to be generally positively related to health service delivery-related outcomes.	11
Quality of governance	3. The extent of corruption is negatively related to health service delivery, including health outcomes.	Corruption was found to be persistently negatively related to a range of health service delivery-related outcomes.	
Quality of governance	4. Good governance helps translate public health spending into a more effective health service delivery.	All of the studies reviewed found that public spending on health was more effective in better-governed countries.	
Impact of PFM reforms	5. The introduction of MTEFs is likely to lead to improvements in health service delivery.	The evidence for the positive impact of MTEF reforms on health service delivery is conflicting, although there is more evidence in support of this hypothesis than against it. One study found that MTEF	3

Table 1. (*Continued*)

Hypothesis		Summary of evidence	Number of studies reviewed
		reform had not prevented a decline in the proportion of budgets allocated to health care. Another study found that the most advanced form of MTEF, i.e. Medium Term Performance Framework (MTPF), was positively related to the cost-effectiveness of public health expenditures. In a third study, MTPFs were found to have a significant positive impact on technical efficiency in the health sector.	
Fiscal and budget transparency	6. Fiscal and budgetary transparencies are positively correlated with health service delivery, particularly in well-governed countries with sufficient institutional capacity.	Several studies found strong evidence of a positive relationship between various indicators of fiscal and budgetary transparency and outcomes related to health service delivery.	11 (8 were of questionable design)
Participatory budgeting and community scorecards	7. Initiatives to increase transparency and accountability, such as participatory budgeting and community scorecards, are positively correlated with health service delivery.	There is some evidence for the positive impact on the health service delivery of initiatives to increase transparency and accountability such as participatory budgeting and community scorecards.	12
Fiscal decentralization	8. Fiscal decentralization is likely to lead to better health service delivery outcomes, although the effect is likely to depend on local institutional capacity.	Fiscal decentralization in general was found to be positively related to good health service delivery outcomes. However, it seems that decentralization is more likely to be effective where there is sufficient local institutional capacity and accountability.	7

(*Continued*)

Table 1. (*Continued*)

	Hypothesis	Summary of evidence	Number of studies reviewed
Fiscal decentralization	9. Activity-based budgeting is likely to be positively related to health service delivery outcomes.	There is limited evidence on the impact of activity-based budgeting on the quality of health service delivery. One study found that activity-based budgeting had only a limited impact on cost-effectiveness and cost containment.	4
Fiscal decentralization	10. The introduction of HMIS is likely to lead to better health service delivery outcomes.	We found no empirical evidence on the impact of FMIS on health service delivery. One study undertaken specifically of HMIS concluded that very little improvement in decision-making in the health sector resulted from the introduction of HMIS.	
Impact of donor-related reforms	11. The introduction of SWAps is likely to be positively correlated with health service delivery, although its predicted impact on aid flow toward health is less certain.	While the scarce available case study evidence provides some initial support for the hypothesis (and for the notion that SWAps can increase resources allocated to the health sector), the lack of studies involving any advanced quantitative analysis does not allow for major conclusions at this stage.	3

3.1. *PFM system quality*

The first identified hypothesis addresses the impact of PFM quality on health service delivery outcomes. The PFM literature postulates that higher quality PFM systems produce a number of benefits that could result in more reliable and better-quality service delivery, including health service delivery (Fritz *et al.*, 2012). For instance, better PFM may be linked to more transparent and accountable governance, which may in turn lead to greater efficiency in public spending (Fonchamnyo and Sama, 2016). The development of more robust budgeting systems, in which stakeholders adhere to formal rules and enforcement mechanisms, may lead to the fiscal system being more stable and reliable. Ultimately, better PFM systems should

- improve overall fiscal discipline, with realistic budgets being executed in a timely fashion;
- improve allocative efficiency, with fund allocations aligned with public priorities;
- maximize social welfare;
- improve operational efficiency, with reduced waste, reduced corruption and other leakages (Fritz *et al.*, 2014).

Within the literature reviewed, two studies (Fritz *et al.*, 2014; Fonchamnyo *et al.*, 2016) attempted to directly evaluate the impact of PFM system quality on health service delivery. Both articles were relatively high-quality econometric studies that relied on cross-country evidence.

3.2. *Quality of governance*

Hypotheses 2–4 in Table 1 consider the quality of PFM systems and the quality of governance, which are likely to be strongly interlinked.[3] It is widely recognized that state-building and PFM progress are mutually interdependent (Fritz *et al.*, 2012), and there is a large body of empirical evidence on the relationship between the effectiveness of public health spending and the quality of governance. The impact of public spending on health is therefore likely to depend on the institutional capacity of the system to convert this investment into improved public services (Filmer and Pritchett, 1999; Fukuda-Parr *et al.*, 2011). This institutional capacity may include well-designed PFM systems. The reasons why high-quality

---

[3] By "quality of governance", we mean the quality of formal institutions (such as formal laws and regulations designed to guarantee transparency and accountability and to prevent corruption), as well as the technical capacity and competence of the bureaucracy.

governance is important for better service delivery are numerous and may include the following factors:

- greater technical capacity of the relevant staff and institutions responsible for managing the delivery and auditing of public funds;
- reduced information asymmetries associated with corruption and resource leakages, for example, through a more transparent budget process and greater accountability in the use of funds (Rajkumar and Swaroop, 2008; Holmberg and Rothstein, 2011; Hu and Mendoza, 2013);
- a more transparent procurement process, leading to lower purchase costs, adjustments in incentive systems to prevent fraud and promote cost-effectiveness (Rajkumar and Swaroop, 2008);
- greater responsiveness to population preferences when setting budgeting priorities.

One important function of well-designed PFM systems is that of reducing or preventing corruption and the misuse of public fund by reducing informational asymmetries or by adjusting incentives for agents. These effects should be achieved because well-designed PFM systems establish and implement rules about who has access to public resources and about the processes for accessing these resources, for example through effective procurement mechanisms (Cabezon and Prakash, 2008). This is challenging, however, since politicians may not necessarily find it in their self-interest to increase transparency and accountability (Sarr, 2015). Higher levels of corruption can also lead to less efficiency in PFM, since even well-designed PFM systems may not function well if bribery, stealing and fraud are widespread (Akin *et al.*, 2005). Governmental transfers designed to encourage greater utilization of health services through reductions in user fees may be ineffective if there are significant resource leakages in the process (Gauthier and Wane, 2009) or if inadequate procurement rules result in the payment of exceedingly high prices.

Eleven empirical studies were reviewed for this section, of which all but one were quantitative. The research design of these studies was generally of good standard, with multivariate regression employed. Several studies applied more advanced methods (e.g. fixed-effects and instrumental variable (IV) regressions). Cross-country data were used in almost all of the studies. While such study designs and data can still produce relevant insights not least due to their wide-ranging, potentially global scope, the extent to which they allow for causal inference tends to be more limited, compared to study designs using ideally randomized designs and/or more fine-grained within-country data.

3.3. *Impact of PFM reforms*

PFM reforms are generally conducted with the goal of improving service delivery, which should ultimately lead to better health outcomes. Thus, according to the framework developed in Fritz *et al.* (2012), PFM reforms can have an impact on service delivery through a number of sequential inputs and outcomes, both intermediate and final. In theory, PFM reforms should lead to changes in intermediate outcomes, including the extent of transparency, oversight and accountability in PFM systems. This is expected to lead to improvements in fiscal discipline, with more efficient allocation of resources and greater efficiency in public spending. For these reasons, PFM reforms are expected to lead to improvements in capacity and accountability, and ultimately to better service delivery and population health. At the same time, however, the effectiveness of PFM reforms, as well as the speed and effectiveness of the transmission of benefits between different links in the chain of assumed relationship, is also expected to depend on contextual factors such as existing income levels and governmental and institutional capacity.

3.3.1. *Impact of PFM reforms: Medium-term-expenditure frameworks*

As mentioned in the Introduction to this review, the defining features of well-functioning PFMs include the timeliness, effectiveness and predictability of the budgeting process. One important reform to improve the long-term budgetary planning ability of governments is the introduction of fiscal commitment devices, known under the umbrella term of MTEFs. When implemented properly, MTEFs can be viewed as a key component of high-quality PFM systems. The intended purposes of these frameworks include reducing volatility in revenue collection and the disbursements of funds, the institution of multiyear expenditure controls, as well as improving overall budgetary discipline and increasing the ability to take future fiscal challenges into account in preparing annual budgets (Bevan and Palomba, 2000; Vlaicu *et al.*, 2014). More than two-thirds of all countries had introduced multiyear MTEFs by 2010 in an effort to improve their budgeting processes (Brumby *et al.*, 2013). MTEFs also serve as a straightforward accountability device, enabling government performance to be checked against previously declared targets. A potential complication, however, is that spending patterns may remain unaffected over the medium-term in spite of changing needs (and hence the need to change targets) (Brumby *et al.*, 2013). This lack of change means that the extent to which improved PFM quality translates into improved health service delivery is not certain, since the allocative efficiency may remain unaffected by MTEF reforms.

Three quantitative studies were evaluated to assess the hypothesis that the introduction of MTEFs leads to improvements in health service delivery. All three were of relatively high quality, relying on a range of estimation techniques, including panel data and IV to deal with endogeneity, though still mostly relying only on cross-country data (hence allowing for only a limited degree of causal inference).

3.3.2. *Impact of PFM reforms: Fiscal and budget transparency*

Transparency is particularly important both as a component and goal of PFM systems as it may help ensure that the benefits of public spending are not distributed only to elites (Bellver and Kaufmann, 2005), and greater transparency may increase public trust in government and thus encourage greater public participation in policy decision-making processes (de Renzio *et al.*, 2005). Greater transparency may also increase allocative efficiency as a result of public officials being subject to increased accountability and gaining greater legitimacy (de Renzio *et al.*, 2005).

One way of enhancing transparency in fiscal policymaking is to undertake open budgeting initiatives aimed at reducing information asymmetries (Fukuda-Parr *et al.*, 2011; Simson, 2014). However, a number of potential contextual factors may limit the gains in service delivery that open budgeting initiatives to improve transparency are intended to facilitate, such as limited ability and/or incentives for individuals to process and act upon complicated financial information. Adequate institutional mechanisms to monitor and punish corrupt public officials may be needed in order for initiatives to be effective (Carlitz, 2013).

Eleven empirical studies were identified to review the hypothesis that fiscal and budgetary transparency are positively correlated with health service delivery (particularly in well-governed countries with sufficient institutional capacity). However, eight of these studies had questionable research design. Weaknesses in the quantitative studies included a lack of controls and/or a reliance on simple correlations. The qualitative studies, meanwhile, included small case studies with findings that are difficult to generalize to other settings.

3.3.3. *Impact of PFM reforms: Participatory budgeting and community scorecards*

Effective PFM systems are supposed to make public spending not only more resistant to the influence of corruption but also more closely aligned with the preferences of the general public. PFM reforms may thus include such initiatives as participatory budgeting and community scorecards, as well as more general monitoring.

Participatory budgeting initiatives were originally inspired by the Porto Alegre experiment to study the potential of citizen participation to influence budgeting and spending priorities in Brazilian municipalities (Robinson, 2006). Such initiatives can be viewed as a potential alternative to fiscal decentralization, with a similar goal of increasing the responsiveness of policymaking to people's preferences and thus ultimately leading to improved allocative efficiency in the delivery of public services (Robinson, 2006). Participatory budgeting is expected to improve health service delivery by enhancing information flows between policymakers and users of health services by strengthening accountability as a commitment device for policymakers and by enabling easier and more frequent checks on policymakers' actions (Gonçalves, 2014). The mechanism of action is thus somewhat similar to open budgeting initiatives aimed at reducing information asymmetries between principals and agents. However, the focus of participatory budgeting is not only on increasing accountability but also on enabling greater information exchange with the aim of increasing responsiveness to voters' preferences.

The use of community scorecards, while not generally viewed as a mechanism aimed at affecting the quality of PFM, is intended to improve transparency and accountability in health service delivery by increasing public participation in policymaking and by holding public officials and service providers to account (Ho et al., 2015). Combining the techniques of social audits and citizen report cards, community scorecards are a monitoring tool that is expected to lead to greater public accountability and responsiveness from the service providers (Mistra and Ramasankar, 2007). While community scorecards may not be viewed as an essential component of well-functioning PFM systems, they can affect their quality in a similar way to the accountability and transparency initiatives discussed before. Another monitoring device is the "balanced scorecard performance system", which is basically a collection of a range of performance indicators in key domains, also described in Edward et al. (2011) as "an integrated management and measurement tool that enables organizations to clarify their vision and strategy and translate them into action". The rationale for using balanced scorecard systems is similar to the rationale for using community scorecards.

Twelve empirical studies were reviewed to assess the hypothesis that transparency and accountability initiatives such as participatory budgeting and community scorecards will be positively correlated with health services delivery. One was a synthesis report summarizing empirical evidence from other studies; three were individual case studies; four were studies with relatively poor design (e.g. lack of controls in regression, or lack of clarity about their empirical approach) and four were relatively high-quality econometric studies. The majority of the studies relied primarily on cross-country data only.

3.4. Fiscal decentralization

Fiscal decentralization has been promoted as a mechanism for increasing the responsiveness of public policy to voters' preferences and for increasing democratic participation in governance. The theoretical argument for greater decentralization is the presumed inability of centralized systems to coordinate large-scale activities due to lack of knowledge about local culture and circumstances (Robalino *et al.*, 2001; Akin *et al.*, 2005). In this view, decentralization may bring about Pareto improvements in aggregate welfare, i.e. improvements that help some people without harming others (Akin *et al.*, 2005). Decentralization is also sometimes theorized to encourage yardstick competition among local governments and thus potentially lead to better-quality public services (Adam *et al.*, 2008), especially if accompanied with appropriate performance management. In relation to health service delivery, fiscal decentralization is expected to bring about improvements in allocative and technical efficiency through the above-mentioned mechanisms (Robalino *et al.*, 2001), as well as by involving local communities in decision-making and implementation processes (Uchimura and Jütting, 2009). However, fiscal decentralization reform will not necessarily lead to greater community participation unless accompanied by additional steps such as the introduction of participatory budgeting and community scorecards, as well, perhaps, as the adoption of SWAps (discussed in the following).

As in the case of transparency, however, the view on the usefulness of fiscal decentralization initiatives is not uniformly positive. A major concern is that decentralization may lead to the capture of decision-making processes by local elites rather than by the communities they represent (Akin *et al.*, 2005), thereby promoting rather than preventing corruption (Vian and Collins, 2006). Another concern is that the poorer regions may suffer if the redistributive powers of central government are reduced (Robalino *et al.*, 2001). The positive impact of decentralization reforms is also viewed sceptically in the context of institutionally weak systems (Lewis, 2006).

Seven empirical studies were reviewed to assess the hypothesis that fiscal decentralization is likely to lead to better health service delivery outcomes, although this effect will depend on the local institutional capacity. Of these, one was a quality-adjusted literature review of other empirical evidence. The remaining six articles all used relatively high-quality econometric approaches based on cross-country data analysis (for which, as mentioned earlier, it is harder to draw causal inferences, even with sophisticated econometric methods).

3.5. *Other PFM reforms*

"Activity-based budgeting" is an MTEF-related reform designed to improve the budgeting process by increasing the capacity to set appropriate priorities and cost activities, which should lead to a greater sense of ownership of the budgeting process. Under activity-based budgeting, changes in funding allocations should be related to changes in activities (Anipa *et al.*, 1999) rather than being based simply on the spending in previous years (Bentes *et al.*, 2004).

"Performance-based budgeting", meanwhile, aims to improve health service delivery through a number of assessment mechanisms designed "to strengthen links between the funds provided [...] and their outcomes/ outputs" (Brumby and Robinson, 2005, p. 5). These assessment mechanisms act as incentives related to achieving certain service quality targets. Although there is an extensive literature on the use of such mechanisms in the financing of health care, almost all of this literature is limited to high-income countries (HICs) (Brumby and Robinson, 2005; Glied and Smith, 2011). Performance-based budgeting is not considered in this review because such budgeting can affect health service delivery not only through changes in PFM quality but also through the provision of strong incentives on organizational behavior focused on the impact of cost-containment incentives.

Another potentially important factor for improving health service delivery is the greater reliability of funding flows. This could be achieved, for example, by a more efficient setup of payroll mechanisms. Additionally, stronger and more competitive open market procurement systems may theoretically result in lower costs, more reliable resource flows and better health service outcomes. As yet, however, there is little to no reliable evidence on this (Andrews *et al.*, 2014). Finally, the introduction of health management information systems (HMIS), of which financial management information systems (FMIS) are a subcomponent, is another reform with the potential to improve health service delivery. Such systems are intended to enable the integration of reliable data which can then be used to measure and ultimately improve the quality of health services (Chaulagai *et al.*, 2005).

There are therefore two hypotheses to be evaluated: first, activity-based budgeting is likely to be positively related to health service delivery outcomes; second, the introduction of HMIS is likely to lead to better health service delivery outcomes.

Four empirical studies were reviewed in this group, none of which were large-N econometric/statistical studies. All four studies relied on case study design, thus limiting their ability to generalize findings to other contexts.

3.5.1. *Impact of donor-related reforms*

Given the importance of donor involvement in the health care and PFM reform agendas of developing countries, the literature review looked specifically at the theoretical and empirical evidence for links between typical donor-related PFM reforms and their impact on health care delivery.

In the context of donor support, SWAps have been adopted in many countries as a strategy to increase the efficiency of health spending. SWAps are designed to improve efficiency by increasing the responsiveness of health policy to local priorities, fostering greater public participation and improving interaction between different key stakeholders (particularly donors) in a fragmented system (Cassels and Janovsky, 1998; Bodart *et al.*, 2001; Chansa *et al.*, 2008). SWAps are expected to strengthen coordination between different players, serve as a mechanism for improved coordination and alignment between donors and partners, improving domestic ownership and accountability, reduce transaction costs, improve planning, improve resource allocation and policy implementation capacity and ultimately to lead to better health service delivery (Dickinson, 2011). However, the implementation of SWAps may also lead to a perception on the part of some donors that they are losing control. For this reason, there is some concern that the implementation of SWAps may lead donors to reduce aid toward health programmes in low-income countries (LICs) (Sweeney *et al.*, 2014).

Three empirical studies were found in the literature relevant to the hypothesis that the introduction of SWAps is likely to be positively correlated with improved health service delivery. However, there is less certainty about the predicted impact of SWAps on aid flow toward health. None of the studies involved advanced quantitative analysis. One was a literature review, while the other two were case studies.

3.6. Reviewing the identified hypotheses

The literature review has reviewed the selected studies in order to draw out more clearly their implicit or explicit hypotheses regarding the relationship between PFM and health service delivery. These hypotheses are summarized here alongside a concluding set of remarks identifying the degree to which the hypotheses have been supported by the reviewed empirical evidence.

3.7. Summary of the evidence

The studies reviewed use different definitions of PFM and health service performance, making it problematic to draw comparisons between them. In addition, while it is preferable to use a direct measure of PFM quality (e.g. a measure that can take into account the ability of PFM systems to ensure the transparency and reliability of the budget process), aggregate scores may suffer from a number of disadvantages. For example, aggregate scores may be unable to take into account separate subdimensions of PFM, or to distinguish between a PFM system that scores highly with the correct "form" but that nevertheless fails to deliver actual functionality. An alternative approach is to consider the impact of proxies for these separate dimensions, such as the extent of transparency, the quality of governance and the responsiveness of PFM and related institutions.

Within this review, empirical evidence on the nature of PFM systems was taken from studies in which the impact of PFM systems was more or less clearly defined and measured (e.g. as CPIA index or PEFA scores) as well as from studies in the health system-strengthening literature that concerned dimensions of health systems in some way related to well-functioning PFM systems, though these latter studies did not explicitly measure PFM quality.

One of the strongest and most consistent findings was the evidence that simply increasing public funding of health programmes is unlikely to be as effective in poorly governed countries as in better governed countries (with "governance" likely to include the quality of PFM). Good governance is also likely to be positively correlated with public sector efficiency in achieving good population health outcomes.

There is some evidence, however, that greater participation of stakeholders in the design, implementation and evaluation of health services may be an effective way to improve their quality so as to maximize the benefit of additional financing. This could be achieved through mechanisms such as participatory budgeting initiatives (Baiocchi *et al.*, 2006; Gonçalves, 2014), community scorecards (Mistra and Ramasankar, 2007; Ho *et al.*, 2015), community-based monitoring of primary care provision (Bjorkman and Svensson, 2007) and SWAps (Bodart *et al.*, 2001; Chansa *et al.*, 2008; Dickinson, 2011).

Fiscal decentralization was found to be generally positively related to population health (Robalino *et al.*, 2001; Uchimura and Jütting, 2009), although this appeared to be dependent on the availability of good local institutional capacity. However, decentralization may also lead to some undesirable results, such as declining proportions of budgets going to primary health care or other public goods (Akin *et al.*, 2005; Brixi *et al.*, 2013). Despite fiscal decentralization being a widely adopted policy in LMICs, the evidence thus does not indicate that decentralization is unambiguously positive for health service delivery. In some cases, therefore, continued central control over the allocation/use of funds may be beneficial, especially in health care.

The studies review found that MTEF reforms usually improve budget reliability and fiscal discipline, and sometimes lead to improvements in the technical efficiency of the health sector (especially in the case of MTPF reforms). However, such reforms may actually lead to lower allocation of funding toward health, especially if there is significant fungibility in health aid financing (Lu *et al.*, 2010; Bevan and Palomba, 2000). The reduced funding of health care observed in some countries may reflect a genuine preference for alternative spending targets, for example on education (as discussed in Bevan and Palomba, 2000), even in countries with apparently well-governed PFM systems.

In some cases, greater public financial accountability can have unintended consequences. For example, some service providers, when placed under pressure, may focus less on the qualities of the services they deliver and opt instead to focus on quantitative outcomes. Nevertheless, as the evidence for this unintended consequence comes only from the USA, which has a highly idiosyncratic health system setup, this finding may not apply in LMICs.

There is evidence of greater allocations of funding toward health (as well as greater reliability of health funding) in countries with greater budget transparency and less corruption (Mauro, 1998; Robinson, 2006; Simson, 2014; Sarr, 2015). In some cases, this was even found to be translated into better health outcomes, including lower rates of infant mortality rates and higher rates of health care utilization (Gupta *et al.*, 2000; Bellver and Kaufmann, 2005; Fukuda-Parr *et al.*, 2011; Sarr, 2015). However, the *reduced* funding of health care observed in some countries may reflect a genuine preference for alternative spending targets, e.g. on education (as discussed in Bevan and Palomba, 2000), even in apparently well-governed PFM systems.

4. Discussion

While the overall evidence in this field appears to be patchy, the evidence in some subfields is much more developed than in others. For example, there were 11 empirical articles on the impact of good governance, most of which were of high-quality design, while only two empirical studies were found on the impact of PFM system quality (measured directly) on health services delivery. A significant proportion of the reviewed articles were single-country case studies, or qualitative articles where it was not completely clear how the conclusion was reached. Many of the quantitative studies we reviewed were also not ideal, with some relying on simple correlations, some using regression analysis without appropriate controls and some employing inappropriate methodological approaches. On the other hand, quite a few of the econometric studies we reviewed relied on more advanced approaches such as panel data analysis and IV regression. Even these better-designed studies, however, often relied on cross-country data only, hence allowing for limited causal claims. Only one study made use of a truly randomized design, implying greater causal inference. Nevertheless, given that this field appears to be in its early stages of development, and given the difficulty of finding relevant articles among hundreds of results generated by the search terms, we believe that the 53 empirical articles that we found (not counting the articles that informed the theoretical part of our review) provided a good basis for this initial review. In the future, it may be useful to have more studies focusing on the specific subdimensions of PFM systems. One way to start doing this would be to break down the analysis of the broad indicators into their component parts.

5. Conclusion

The theoretical literature predicts that high-quality PFM systems will have a positive impact on the various dimensions of performance, whereas evidence from empirical studies is more limited, though generally positive. Overall, evidence shows good governance has an important role in health service delivery. Increased public funding of health programmes is likely to be more effective in countries with better governance, but what this means in practice is highly context-specific.

Acknowledgments

This review was undertaken by the University of York Centre for Health Economics in April–June 2016. It was overseen by the Overseas Development Institute (ODI) staff members Tom Hart and Bryn Welham. This research was funded through a grant from the Bill and Melinda Gates Foundation. It was originally published as an ODI paper. The study has contributed to a wider research project on the nature of the relationship between PFM and health care delivery that considers the issue from a number of methodological lenses.

References

Adam, A., Delis, M. D., Kammas, P. (2008). Fiscal decentralization and public sector efficiency: Evidence from OECD countries. CESifo Working Paper No. 2364.

Akin, J., Hutchinson, P., Strumpf, K. (2005). Decentralisation and government provision of public goods: The public health sector in Uganda. *Journal of Development Studies*, 41(8): 1417–1443.

Andrews, M., Cangiano, M., Cole, N., De Renzio, P., Krause, P., Seligmann, R. (2014). This is PFM. CID Working Paper No. 285. Cambridge, MA: Centre for International Development, Harvard University.

Anipa, S., Kaluma, F., Muggeridge, E. (1999). DFID seminar on best practice in public expenditure management: Case study on MTEF in Malawi and Ghana. Consulting Africa Limited. Background Papers for OPM Conference on Good Practice in Public Expenditure Management. Eyesham Hall, Oxford.

Baiocchi, G., Heller, P., Chaudhuri, S., Silva, M. K. (2006). Evaluating empowerment: Participatory budgeting in Brazilian municipalities. In: Alsop R., Bertelsen M. and Holland J., eds., *Empowerment in Practice: From Analysis to Implementation*. Washington DC: The World Bank. pp. 95–128.

Bellver, A. and Kaufmann, D. (2005). Transparenting transparency: Initial empirics and policy applications. World Bank Policy Research Working Paper. pp. 1–72.

Bentes, M., Dias, C. M., Sakellarides, C., Bankauskaite, V. (2004). Health care systems in transition: Portugal. European Observatory on Health Systems and Policies.

Bevan, D., Palomba, G. (2000). Uganda: The budget and medium-term expenditure framework set in a wider context. Background paper for Poverty Reduction Support Credit with DFID Finance. London.

Bjorkman, M., Svensson, J. (2007). Power to the people: Evidence from a randomized field experiment of a community-based monitoring project in Uganda. World Bank Policy Research Working Paper 4268. Washington DC: World Bank.

Bodart, C., Servais, G., Mohamed, Y. L., Schmidt-Ehry, B. (2001). The influence of health sector reform and external assistance in Burkina Faso. *Health Policy and Planning*, 16(1): 74–86.

Brixi, H., Mu, Y., Targa, B., Hipgrave, D. (2013). Engaging sub-national governments in addressing health equities: Challenges and opportunities in China's health system reform. *Health Policy and Planning*, 28(8): 809–824.

Brumby, J., Biletska, N., Grigoli, F., Hemming, R., Kang, Y., Lee, J. W., Mills, Z., Min, S. Y., Moreno-Dodson, B., Vlaicu, R. (2013). *Beyond the Annual Budget: Global Experience with Medium-Term Expenditure Frameworks*. Washington DC: World Bank.

Brumby, J., Robinson, M. (2005). Does performance budgeting work? An analytical review of the empirical literature. IMF Working Paper WP/05/210. Washington DC: International Monetary Fund.

Cabezon, E., Prakash, T. (2008). Public financial management and fiscal outcomes in sub-Saharan African heavily-indebted poor countries. IMF Working Paper (WP/08/217). International Monetary Fund.

Carlitz, R. (2013). Improving transparency and accountability in the budget process: An assessment of recent initiatives. *Development Policy Review*, 31(S1): s49–s67.

Cassels, A., Janovsky, K. (1998). Better health in developing countries: Are sector-wide approaches the way of the future? *The Lancet*, 352(9142): 1777–1779.

Chansa, C., Sundewall, J., Mcintyre, D., Tomson, G., Forsberg, B. C. (2008). Exploring SWAp's contribution to the efficient allocation and use of resources in the health sector in Zambia. *Health Policy and Planning*, 23(4): 244–251.

Chaulagai, C. N., Moyo, C. M., Koot, J., Moyo, H. B., Sambakunsi, T. C., Khunga, F. M., Naphini, P. D. (2005). Design and implementation of a health management information system in Malawi: Issues, innovations and results. *Health Policy and Planning*, 20(6): 375–384.

de Renzio, P. (2006). Aid, budgets and accountability: A survey article. *Development Policy Review*, 24(6): 627–645.

de Renzio, P., Andrews, M., Mills, Z. (2010). Evaluation of donor support to public financial management (PFM) reform in developing countries. Analytical study of quantitative cross-country evidence. Final Report. Sida Evaluation (2010:5). Stockholm: SIDA.

de Renzio, P., Andrews, M., Mills, Z. (2011). Does donor support to public financial management reforms in developing countries work? An analytical study of quantitative cross-country evidence. Working Paper 329. London: Overseas Development Institute.

de Renzio, P., Gomez, P., Sheppard, J. (2005). Budget transparency and development in resource-dependent countries. *International Social Science Journal*, 57(s1): 57–69.

Dickinson, C. (2011). *Is Aid Effectiveness Giving Us Better Health Results?* London: HLSP Institute.

Edward, A., Kumar, B., Kakar, F., Salehi, A. S., Burnham, G., Peters, D. H. (2011). Configuring balanced scorecards for measuring health system performance: Evidence from 5 years' evaluation in Afghanistan. *PLoS Medicine*, 8(7): e1001066.

Filmer, D., Pritchett, L. (1999). The impact of public spending on health: Does money matter? *Social Science & Medicine*, 49(10): 1309–1323.

Fonchamnyo, D. C., Sama, M. C. (2016). Determinants of public spending efficiency in education and health: Evidence from selected CEMAC countries. *Journal of Economics and Finance*, 40(1): 199–210.

Fritz, V., Lopez, A. P. F., Hedger, E., Tavakoli, H., Krause, P. (2012). Public financial management reforms in post-conflict countries. Synthesis Report. Washington, DC: World Bank.

Fritz, V., Sweet, S., Verhoeven, M. (2014). Strengthening public financial management: Exploring drivers and effects. World Bank Policy Research Working Paper (WPS7084).

Fukuda-Parr, S., Guyer, P., Lawson-Remer, T. (2011). Does budget transparency lead to stronger human development outcomes and commitments to economic and social rights? IBP Working Paper 4. Washington: International Budget Partnership.

Gauthier, B. (2006). PETS-QSDS in sub-Saharan Africa: A stocktaking study. Report for the Project 'Measuring Progress in Public Services Delivery'. Washington DC: World Bank.

Gauthier, B., Wane, W. (2009). Leakage of public resources in the health sector: An empirical investigation of Chad. *Journal of African Economies*, 18(1): 52–83.

Glied, S., Smith, P. C. (eds.) (2011). *The Oxford Handbook of Health Economics*. Oxford: Oxford University Press.

Gonçalves, S. (2014). The effects of participatory budgeting on municipal expenditures and infant mortality in Brazil. *World Development*, 53: 94–110.

Goryakin, Y., Revill, P., Mirelman, A., Sweeney, R., Ochalek, J., Suhrcke, M. (2017). Public financial management and health service delivery. A literature review. London.

Gupta, S., Davoodi, H. R., Tiongson, E. (2000). Corruption and the provision of health care and education services. IMF Working Paper (WP/00/116). International Monetary Fund.

Ho, L. S., Labrecque, G., Batonon, I., Salsi, V., Ratnayake, R. (2015). Effects of a community scorecard on improving the local health system in Eastern Democratic Republic of Congo: Qualitative evidence using the most significant change technique. *Conflict and Health*, 9(1): 1.

Holmberg, S., Rothstein, B. (2011). Dying of corruption. *Health Economics, Policy and Law*, 6(04): 529–547.

Hu, B., Mendoza, R. U. (2013). Public health spending, governance and child health outcomes: Revisiting the links. *Journal of Human Development and Capabilities*, 14(2): 285–311.

Lewis, M. (2006). Governance and corruption in public health care systems. Working Paper 78. Center for Global Development.

Lu, C., Schneider, M. T., Gubbins, P., Leach-Kemon, K., Jamison, D., Murray, C. J. (2010). Public financing of health in developing countries: A cross-national systematic analysis. *The Lancet*, 375(9723): 1375–1387.

Mauro, P. (1998). Corruption and the composition of government expenditure. *Journal of Public Economics*, 69(2): 263–279.

Mistra, V., Ramasankar, P. (2007). Andhra Pradesh, India: Improving health services through community score cards. Social Accountability Series Note 1. Washington DC: World Bank.

OECD (2015). *Health at a Glance 2015*. OECD Publishing.

Rajkumar, A. S., Swaroop, V. (2008). Public spending and outcomes: Does governance matter? *Journal of Development Economics*, 86(1): 96–111.

Robalino, D. A., Picazo, O. F., Voetberg, A. (2001). Does fiscal decentralization improve health outcomes? Evidence from a cross-country analysis. World Bank Policy Research Working Paper 2565. Washington DC: World Bank Publications.

Robinson, M. (2006). Budget analysis and policy advocacy: The role of non-governmental public action. University of Sussex Institute of Development Studies Working Paper 279.

Robinson, M. (2007). Does decentralisation improve equity and efficiency in public service delivery provision? *IDS Bulletin*, 38(1): 7–17.

Sarr, B. (2015). Credibility and reliability of government budgets: Does fiscal transparency matter? International Budget Partnership Working Paper 5. Washington DC: International Budget Partnership.

Simson, R. (2014). Transparency for development: Examining the relationship between budget transparency, MDG expenditure, and results. IBP Working Paper: Applied research on open and accountable public finance management and civil society budget advocacy. Washington DC: International Budget Partnership.

Sweeney, R., Mortimer, D., Johnston, D. W. (2014). Do sector wide approaches for health aid delivery lead to 'donor-flight'? A comparison of 46 low-income countries. *Social Science & Medicine*, 105(2014): 38–46.

Uchimura, H., Jütting, J. P. (2009). Fiscal decentralization, Chinese style: Good for health outcomes? *World Development*, 37(12): 1926–1934.

Vian, T., Collins, D. (2006). Using financial performance indicators to promote transparency and accountability in health systems. *U4 Brief* 1. Bergen, Norway: Anti-Corruption Resource Centre, Chr. Michelsen Institute.

Vlaicu, R., Verhoeven, M., Grigoli, F., Mills, Z. (2014). Multiyear budgets and fiscal performance: Panel data evidence. *Journal of Public Economics*, 111(2014): 79–95.

Chapter 8

Demand-Side Financing in Health in Low-Resource Settings

Tim Ensor and Suresh Tiwari

Abstract

In this chapter, we discuss the use of demand-side financing (DSF) mechanisms as a way to increase access to health services and improve health outcomes. The discussion makes use of a range of evidence including a series of systematic reviews focused on low-resource settings and detailed experience of developing DSF for maternal health in Nepal.

1. Introduction

Public health systems traditionally focus efforts on extending population coverage through the supply side, boosting funding to public services, training staff and improving supply chains. The neglect of the demand side is recognized as a weakness in public health policy in high- and, particularly, low-resource contexts (Ensor and Cooper, 2004; O'Donnell, 2007). Study of the demand side has at least two components (Table 1). The first is a recognition that many barriers to accessing services operate before an individual arrives at a health facility. The three delays — the delay in deciding to seek care, delay in arriving at a health service and delay in obtaining treatment once at a facility — are well recognized in

217

Table 1.   Supply- and demand-side barriers and financing.

	Example of barrier	Supply-side financing	Demand-side financing
Supply-side barrier	Lack of medicines/ staff at public facilities	Improved funding and better supply chain management	Payments/vouchers to patients to purchase services from alternative providers
Demand-side barrier	Difficulty in getting to a health facility	Patient transport systems	Vouchers or cash payments to patients for transport

the maternal health literature but equally applicable to most health care (Thaddeus and Maine, 1994; Ensor and Cooper, 2004). The first and second delays are substantially influenced by non-health service issues, including knowledge of services, proximity to a facility and cost of transport. All these might be considered as potential demand-side barriers.

The second component is that funding for public services is typically focused directly on the supply side rather than on increasing the purchasing power of individuals to demand services. Many barriers, whether associated with demand or supply, can be mitigated through action on the supply side. These typically address well-known market failures, including information asymmetries (individuals cannot judge service quality), natural monopolies and externalities (Donaldson and Gerard, 1993). Increasingly, health services introduce a separation between purchaser and provider to make it more likely that services match patient needs. Funding, however, still remains largely outside the control of individual patients. Consumer-led demand-side financing (DSF) is designed to put purchasing power into the hands of consumers in a controlled way that attempts to mitigate information asymmetry (Ensor, 2004). Providing consumers with the purchasing power to seek their own services in a controlled way has a number of potential advantages, including:

1. Greater choice and more competition — allowing consumers to buy from non-government providers that may offer better or closer services. This can be done in a regulated way through certification of those providers qualifying into the scheme.

2. Promoting behaviour change — providing consumers an incentive or "nudge" to encourage consumption of a service (merit good) that is deemed beneficial. This can be seen as a way of overcoming information asymmetries that would otherwise take considerable time to circumvent through other mechanisms such as improved general education.

3. Better targeting — supply-side actions often benefit all that use services. Evidence suggests that public services often disproportionately benefit the non-poor (Demery, 2000; Rannan-Eliya and Somanathan, 2006). At a minimum, supply-side funding can get diluted across many beneficiaries so that those that are least able to pay still end up contributing to the cost of their care. If the aim is to concentrate resources on the vulnerable, then it may be necessary to refocus resources on these groups.

4. Funding for demand-side costs — providing consumers with purchasing power to mitigate costs incurred outside the health service such as transport, time lost from work and costs incurred by those accompanying the patient.

5. Activity-based funding — funding follows the patient so in principle should have a more direct impact on service delivery. For health services, similar effects can be obtained through different provider payment systems including performance-based funding.

1.1. *DSF in Nepal 1 barriers to maternal services and the need for DSF in Nepal*

In the late 1990s, the maternal mortality ratio in Nepal was second only to Afghanistan in Asia[1] at around 550 (maternal deaths per 100,000 live births), compared to the average for South Asia of 388. Consequently, improvement of maternal and eonatal health has been a major focus of Nepalese health policy since the 1990s, aimed to achieve both national and international outcome targets (e.g. Millennium Development Goals (MDGs)). Substantial investment was undertaken in the supply of services

---

[1] The Maternal Mortality Ratio was 550 in Nepal in 2000 compared to the average for South Asia of 388, World Development Indicators, http://databank.worldbank.org/data/.

for pregnant women in communities and in hospitals. Despite these changes delivery with a skilled provider remained low, less than 10% in rural areas by 2001 (HMGN, 2001), and the cost of delivery care was identified as a persistent barrier to use of services. The Demographic and Health Survey (DHS) found that two-thirds of women suggested that "getting money for treatment" was a major problem in accessing health care for themselves or their children (HMGN, 2001). A study carried out in 2004 found that while the supply-side costs of a home or facility vaginal delivery were comparable, costs incurred by households of getting to a facility made the option of a facility birth much more expensive (Borghi *et al.*, 2006). Transport to a facility was found to make up more than 70% of the cost. For the poorest households, the cost, including transport, exceeded 3.5 times monthly cash household income.

While home delivery was chosen by most women for an expected normal delivery, the terrain in most parts of the country meant that later referral in the case of emergency would not be possible. Hence, a strategy to encourage as many women as possible to attend a facility for delivery was suggested that expanded the use of services beyond what investment in facilities had already achieved.

2. Demand-Side Financing Mechanisms

A number of mechanisms have been used in practice to increase the role of demand-side funding, including unconditional and conditional cash transfers, targeted transfers and vouchers. These mechanisms have a variety of goals although in practice it is not always clear which ones are thought of as most important in a specific context.

Unconditional and conditional cash transfers in cash or in kind are an increasingly popular way of boosting demand for health and other services. In high-income countries (HICs), transfers of funding to priority groups serve both to boost the overall disposable income of vulnerable groups and put the purchasing power in the hands of household members who have greater needs or are thought to be better able to manage household resources effectively (UK child benefit). There is evidence, for example, that women are more likely to buy welfare enhancing goods such as health care and education, and so transferring purchasing power from men to women may boost spending on these items (Quisumbing and Maluccio, 2003; Pahl, 2008). Unconditional transfers to women increase the probability that at similar levels of income, a household will spend resources on items such as food particularly on children (Schady and Rosero, 2008; Yoong *et al.*, 2012).

Transfers that are conditioned on particular behaviors are justified on the basis that there are market failures occurring either in the delivery of services by government, by individuals in understanding their own needs or in the results of "imperfect altruism" where some household decision-makers (e.g. parents) take decisions on behalf of other members (e.g. children) (Fiszbein and Schaby, 2009, p. 2).

Conditional Cash Transfers (CCTs) are typically paid to families on condition that a package of services is consumed, usually including both education — for example, sending children to school regularly — and health — for example, attending for child health checks and vaccinations requirements. CCTs explicitly acknowledge that "embedding different outcomes in a package of services could increase demand for individual outcomes more than if they are provided as separates services" (Thomas, 2012). Payments may be withheld if attendance falls below a target level.

Targeted transfers are a type of cash transfer that are allocated for specific activity rather than a general target. Payments mitigate demand-side costs, help increase treatment compliance where the benefits are not clear to users and promote health behavior change. In high- and low-resource settings, for example, there is an extensive literature on the use of small financial and non-financial payments to adhere to tuberculosis (TB) chemotherapy which requires a regular, and to patients often unnecessary, regime of regular drugs that persist past the time disease symptoms appear to have disappeared. A variation on this idea is to provide an incentive to a treatment supporter such as a relative or community health worker (Kliner *et al.*, 2013). The latter is almost indistinguishable from supply-side performance-based financing (PBF) as an activity-based incentive paid to a health care provider.

Targeted transfers may be in cash or in kind. Examples include the Jani Suraksha Yojana (JSY) programme in India which provides a cash payment to women to deliver in a facility, snack and subway vouchers given to TB patients in New York in return for treatment compliance, incentives in cash and in kind to accept male circumcision to reduce HIV transmission in countries of Sub-Saharan Africa and preferential loans given to villagers for selecting long-lasting (particularly permanent) contraceptive methods in Thailand (Weeden *et al.*, 1986; Davidson *et al.*, 2000; Lim *et al.*, 2010; Ensor *et al.*, 2019). Payments to patients remain controversial partly because there is a fine line between offsetting a patient's demand-side cost of treatment and actively providing incentives to obtain care. The issue has stirred an active debate among ethicists and the general public about whether such incentives are likely to lead to harms and unintended consequences that exceed the benefits from increase in service use (Burns, 2007; Shaw, 2007). In LMICs, discussion of perverse incentives in the context of mechanisms focusing on maternal health often focus on inducements to women to increase fertility. In practice, such outcomes are rare with one meta-analysis finding an overall neutral effect on fertility with only one country showing a statistically significant although very small increase (Glassman *et al.*, 2013).

Voucher programmes are generally suitable only for services that have a high probability of being needed by the target population, otherwise efforts will be wasted in distributing them to a population the majority of whom will make no use of them. Examples include vouchers for delivery care in Bangladesh, China and India targeted at women in antenatal clinics, bed-nets aimed at pregnant women in Tanzania and vouchers for Sexually Transmitted Infection (STI) treatment in Nicaragua targeted at adolescents in Managua (Marchant *et al.*, 2002; Meuwissen *et al.* 2006; Brody *et al.*, 2013). For more uncertain services, vouchers are only appropriate if they can be cashed in for a general insurance entitlement. In Georgia, for example, the market-focused government of Saakashvili distributed vouchers to the poor that could be redeemed for insurance coverage with a private insurance company (Gotsadze *et al.*, 2015).

2.1. *DSF in Nepal 2: The government's policy response*

The Government of Nepal's response to the findings on the cost of delivery care, particularly high cost of transport, was rapid for a number of reasons. Imminent elections meant that the government wanted something that was publicly popular, development partners were keen to act and finance action to improve dismal maternal health indicators, and a number of senior officials and other influential citizens acted as powerful advocates for the development of policy (Ensor *et al.*, 2008). Initial plans to develop an intervention that could be tested in pilot areas focusing mainly on the poorer people and regions before a general rollout were scrapped in favor of a national scheme that would immediately benefit the entire country and electorate.

The policy comprised demand-side payments to women for attending a facility for a delivery and supply-side payments to facilities and skilled birth attendants for deliveries at home. The payments to women were envisaged to reduce but not fully cover travel costs since there was sensitivity about seeing the payments as incentives or payments to treat. Costs were shown to be the highest for those living in mountain areas. In 2005, a graduated payment known as the Maternal Incentive Scheme (MIS) was introduced, paying 1,500 Nepali Rupees (NPR) to women delivering at facilities in mountain, NPR 1,000 in hills and NPR 500 in the tarai (flat) areas Table 2). Supply-side payments to hospitals were also introduced in 2006 in the 25 most deprived districts, as assessed by a country version of the Human Development Index (HDI), including all mountain and some hill areas. Smaller payments of NPR 200 were made

Table 2. DSF policies for maternal health in Nepal.

	Maternal incentive scheme (June 2005)	Safe delivery incentive programme (July 2006)	Aama programme (January 2009)
Tarai	NPR 500 transport payment	NPR 500 transport payment	NPR 500 transport payment + free delivery**
Hill (High HDI)	NPR 1,000 transport payment	NPR 1,000 transport payment	NPR 1,000 transport payment + free delivery**
Hill (Low HDI)	NPR 1,000 transport payment	NPR 1,000 transport payment + free delivery*	NPR 1,000 transport payment + free delivery**
Mountain	NPR 1,500 transport payment	NPR 1,500 transport payment + free delivery*	NPR 1,500 transport payment + free delivery**

Notes: * Enabled by a fixed payment to facilities of NPR 1,000 per delivery (vaginal, instrumental and surgical).
** Enabled by fixed payments of NPR 1,000–1,500 for a normal delivery, NPR 3,000 for instrumental delivery and NPR 7,000 for a caesarean section.

to birth attendants undertaking deliveries in homes. These latter payments for home deliveries in some ways contradicted the policy of trying to get women to deliver in facilities, but recognized that facility capacity would be unable to cope if all women immediately sought care facilities.

3. Evidence on DSF Effectiveness and Impact

There is growing evidence on the effectiveness of DSF programmes. Rapid scale-up and national scope of many programmes has meant that many evaluations have utilized quasi-experimental designs although there are some examples of (cluster) randomized control trials (RCT).

Quasi-experimental methods exploiting the gradual rollout of an unconditional cash transfer programme in South Africa found that transferring cash to women was associated with improved nutritional outcomes and yielded long-term economic returns (Aguero *et al.*, 2006). An RCT of cash transfers in Zimbabwe found that unconditional transfers had a significant and similar impact on child attendance at school as the conditional transfers and a significant impact on vaccinations, although one that was more modest than for conditional transfers (Robertson *et al.*, 2013).

Much of the evidence of CCT impact comes from Latin America where the Opportunidades (formerly Progresa) programme in Mexico led the way and offered a model for other similar schemes in neighboring countries. These CCTs offer monthly cash benefits to families in proportion to the number of school-age children as a way to improve education and health outcomes. In return, they require that children are sent to school, receive regular health visits and are fully vaccinated and pregnant women receive maternity services.

Randomised control trials of CCTs have been undertaken across Central America in Mexico, Nicaragua and Honduras as well as in Malawi. These show substantial treatment effects on health-seeking behavior including consultations with public facilities, antenatal visits and postpartum care and child health checks (Lagarde *et al.*, 2007). The impact on health outcomes is more mixed in some cases because studies are not powered to measure them. This is particularly the case with maternal outcomes which require a large sample to demonstrate effect (Murray *et al.*, 2014). Health impacts have been extensively studied in the Opportunidades programme. These indicate significant effect on levels of childhood anaemia and anthropomorphic measures such as child height (Rivera *et al.*, 2004). One of the difficulties in assessing these programmes is that they are complex incorporating multiple interventions and it is often difficult to disentangle the "relative importance of different components" (Lagarde *et al.*, 2007). More complex RCT designs can help but there is also a need for process evaluation to help policymakers understand which elements and in what context interventions work.

Systematic reviews suggest that vouchers are an effective way of boosting utilization of targeted services (Bellows *et al.*, 2011; Brody *et al.*, 2013; Murray *et al.*, 2014). Tracking this to improved outcomes has been hampered by relatively short evaluation periods and an inability to control for other policies. There is also some evidence that vouchers can boost quality of the service as measured by, for example, number of services delivered during an antenatal care (ANC) appointment, reliability of diagnostic testing and appropriateness of treatment given (Brody *et al.*, 2013).

In the education sector, randomizing receipt of vouchers is not uncommon. In the US particularly, the random distribution of vouchers to access private or charter schools have been widely evaluated. Meta-analyses of high-quality RCTs suggest that in general they have a positive impact on performance as measured by reading, language and maths scores although the results across studies are variable (Shakeel *et al.*, 2016). Randomization is less common in low-income contexts although there are examples with positive effects reported in Colombia and Delhi and Andhra (Morgan *et al.*, 2013a, 2013b; Shakeel *et al.*, 2016).

Although there is general evidence of positive impact of DSF mechanisms, the types of impacts measured and effect sizes are extremely varied. Glassman's review study of CCTs is one of the few to undertake a meta-analysis finding average percentage point (pp) increases for a range of outcomes. For maternal health, for example, the study reported effect sizes of 11.6 pp for delivery with skilled provider and 8.4 pp for prenatal monitoring (Glassman *et al.*, 2013). There appears to be little clear relationship between the payment level (in absolute terms or as % of GDP) and effect size (Figure 1). Similarly, although the impact of voucher schemes is generally positive, the reported effect sizes vary substantially. In Bangladesh, delivery with a skilled provider was reported to increase by 42 pp, in Cambodia, a similar scheme had a 14-pp impact, while in

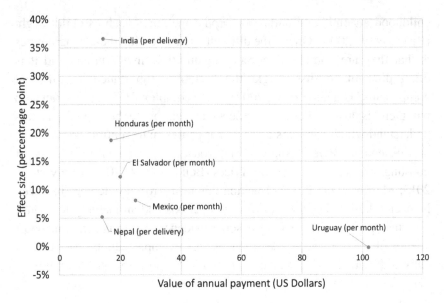

Figure 1. pp increase in delivery with skilled health work and size of payment (US dollars).

Source: Adapted from Glassman *et al.* (2013).

Kenya, maternal vouchers had a much more modest impact on skilled delivery around 5 pp (Hatt *et al.*, 2010; Ir *et al.*, 2010; Obare *et al.*, 2014).

There is relatively little of evidence on the cost-effectiveness and the sustainability of DSF mechanisms with few evaluations undertaking an economic evaluation (Murray *et al.*, 2014). A recent review of voucher programmes, for example, found only one study (out of 24) that undertook an efficiency (unit cost) analysis (Brody *et al.*, 2013). Evaluations also often do not compare the intervention with the cost-effectiveness of a similar sized investment on the supply side which might be regarded as the correct counterfactual (Lagarde *et al.*, 2007).

3.1. DSF in Nepal 3: Assessing the effectiveness of DSF

Use of delivery with a skilled provider at a government facility has increased in all ecological zones of Nepal since the start of the national safe-motherhood strategy in the late 1990s. Trends in use of a facility appear to have increased more steeply since the introduction of the DSF mechanisms particularly in tarai and hill areas (Figure 2).

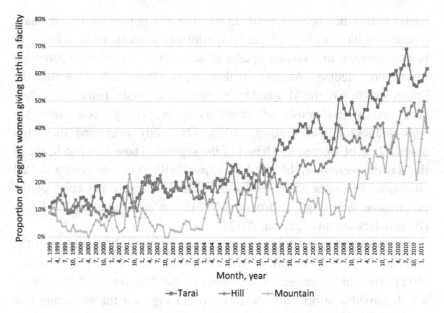

Figure 2.   Trends in facility delivery by zone.

One of the difficulties with evaluating policies of this type is that policy practice can diverge quite substantially from the intention to treat, policy takes time to have impact and in turn can vary substantially across the country and population. A number of evaluations have been undertaken of the delivery-incentive mechanisms in Nepal. An early qualitative assessment of the policy found that there was huge variation in implementation including the amount of cash provided to women and circumstances of payment (Powell-Jackson *et al.*, 2009). Implementation was influenced by interpretation of guidelines by staff and by the delays in money reaching districts. Even though delays in the central disbursement of funds was common across the country, district coping mechanisms varied with some providing pre-funding from other funds while others simply stopped allocations to facilities. Powell-Jackson and Hanson (2012) show that there was a substantial gap between knowledge of the scheme and receipt of the incentive, and this gap tends to be larger for poorer households.

For political reasons, the mechanisms in Nepal were introduced quickly and to the entire country. This mitigated against a randomized evaluation. The relative rareness of maternal mortality in the population meant that it has been difficult to monitor the impact on this primary outcome of interest. Several quasi-experimental evaluations have however been conducted to focus on uptake of services as a marker for eventual impact on outcomes. An early evaluation, conducted 2.5 years after the implementation of the MIS and based on a survey in six districts, matched beneficiaries and non-beneficiaries using propensity score matching (Powell-Jackson and Hanson, 2012). The study suggested that only around 25% of women had heard of the scheme. Those that had heard of the scheme were more likely (4.2 pp, $p < 0.01$) to deliver with a skilled attendant. The same study, suggested that the incremental costs of the programme were high at around US\$210 for each additional delivery (Powell-Jackson and Hanson, 2012).

A recent interrupted time series approach assessed the impact of the evolution of the three policy variants across the country (Ensor *et al.*, 2017). The study merged three rounds of the five-yearly DHS each of which provides information on births occurring over the preceding five years. Given the findings from earlier studies that the intervention effects took time to build-up due to delays in information acquisition and policy implementation, the study design incorporated the possibility for both immediate and gradual effects through the use of intercept and slope dummies. The results suggest that the combined policies are associated with different changes by income and geographic group. For the richest 50% of the population, the use of delivery increased by around 30 pp in the tarai and hill areas and 17 pp in mountainous areas. For the poorest 50%, the increase was 14 pp in the tarai while no statistically significant change was found for the poor in hill and mountain areas. The study suggests that although the policy has had an overall effect that is substantial, the lack of impact on the poorest income groups implies that much more direct targeting will be required to deliver services to the poor living in the least accessible areas.

4. Lessons from DSF Experience in Low-Income Contexts

DSF mechanisms have been introduced for a variety of reasons in low-resource settings. The multiple possible reasons for utilizing DSF can make it difficult to understand the main objective for introducing the mechanism in a particular context. In Cambodia, a maternal voucher scheme was used to target resources at poorer households to reduce their costs at the facility (Van de Poel *et al.*, 2014). In Bangladesh, maternal vouchers were seen as a way of "stimulating increased utilization of maternal health services by poor pregnant women" (Hatt *et al.*, 2010). Allowing choice of facility, was thought to encourage greater competition and improved quality across providers (Ahmed and Khan, 2011a, 2011b). The Kenyan output-based (voucher) scheme, aimed to incentivize demand amongst the poor (Obare *et al.*, 2013). In Nepal, the MIS and then Aama programme were principally introduced to mitigate the costs of transport across the country with some targeting based on geography rather than individual wealth (Department of Health Services, 2007). A number of policy issues are apparent from this experience.

4.1. *Demand-side funding complements well-funded service provision*

DSF mechanisms work best where there is an already well-functioning supply of services so that the focus is on assisting people to use services. Although funding allocated through DSF mechanisms can be substantial it is often directed at non-health service components (e.g. transport, food). Where funding is allocated directly to facilities, in the form for example of vouchers that facilities can exchange for cash, the sums involved generally only cover part of the costs of running the facilities. Adequate funding for overheads, staffing and other aspects of services are still required. While the maternal voucher programme in Bangladesh was associated with an increase in use of services, the overall utilization remained low, particularly amongst the poor who largely rely on public services, because public services remained poor quality (Ahmed and Khan, 2011a, 2011b).

Supply-side investment is particularly important given that incentivizing the demand side is designed to boost the use of services which need to be able to cope with the influx of new users. Indeed, many DSF mechanisms have provided parallel support to the service delivery. There is, however, evidence, in some countries, India and Nicaragua for example, that the necessary investment in infrastructure or additional supplies required are often not in place to support this increased demand (Gopalan *et al.*, 2014a, 2014b). Similarly, a continued wealth gradient between the use of maternal health services in voucher areas in Kenya is partly attributed to the continued lack of access to services by poorer populations (Obare *et al.*, 2013).

In systems with a weak service network, there is relatively little evidence that choice is substantially enhanced by DSF mechanisms. The maternal voucher programme in Bangladesh was touted as offering choice to women of public and non-public providers while the reality was that in many poorer areas only one facility continued to provide services (Schmidt *et al.*, 2010; Ahmed and Khan, 2011a, 2011b). Attempts to expand choice of delivery facility in Nepal have been frustrated by the lack of for-profit providers who have been willing to accept rates of remuneration that do not fully fund their costs (Tiwari *et al.*, 2015). In contrast, in Kenya, maternal health vouchers appear to have expanded the use of non-government services with providers using the funding creatively to improve services (Njuki *et al.*, 2015).

In Nepal, the lack of functional services was and remains an important issue particularly in mountain areas. It led to an early modification of the DSF policy to provide incentives to skilled birth attendants to provide deliveries at home. This contributed to a problem of fraudulent or "phantom" deliveries at home, something that is much harder to monitor than in facilities (Powell-Jackson *et al.*, 2009). A further supply issue, has been that the pressure placed on facilities to provide deliveries crowd out other services that are not similarly incentivized (Mehata *et al.*, 2017).

4.2. How sustainable are DSF mechanisms?

An important criticism of DSF mechanisms relates to sustainability. Mechanisms in LMICs are often supported by international development partners and operated by international not-for-profit organizations (NGOs). When the funding runs out, these mechanisms may collapse. It is easy, however, to overstate the sustainability problem. An unpublished study found that of 40 reproductive health voucher programmes reviewed, only seven had ceased to operate (Gorter *et al.*, 2012). A number of schemes have received multiple rounds of funding from donors and some integrated into national programmes.

A learning or normalization effect is suggested in some studies when use of services goes beyond the remit of services that are incentivized. Women, for example, are reported to be more likely to use a provider for delivery care in studies of Opportunidades in Mexico even though CCTs only condition the use of antenatal care (Glassman *et al.*, 2013). There is paucity of research on this issue, partly because evaluations are rarely long term enough to examine what happens substantially beyond the end of a programme.

4.3. Does DSF encourage unhealthy behavior?

A persistent criticism of DSF, particularly funding that appears to exceed the user cost of care, is that it encourages undesirable behavior. In Bangladesh, there was a concern that the value of a maternal voucher was higher for caesarean section and would therefore encourage excessive surgical deliveries. Although there was some evidence that the rate of surgical deliveries increased after the introduction of the mechanism, this was from a very low base and the rate was still recorded at a lower level than in areas without the voucher funding (Schmidt *et al.*, 2010). A similar worry is that providing funding for maternal care could incentivize fertility. Again, reviews suggest there is little evidence for this with the mechanisms in some countries showing small decreases in fertility and in others small increases (Morgan *et al.*, 2013a, 2013b).

4.4. Do DSF mechanisms swap one information asymmetry for another?

DSF mechanisms can generally help overcome information asymmetries by nudging service users into particular health-seeking behaviors and service use patterns. However, the mechanisms themselves need publicizing and often explaining which may lead to other information shortfalls. In the early days of the MIS in Nepal, for example, the low take-up was attributed to lack of knowledge about the operation of the scheme (Powell-Jackson and Hanson, 2012). A systematic review using a realist synthesis noted that not only does it take some time for DSF programmes to impact on behavior but that misconceptions about programme operation can lead to perverse behaviors; for example, in Mexico, the worry that improved child nutritional status might lead to reduced programme benefits caused some mothers to withhold food from their children (Gopalan *et al.*, 2014a, 2014b). Similarly, service providers must learn the rules governing the new system which can be complex where many but not all services and groups are covered. In Kenya, this knowledge was unequally spread with workers in larger facilities having access to more training and knowledge than those working in more remote dispensaries with a likely knock-on impact on population access (Njuki *et al.*, 2015).

5. Conclusion

The maternal DSF in Nepal is illustrative of a class of financing mechanisms that have now become a routine part of the international health policy dialogue. They have the potential to impact health service behavior and ultimately outcomes, and fill the gap left by initiatives operating only the supply side. That these mechanisms can achieve multiple objectives not only increases their potential power but also means that objectives can be muddled and their implementation in practice may diverge from theoretical expectations. The long-term effect and cost-effectiveness of DSF remain under-researched, partly because in most countries, these mechanisms remain relatively novel and partly because most evaluations are undertaken during periods of donor support and relatively soon after implementation. Future research could focus on longer term sustainability and the degree to which these mechanisms encourage normalization of health behavior change. The wide range of mechanisms implemented in different countries with diverse results also suggests the need to focus further on the contextual factors that influence the impact of each mechanism.

References

Aguero, J. M., Carter, M. R., Woodward, I. (2006). The impact of unconditional cash transfers on nutrition: The South African child support grant. Labour and Development Research Unit Working Paper Number 06/08. Cape Town, South Africa.

Ahmed, S., Khan, M. M. (2011a). Is demand-side financing equity enhancing? Lessons from a maternal health voucher scheme in Bangladesh. *Social Science & Medicine*, 72(10): 1704–1710.

Ahmed, S., Khan, M. M. (2011b). A maternal health voucher scheme: What have we learned from the demand-side financing scheme in Bangladesh? *Health Policy and Planning*, 26(1): 25–32.

Bellows, N. M., Bellows, B. W., Warren, C. (2011). Systematic review: The use of vouchers for reproductive health services in developing countries: Systematic review. *Tropical Medicine & International Health*, 16(1): 84–96.

Borghi, J., Ensor, T., Neupane, B. D., Tiwari, S. (2006). Financial implications of skilled attendance at delivery in Nepal. *Tropical Medicine & International Health*, 11(2): 228–237.

Brody, C. M., Bellows, N., Campbell, M., Potts, M. (2013). The impact of vouchers on the use and quality of health care in developing countries: A systematic review. *Global Public Health*, 8(4): 363–388.

Burns, T. (2007). Is it acceptable for people to be paid to adhere to medication? Yes. *British Medical Journal*, 335(7613): 232.

Davidson, H., Schluger, N. W., Feldman, P. H., Valentine, D. P., Telzak, E. E., Laufer, F. N. (2000). The effects of increasing incentives on adherence to tuberculosis directly observed therapy. *The International Journal of Tuberculosis and Lung Disease*, 4(9): 860–865.

Demery, L. (2000). *Benefits Incidence: A Practitioner's Guide*. Washington: World Bank.

Department of Health Services (2007). Nepal Department of Health Services Annual Report 2006–2007. Kathmandu: Ministry of Health and Population.

Donaldson, C., Gerard, K. (1993). Market failure in health care. In: *Economics of Health Care Financing: The Visible Hand*, Economic Issues in Health Care. London: Palgrave.

Ensor S, Davies, B., Rai, T., Ward, H. (2019). The effectiveness of demand creation interventions for voluntary male medical circumcision for HIV prevention in sub-Saharan Africa: A mixed methods systematic review. *Journal of the International AIDS Society*, 22, Supplement 4: 40–53.

Ensor, T. (2004). Consumer-led demand side financing in health and education and its relevance for low and middle income countries. *International Journal of Health and Planning Management*, 19: 267–285.

Ensor, T., Cooper, S. (2004). Overcoming barriers to health service access: Influencing the demand side. *Health Policy and Planning*, 19(2): 69–79.

Ensor, T., Clapham, S., Prasai, D. P. (2008). What drives health policy formulation: Insights from the Nepal maternity incentive scheme? *Health Policy*, 90(2–3):247–253.

Ensor, T., Bhatt, H., Tiwari, S. (2017). Incentivizing universal safe delivery in Nepal: 10 years of experience. *Health Policy and Planning*, 32(8): 1185–1192.

Fiszbein, A., Schaby, N. (2009). *Conditional Cash Transfers: Reducing Present and Future Poverty*. Washington: The World Bank.

Glassman, A., Duran, D., Fleisher, L., Singer, D., Sturke, R., Angeles, G., Charles, J., Emrey, B., Gleason, J., Mwebsa, W., Saldana, K., Yarrow, K., Koblinsky, M. (2013). Impact of conditional cash transfers on maternal and newborn health. *Journal of Health, Population and Nutrition*, 31(4 Suppl 2): 48–66.

Gopalan, S. S., Das, A., Mutasa, R. (2014a). What makes health demand-side financing schemes work in low- and middle-income countries? A realist review. *Journal of Public Health Research*, 3(3): 304.

Gopalan, S. S., Mutasa, R., Friedman, J., Das, A. (2014b). Health sector demand-side financial incentives in low- and middle-income countries: A systematic review on demand- and supply-side effects. *Social Science & Medicine*, 100: 72–83.

Gorter, A., Grainger, C., Okal, J., Bellows, B. (2012). *Systematic Review of Structural and Implementation Issues of Voucher Programs: Analysis of 40 Voucher Programs In-Depth Analysis of 20 Programs*. Nairobi, Kenya: Population Council.

Gotsadze, G., Zoidze, A., Rukhadze, N., Shengelia, N., Chkhaidze, N. (2015). An impact evaluation of medical insurance for poor in Georgia: Preliminary results and policy implications. *Health Policy and Planning*, 30 (Suppl 1): i2–13.

Gregson, S. (2013). Effects of unconditional and conditional cash transfers on child health and development in Zimbabwe: A cluster-randomised trial. *The Lancet*, 381(9874): 1283–1292.

Hatt, L., Nguyen, H., Sloan, N., Miner, S., Magvanjav, O., Sharma, A., Chowdhury, J., Chowdhury, R., Paul, D., Islam, M., Wang, H. (2010). Economic evaluation of demand-side financing (DSF) for maternal health in Bangladesh. In: *Review, Analysis and Assessment of Issues Related to Health Care Financing and Health Economics in Bangladesh*. Bethesda, MD: Abt Associates Inc.

HMGN (2001). Nepal Demographic and Health Survey. Kathmandu, Nepal: New ERA and Maryland, USA: ORC Macro.

Ir, P., Horemans, D., Souk, N., Van Damme, W. (2010). Using targeted vouchers and health equity funds to improve access to skilled birth attendants for poor women: A case study in three rural health districts in Cambodia. *BMC Pregnancy Childbirth*, 10: 1.

Kliner, M., Knight, A., Elston, J., Humphreys, C., Mamvura, C., Wright, J., Walley, J. (2013). Development and testing of models of tuberculosis contact tracing in rural southern Africa. *Public Health Action*, 3(4): 299–303.

Lagarde, M., Haines, A., Palmer, N. (2007). Conditional cash transfers for improving uptake of health interventions in low- and middle-income countries: A systematic review. *The Journal of the American Medical Association*, 298(16): 1900–1910.

Lim, S. S., Dandona, L., Hoisington, J. A., James, S. L., Hogan, M. C., Gakidou, E. (2010). India's Janani Suraksha yojana, a conditional cash transfer programme to increase births in health facilities: An impact evaluation. *The Lancet*, 375(9730): 2009–2023.

Marchant, T., Schellenbeg, J. A., Edgar, T., Nathan, R., Abdulla, S., Mukasa, O., Mponda, H., Lengeler, C. (2002). Socially marketed insecticide-treated nets improve malaria and anaemia in pregnancy in southern Tanzania. *Tropical Medicine & International Health*, 7(2): 149–158.

Mehata, S., Paudel, Y. R., Dariang, M., Aryal, K. K., Paudel, S., Mehta, R., King, S., Barnett, S. (2017). Factors determining satisfaction among facility-based maternity clients in Nepal. *BMC Pregnancy and Childbirth*, 17(319).

Meuwissen, L. E., Gorter, A. C., Knottnerus, A. J. A. (2006). Impact of accessible sexual and reproductive health care on poor and underserved adolescents in Managua, Nicaragua: A quasi-experimental intervention study. *Journal of Adolescent Health*, 38(1): 56.e51–56.e59.

Morgan, C., Petrosino, A., Fronius, T. (2013a). *A Systematic Review of the Evidence of the Impact of School Voucher Programmes in Developing Countries*. London: EPPI-Centre, Social Science Research Unit, Institute of Education, University of London.

Morgan, L., Stanton, M. E., Higgs, E. S., Balster, R. L., Bellows, B. W., Brandes, N., Comfort, A. B., Eichler, R., Glassman, A., Hatt, L. E., Conlon, C. M., Koblinsky, M. (2013b). Financial incentives and maternal health: Where do we go from here? *Journal of Health, Population and Nutrition*, 31(4 Suppl 2): 8–22.

Murray, S. F., Hunter, B. M., Bisht, R., Ensor, T., Bick, D. (2014). Effects of demand-side financing on utilisation, experiences and outcomes of maternity care in low- and middle-income countries: A systematic review. *BMC Pregnancy Childbirth*, 14: 30.

Njuki, R., Abuya, T., Kimani, J., Kanya, L., Korongo, A., Mukanya, C., Bracke, P., Bellows, B., Warren, C. E. (2015). Does a voucher program improve reproductive health service delivery and access in Kenya? *BMC Health Services Research*, 15: 206.

Obare, F., Warren, C., Njuki, R., Abuya, T., Sunday, J., Askew, I., Bellows, B. (2013). Community-level impact of the reproductive health vouchers programme on service utilization in Kenya. *Health Policy and Planning*, 28(2): 165–175.

Obare, F., Warren, C., Abuya, T., Askew, I., Bellows, B. (2014). Assessing the population-level impact of vouchers on access to health facility delivery for women in Kenya. *Social Science & Medicine*, 102: 183–189.

O'Donnell, O. (2007). Access to health care in developing countries: Breaking down demand side barriers. *Cadernos de Saúde Pública*, 23: 2820–2834.

Pahl, J. (2008). Family finances, individualisation, spending patterns and access to credit. *The Journal of Socio-Economics*, 37(2): 577–591.

Powell-Jackson, T., Morrison, J., Tiwari, S., Neupane, B. D., Costello, A. M. (2009). The experiences of districts in implementing a national incentive programme to promote safe delivery in Nepal. *BMC Health Services Research*, 9(97).

Powell-Jackson, T., Hanson, K. (2012). Financial incentives for maternal health: Impact of a national programme in Nepal. *Journal of Health Economics*, 31(1): 271–284.

Quisumbing, A. R., Maluccio, J. A. (2003). Resources at marriage and intrahousehold allocation: Evidence from Bangladesh, Ethiopia, Indonesia, and South Africa. *Oxford Bulletin of Economics and Statistics*, 65(5): 283–327.

Rannan-Eliya, R., Somanathan, A. (2006). Equity in health and health care systems in Asia. In: *The Elgar Companion to Health Economics*. Edward Elgar Publishing.

Rivera, J. A., Sotres-Alvarez, D., Habicht, J. P., Shamah, T.,Villalpando, S. (2004). Impact of the Mexican program for education, health, and nutrition (Progresa) on rates of growth and anemia in infants and young children: A randomized effectiveness study. *The Journal of the American Medical Association*, 291(21): 2563–2570.

Robertson, L., Mushati, P., Eaton, J. W., Dumba, L., Mavise, G., Makoni, J., Schumacher, C., Crea, T., Monasch, R., Sherr, L., Garnett, G. P., Nyamukapa, C., Schady, N., Rosero, J. (2008). Are cash transfers made to women spent like other sources of income? *Economics Letters*, 101(3): 246–248.

Schady, N., Rosero, J. (2008). Are cash transfers made to women spent like other sources of income? *Economics Letters*, 101(3): 246–248.

Schmidt, J. O., Ensor, T., Hossain, A., Khan, S. (2010). Vouchers as demand side financing instruments for health care: A review of the Bangladesh maternal voucher scheme. *Health Policy,* 96(2): 98–107.

Shakeel, M. D., Anderson, K. P., Wolf, P. J. (2016). *The Participant Effects of Private School Vouchers Across the Globe: A Meta-Analytic and Systematic Review.* Department of Education Reform, University of Arkansas.

Shaw, J. (2007). Is it acceptable for people to be paid to adhere to medication? No. *British Medical Journal,* 335(7613): 233.

Thaddeus, S., Maine, D. (1994). Too far to walk: Maternal mortality in context. *Social Science & Medicine,* 38(8): 1091–1110.

Thomas, R. (2012). Conditional cash transfers to improve education and health: An ex ante evaluation of Red de Proteccion Social, Nicaragua. *Health Econ,* 21(10): 1136–1154.

Tiwari, S., Bhatt, H., Ensor, T., Suvedi, B., Lievens, T., James, C., Sharma, S. K. (2015). *Unit Cost Analysis of the Health Facility Reimbursement Made Under the Aama Programme.* Kathmandu: Ministry of Health and Population, Family Health Division and Nepal Health Sector Support Programme.

Van de Poel, E., Flores, G., Ir, P., O'Donnell, O., Van Doorslaer, E. (2014). Can vouchers deliver? An evaluation of subsidies for maternal health care in Cambodia. *Bulletin of the World Health Organization,* 92(5): 331–339.

Weeden, D., Bennett, A., Lauro, D., Viravaidya, M. (1986). An incentives program to increase contraceptive prevalence in rural Thailand. *International Family Planning Perspectives,* 12(1): 11–16.

Yoong, J., Rabinovich, L., Diepeveen, S. (2012). *The Impact of Economic Resource Transfers to Women Versus Men: A Systematic Review.* London: EPPI-Centre, Social Science Research Unit, Institute of Education, University of London.

Chapter 9

A New Approach to Measuring Health Development: From National Income Toward Health Coverage (and Beyond)

Rodrigo Moreno-Serra, Arne Hole and Peter C. Smith

Abstract

This chapter proposes an alternative approach to identify and constraints in countries, based on indicators that are broader than national income and more relevant to assess the stage of national development in health. A conceptual framework of "health coverage" underpins the construction of sub-indices of national performance in the dimensions of access to care, financial risk protection in health and domestic financial constraints, which are then used to construct overall indices of national health development. Country rankings in the health development scale vary substantially when the conditions of access to care, financial protection and domestic capacity to finance the health system are considered, compared to conventional income rankings. Furthermore, the decomposition of our health development indices sheds light on important aspects for health policy, including the identification of cases where there is a need for external support to maintain and expand current health coverage levels, as well as preliminary insights into specific support modalities by donor agencies that may be more efficient to promote health development in a particular setting. This chapter also demonstrates how our proposed indices can inform policy decisions at a higher granularity level subject to the availability of subnational level data.

1. Introduction

Historically, national income has been chosen in practice as the key (or only) indicator of a country's development achievement by multilateral organizations and countries that provide development assistance (Equitable Access Initiative, 2016). This choice is mainly due to pragmatic reasons. Average income levels — measured usually through Gross National Income (GNI) or Gross Domestic Product (GDP) per capita (pc) — are considered to be reasonably good indicators of a country's economic welfare. Measures such as GNI pc are simple, well understood and widely available for almost every country in the world.

Yet, the simplicity of GNI or GDP pc indicators means that many aspects of a country's development that may be deemed relevant for the assessment of population welfare are not satisfactorily captured in the measurements. In the health area, countries that make progress in terms of average income may do so with a persistent and very significant overall burden of disease, and this has been the situation in most low- and middle-income countries (LMICs) — including many of the countries that transitioned to the "middle-income" status in recent years and suffered a consequent reduction in aid flows to their health sectors based on their revised GNI pc levels (Equitable Access Initiative, 2016). Despite the rise in average incomes, some of these countries may still need a strong international contribution to remedy the lack of their health system's capacity to cope with a large and changing burden of disease.

Multilateral institutions such as World Health Organization (WHO), the World Bank and others have been urging countries to take concrete steps toward the achievement of universal health coverage, which in its simplest formulation means providing all people with access to needed health services of sufficient quality, which should be effective, without imposing financial hardship (WHO, 2010). Effective access to the health system accompanied (and enabled) by higher reliance on prepaid health spending and risk pooling mechanisms are regarded as key conditions for actual progress in terms of population health coverage, and expansions in coverage have become a fundamental development objective in the health sector (Backman *et al.*, 2008; Garrett *et al.*, 2009). Countries where the average income has been increasing may still experience major challenges in meeting the fundamental development goal of expanding health coverage, facing growing and changing population's health needs in situations, for example, where a very limited tax and contributory base acts as a major constraint to reduce large shares of private out-of-pocket (OOP) spending in the total financing of the health system. Ideally then, the information included in assessing a country's development in health should reflect the national situation concerning the key strategic objective of health coverage. Sustaining and increasing the pool of funds available for health is crucial to promote equity of access to and quality of health services, ultimately improving population health.

The aim of this chapter is to propose an approach to identify health needs and constraints in countries, based on indicators that are broader than national income and more relevant to assess the stage of national development in health. In Section 2, we propose a framework that examines health needs and system performance jointly under the overarching concept of "health coverage". We then suggest methodologies for constructing measures of national development in health based on relevant indicators that are of comparable definition and measurement across countries, measured in an acceptably reliable way, not easily manipulated and publicly available for most countries. Section 3 presents the results for the computations of our health development indices, contrasting these results with country development assessments based solely on income pc, and showcases the flexibility of our suggested approach for broader assessments of development in health based both on national- and subnational-level data. Section 4 discusses the main implications for policy arising from our analyses and concludes.

2. Methods

2.1. *Theoretical background and data sources*

Elsewhere, we propose a simple theoretical framework to underpin discussions and measurement of national health development based on the underlying degree of health system coverage (see details in Moreno-Serra and Smith, 2012a). Our framework examines the notions of health needs and system performance jointly from a conventional microeconomic perspective. It implies that an operational health development index requires a count of people with adequate access to necessary services in a country, with the associated health benefits obtained. It also requires an assessment of the countries' performance on financial risk protection in health, i.e. the level of protection achieved against financial hardship caused by securing access to necessary care.

Most data we use in our empirical work come from major international, publicly available sources. These include the World Bank World Development Indicators (WDI), the WHO Global Health Observatory repository, UNICEF Childinfo and Global Burden of Disease estimates from Institute for Health Metrics and Evaluation (University of Washington). The indicators used are described in the following, and their sources are given in Table 1. The time period for which we have been able to collect the relevant country information is 1995–2013.

2.2. Measuring access to care and health needs

Rates of utilisation of services that should be provided to entire population groups (e.g. pregnant women, children) can be used as proxies for the conditions of access to needed services in a health system. Here we use the proportion of births attended by skilled health staff (% of total births in the most recent year). Skilled birth attendance represents a good proxy

Table 1. Indicator definitions and sources.

Indicator	Description	Source
Skilled birth attendance	Births attended by skilled health staff (% of total)	World Bank; WHO; UNICEF
DALYs lost	Total number of DALYs lost for all causes, all ages (per 100,000)	Institute for Health Metrics and Evaluation
Pooled prepaid health expenditure	Pooled prepaid health expenditure (= total minus out-of-pocket) as share of total health expenditure (%)	WHO
GNI per capita	GNI per capita, PPP (international dollars)	World Bank
Tax revenue	Tax revenue (% of GDP)	World Bank

for the conditions of access to the broader basket of services provided in a health system (WHO, 2008). It refers to a service that should be provided in clinical facilities to all pregnant women; thus, shortages from the 100% rate tend to indicate general deficiencies in access to the health system.

A rough estimate of the health benefits gained from adequate access to necessary treatments can be obtained in terms of disability-adjusted life years (DALYs). DALYs are a measure of overall disease burden, expressed as the number of years lost due to ill-health, disability or early death. In our application, we use the total number of DALYs lost for all causes (communicable diseases, non-communicable diseases (NCDs) and injuries) in the country in 2013, per 100,000 population. Since in this application we will be constructing an index that is intended to be a positive function of health development — i.e. the higher the index, the higher the level of development — we use in the computations the *inverse* of the total number of DALYs lost in a country.

2.3. *Measuring financial protection in health*

Given that conventional financial protection indicators such as catastrophic health spending incidence have been produced only sporadically and for a reduced number of countries (cf. e.g. WHO, 2015), simpler proxies must be used in this application. We have collected data on OOP health spending as a share of total, which has been found to be highly and positively correlated with indicators of catastrophic health spending (Xu *et al.*, 2007; Moreno-Serra *et al.*, 2013). We then construct a measure of pooled prepaid health spending as a share of total health spending, by subtracting the share of OOP health spending from the total. Pooled prepaid spending refers to funds paid by individuals before the need for medical care, through channels such as general taxation, social insurance contributions and private voluntary insurance payments. Higher reliance on pooled sources of health financing (as opposed to OOP funding) has been found to greatly enhance the positive population impacts brought about by additional resources pumped into the health system, through broader access to health services and improved protection against catastrophic health payments (Escobar *et al.*, 2010; Moreno-Serra and

Smith, 2012b, 2014). Therefore, the inclusion of the pooled spending measure in the computation of our health development index can also provide valuable information for policy on how effective additional domestic and donor funds are likely to be for spurring health improvements in a given country.

2.4. A flexible approach: Incorporating information on financial constraints

The operationalisation of our theoretical index can be flexible enough to incorporate information on other country factors beyond — but associated with — health needs, access and financial protection, that may be seen as relevant for welfare assessments in the health domain. These factors include perceived constraints for development in health. The importance of the latter aspect for global health policy debates is reflected, among others, by its inclusion (in various capacities) within the funding allocation formulas adopted by many international agencies, including the World Bank International Development Association (IDA) and the Global Fund to Fight AIDS, Tuberculosis and Malaria (GFATM) (Equitable Access Initiative, 2016).

Here we explore the possibility of accounting for national capacity to finance health domestically. We focus on two related indicators to obtain a broad picture of such financing capacity. The first one is the traditionally used indicator of income per person, GNI pc, measured in purchasing power parity-adjusted (international) dollars. The second indicator is tax revenue as a proportion of GDP. The latter provides good information about the available domestic contributory base to support expansions in pooled health financing and — particularly in LMICs — the extension of the informal economy as an associated constraint for raising health revenues (Johnson *et al.*, 1997).

2.5. The computation of health development indices

The general approach we choose for index construction is close in spirit to the mechanics behind the Human Development Index (UNDP, 2015). We seek to construct indices of health development that are comparable across countries, for each of the three dimensions: (a) access to care; (b) financial protection and (c) domestic constraints to expansions in health system coverage. After computation of these dimension-specific indices, we proceed to construct composite measures of health development combining all components (a), (b) and (c).

Since dimensions (a) and (b) correspond more closely to the notion of health development based on coverage as derived from our theoretical framework, we first compute a *strict* health development index encompassing only the dimension-specific indices of access to care and financial protection, under equal weights for each of the components. Finally, in a separate computation, we construct an *extended* health development index for each country, which is an overall measure combining country performance in all three dimension-specific indices for components (a), (b) and (c). Figure 1 summarizes our approach.

2.5.1. *Access to care index*

As shown in Table 2, the access to care index is constructed as the geometric mean of two normalized sub-indices reflecting performance in unmet health needs (the skilled birth attendance rate) and total health needs (total DALYs lost). For the normalization of the sub-indices, a minimum value of 0 and a maximum of 100 are set for skilled birth attendance. This of course means that the unmet needs sub-index is given by the observed ratio of skilled birth attendance itself. For total health needs, on the other hand, we

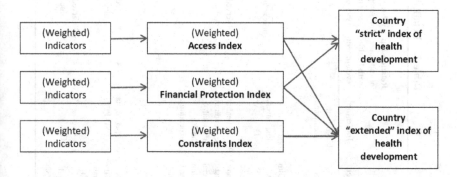

Figure 1. An overview of our approach to constructing health development indices.

Table 2. Detailed methodology for computation of health development indices.

Dimension	Aspect	Indicator	Relationship of indicator with health development	Minimum value (full = full sample, all countries, 1995–2013)	Maximum value (full = full sample, all countries, 1995–2013)	From indicator to sub-index (t = 2013 = latest year) (full = full sample, all countries, 1995–2013)	Dimension-specific index (geo mean = geometric mean) (t = 2013 = latest year) (full = full sample, all countries, 1995–2013)	Health development index strict	Health development index extended
Access to care	Unmet health needs	Skilled birth attendance (%)	+	0	100	(1) $\dfrac{actual\ value(t) - min\ value(full)}{max\ value(full) - min\ value(full)}$	(a) $\dfrac{geo\ mean(1,2)(t)}{max\ value(geo\ mean(1,2))(full)}$ $=$ $\dfrac{\sqrt{index(1)(t) \times index(2)(t)}}{max\ value(geo\ mean(1,2))(full)}$	$\sqrt{a \times b}$	$\sqrt[3]{a \times b \times c}$
	Total health needs	Total DALYs lost (inverse of)	+	$\dfrac{1}{max\ value\ (full)}$	$\dfrac{1}{min\ value\ (full)}$	(2) $\dfrac{\frac{1}{actual\ value(t)} - \frac{1}{max\ value(full)}}{\frac{1}{min\ value(full)} - \frac{1}{max\ value(full)}}$			
Financial protection	Protection against financial hardship caused by out-of-pocket health payments	Pooled health expenditure (% total health expenditure)	+	Observed min value (full)	Observed max value (full)	(3) $\dfrac{actual\ value(t) - min\ value(full)}{max\ value(full) - min\ value(full)}$	(b) Same as (3)		
Constraints	Domestic capacity to finance health and expand coverage	GNI per capita (USD PPP)	+	Observed min value (full)	Observed max value (full)	(4) $\dfrac{actual\ value(t) - min\ value(full)}{max\ value(full) - min\ value(full)}$	(c) $\dfrac{geo\ mean(4,5)(t)}{max\ value(geo\ mean(4,5))(full)}$ $=$ $\dfrac{\sqrt{index(4)(t) \times index(5)(t)}}{max\ value(geo\ mean(4,5))(full)}$		
		Tax revenue (% GDP)	+	Observed min value (full)	Observed max value (full)	(5) $\dfrac{actual\ value(t) - min\ value(full)}{max\ value(full) - min\ value(full)}$			

use the inverse of the number of DALYs lost (as explained before), and the corresponding minimum and maximum values are those observed in the entire sample of countries for the available period 1995–2013.

Having calculated the normalized unmet needs and total health needs sub-indices, the geometric mean of these sub-indices is computed. The final access to care index for a given country is then computed as the normalized value of its sub-indices' geometric mean, using the minimum value of 0 and, as maximum value, the highest geometric mean of the sub-indices for all countries and years under consideration. As with all other indices computed in this application, the normalization employed ensures the access index lies between 0 and 1, with higher values of the index indicating better conditions of access to care given health needs in a country.

2.5.2. Financial protection index

The financial protection index is constructed based on the share of pooled health spending in the total health financing (Table 2). It is computed as the normalized value of a country's pooled spending share, where the minimum and maximum values used in the normalization procedure correspond, respectively, to the lowest and highest values of the pooled spending share observed for the entire sample of countries and years under consideration. Higher values of the index indicate higher degrees of protection against financial risk due to health care payments.

2.5.3. Constraints index

The constraints index is computed as the geometric mean of normalized sub-indices for GNI pc and tax revenue as a share of GDP (Table 2). The normalization of these two sub-indices is based on the corresponding minimum and maximum values for each indicator observed in the entire sample of countries for the available period 1995–2013. Having computed the normalized GNI and tax revenue sub-indices, the geometric mean of these sub-indices is computed. The final constraints index for a given country is then given by the normalized value of the GNI and tax revenue sub-indices' geometric mean, where the minimum value used for the normalization is 0 and the highest geometric mean of the sub-indices for all countries and years under consideration is used as the maximum value. A higher value of the constraints index suggests a higher domestic capacity to finance health and improve coverage.

3. Results

3.1. Overview

The full results for the computations of the health development indices described above are shown in Table S1 (see Supplementary Data). All analyses in this chapter refer to the results for the 165 countries with data on GNI pc and for which at least the "strict" health development index could be calculated, given data availability. The additional information required to account for the *constraints* dimension as defined above means that the "extended" index could only be calculated for a smaller number of countries (141). All indices refer to year 2013, the most recent year available at the time of analysis. Further breakdowns of the analyses presented in the following, as well as computation of health development indices using additional measures of access to care, are presented in the Supplementary Data.

We start by examining the distribution of the "strict" and "extended" health development indices according to income groups (defined as per the World Bank classification of countries). Figure 2 shows the composition of each quartile of the "strict" index (1 = first quartile, countries with the 25% lowest values of the "strict" index"; going up to 4 = fourth quartile, countries with the 25% highest values of the "strict" index) by income group. Half of the first quartile is made of low-income countries (LICs) (21), followed in composition by 39% of lower-middle-income countries (l-MICs). All remaining LICs and most of the remaining l-MICs belong to the second quartile of the "strict" index distribution. Interestingly, many upper middle-income countries (u-MICs) (16) — and even some non-Organization for Economic Cooperation and Development (non-OECD) countries classified as high-income — rank in the bottom 50% of health development levels measured by the "strict" index.

Figure 3 shows a similar analysis, but for the composition of our "extended" index of health development. A clear message that arises is that all 21 LICs for which the "extended" index could be calculated

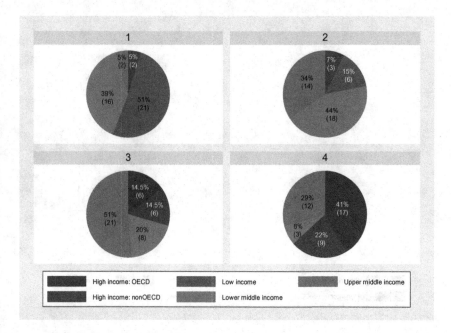

Figure 2. Composition of the four quartiles of the "strict" index of health development, by income groups.

Note: Number of countries in parentheses.

belong to the first quartile; in other words, all LICs present poor health development performance if domestic constraints to finance health and coverage expansions are taken into account. Similarly, all l-MICs fall in the lowest two quartiles of health development when financial constraints are considered, accompanied by eight u-MICs. Since the "extended" index includes the GNI pc indicator, it is not that surprising to see the composition of quartiles and ranking of countries according to the "extended" index to be closer to the simple GNI pc ranking, in contrast to what was observed for the "strict" health development index.

The information conveyed by our original "strict" and "extended" indices can be summarized through maps showing the comparative performance of each country according to performance bands (quartiles). Figures 4 and 5 show country rankings where lower rankings (closer to 1) represent lower health development (according to the "strict" index) and lower health development and higher financial constraints ("extended" index).

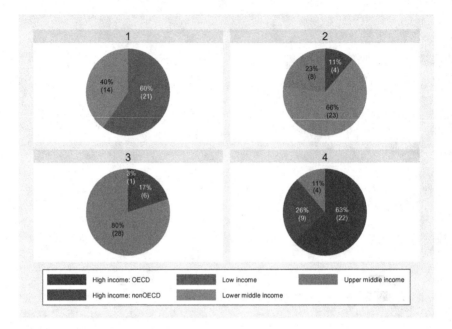

Figure 3. Composition of the four quartiles of the "extended" index of health development, by income groups.

Note: Number of countries in parentheses.

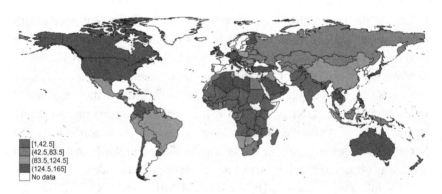

Figure 4.   Country rankings according to the "strict" index (165 countries).

Although most bad performers according to the "strict" index are in sub-Saharan Africa and South Asia, some u-MICs and even high-income countries (HICs) such as Russia and Venezuela also belong to the two bottom groups in terms of health development performance (Figure 4). If

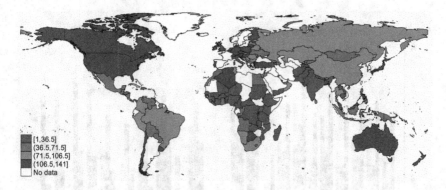

Figure 5. Country rankings according to the "extended" index (141 countries).

in addition to health development *per se* we also take into consideration domestic financial constraints measured by the "extended" index, the map in Figure 5 shows that the LICs in Africa and South Asia are still among the lowest-ranked nations, reflecting prevalent domestic financial constraints. Other countries such as South Africa, Russia and Venezuela climb in the rankings due to their relatively high capacity to finance health coverage expansions domestically. Arguably, for the latter group of countries, there is at least some degree of mismatch between their relatively high ability to pay for health coverage improvements and their relatively poor observed performance in ensuring adequate access and financial protection for their populations.

3.2. A closer look: Comparisons of health development indices and GNI classification for selected countries

We now turn to a closer examination of how the rankings of specific countries change in the health development scale when the latter is evaluated by our proposed "strict" and "extended" indices, compared to the commonly used GNI pc indicator.

Figure 6 shows country rankings according to GNI pc and the resulting rankings using our indices. We select for this analysis the 10 countries (or 11 countries in case of a tie) whose rankings change the most moving "from higher development to lower" (i.e. those with the largest negative changes in ranking when moving from the GNI indicator to the "strict" index, reflecting a deterioration in measured health

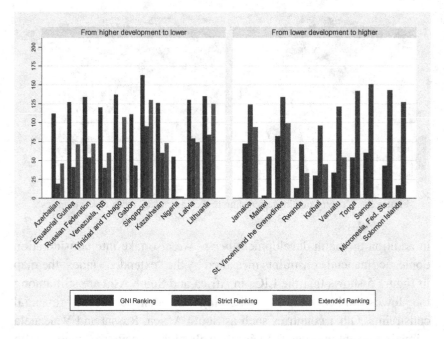

Figure 6. Changes in health development rankings using different indices, selected countries.

Note: The vertical axis denotes the country ranking according to the corresponding index. Lower ranking (closer to 1) = worse health development performance.

development from the former to the latter), as well as the 10 countries whose rankings change the most "from lower development to higher" (i.e. those with the largest positive changes in ranking between the GNI indicator and the "strict" index, reflecting an improvement in measured health development from the former to the latter).

Among the countries whose health development deteriorates when measured by our proposed indices, the majority are economies largely driven by oil production revenues. Countries such as Azerbaijan, Equatorial Guinea and Nigeria experience quite dramatic departures from their higher levels of health development measured solely by GNI, moving to the group of countries with the lowest health development rankings measured by the "strict" and "extended" indices. Beyond a simple reclassification of countries, the decomposition of changes in ranking between a GNI criterion and our health development indices also sheds light on some potentially important aspects for health policy. For example, for the majority of countries whose health development ranking worsens the most when our proposed indices are used instead of GNI only, such deterioration is driven mostly by accounting for their situation regarding access to care and financial risk protection in health (reflected in the "strict" index version). Accounting for financial constraints (the "extended" index version) tends to improve the ranking of these countries. Thus, policy measures aimed at advancing health development in these countries could do well by ensuring that the relatively adequate domestic capacity to finance health care is channelled through pooled prepaid sources and effectively expands access to needed health services. Of course, the major bottlenecks for health development in a specific country may lie on financial/non-financial barriers to access and/or financial hardship caused by health care payments. To shed light on this, the changes from GNI ranking to the "strict" health development index ranking can be further decomposed by access to care and financial protection dimensions as well. We perform such analyses in Section 3.3.

Figure 6 also shows information for the 10 countries whose health development ranking improves the most when measured by our proposed indices ("from lower development to higher"). Once again, the main drivers behind ranking changes are access to care and financial protection in health, whereas accounting for financial constraints through the "extended" index brings country rankings closer to their GNI-only rankings. The "strict" index rightly reflects health development progress achieved by countries known to have implemented wide-ranging health system reforms geared toward coverage expansions. As an example, Rwanda achieved great progress in terms of population coverage by formal health insurance arrangements in the last decade, based on increased reliance on pooled sources of health financing through a combination of enhanced government budget support and community-based health insurance schemes. This progress has been followed by measured improvements in access to services by disadvantaged populations and reductions in the incidence of catastrophic health expenditures (Saksena et al., 2010), which are reflected in our "strict" health development index.

3.3. Relative importance of access to care and financial protection for measured levels of health development

From a policy perspective, it seems relevant to disentangle the particular impact of each of the components of the health development indices for the resulting country rankings. In what follows, we present analyses for the components of the "strict" index.

Figure 7 shows the variation in country rankings when we measure health development solely by GNI, then separately by each dimension of the "strict" index — access to care and financial protection — and finally by the resulting overall "strict" index. The selected countries are the 10 countries with the largest negative changes in ranking from GNI-only to "strict" indices, and also the 10 countries with the corresponding largest positive changes in ranking, as defined in Section 3.2.

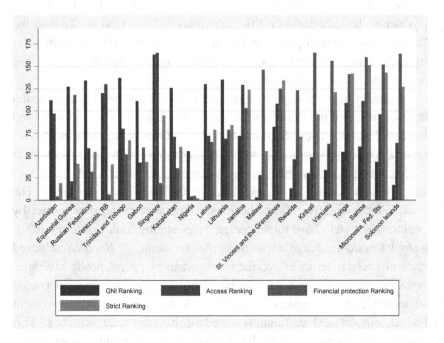

Figure 7.   Changes in health development rankings using different sub-indices, selected countries.

Note: The vertical axis denotes the country ranking according to the corresponding index. Lower ranking (closer to 1) = worse health development performance.

The examination of components of the "strict" index produces valuable insights about the main bottlenecks for health development — and consequently potential policy responses — across the selected group of countries. As an illustration, Azerbaijan's substantial fall in the health development ranking when the latter is measured by the "strict" index instead of GNI pc is led primarily by low performance in the financial protection dimension. This may suggest a situation where improvements in the utilization of needed health services by its population have been achieved at the cost of relatively high private OOP payments associated with access to those services, potentially exposing large population groups to financially catastrophic health payments. The panorama looks somewhat different in Equatorial Guinea, another country with a significant drop in the health development ranking as measured by the "strict" index. The major driver behind this drop in Equatorial Guinea's health development ranking is in fact poor performance in the access to care dimension, which suggests a situation where access to services is inadequate given the burden of disease in the population, possibly due to barriers to access beyond a lack of reliance in pooled health financing (such as physical availability of services for instance). Of course, more detailed analyses specific to each country should be conducted to validate the conjectures above and define policy responses, but the examination of our simple indices provides useful insights on where the main hurdles for health development may lie.

3.4. Computation of health development indices using subnational data: The case of India

We now present exploratory work on the computation of our health development indices using data at the subnational level. This exercise is useful to showcase the flexibility of the suggested methodological framework to provide policy insights at a higher granularity level. There are also important practical reasons why the calculation of health development indices with subnational data is relevant from a policy standpoint. National governments may be interested in using the information on health needs, access to care and financial risk protection available across jurisdictions to inform their decisions about transfers from the central health budget to subnational levels of government. Such information could be incorporated, for instance, as further risk-adjusters — in addition to more traditional measures such as population size — into the capitated funding allocation models used by some national governments. From a different perspective, an international donor agency may wish to focus their efforts on the particular geographic areas that exhibit the lowest levels of health development within a given country, as opposed to supporting activities for the whole country population. This could contribute to the achievement of maximum value-for-money for a given pot of resources according to the agency's specific objectives.

We choose India, one of the most populated countries in the world, as a case study to illustrate the issues above. Although India belongs to the middle-income World Bank category classification as indicated by its GNI pc (US$5,180 in 2013), the country's ranking in the health development scale drops substantially if our "strict" index is used instead of GNI pc. India becomes the 18th least-developed country in the world with a measured "strict" index of just 0.409 (Table S1), driven by relatively similar poor performance on both the access to care given health needs and financial protection dimensions.

In what follows, we use our proposed methodology to examine how such health development performance varies across Indian states. The subnational-level indicators used for this exercise are similar to the ones used for the cross-country analyses and are described in the Supplementary Data (Table S2). Given the availability of data, we are able to compute the indices for 28 states; the full results are shown in Supplementary Data Table S3.

Figure 8 illustrates how health development rankings for Indian states change from when we use GDP pc as the single criterion, moving to assessing health development separately by access to care and financial risk protection, and by the overall "strict" index. For the sake of comparison, we select the seven states in the bottom and top quartiles of the "strict" index. This exercise demonstrates how the flexible nature of the "strict" index may be used to generate insights into the major obstacles for health development, beyond what can be provided by a simple examination of income levels, and this time with more disaggregated data. For example, among the 25% worse performers according to the "strict" index, there are cases of relatively wealthy states such as Madhya Pradesh and West Bengal, alongside very poor states such as Bihar and Uttar

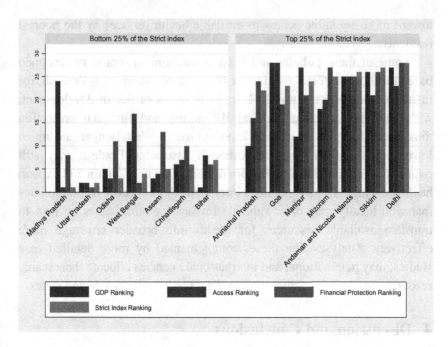

Figure 8. Changes in health development rankings using different sub-indices, Indian states.

Note: The vertical axis denotes the state ranking according to the corresponding index. Lower ranking (closer to 1) = worse health development performance.

Pradesh. The low levels of health development found in the latter two states are compounded by the relative scarcity of local resources to pay for health services, a situation that may be regarded as deserving particular attention by central government policies and international donor agencies, involving both financial and non-financial support mechanisms.

By contrast, the relatively higher ability to pay for health care in Madhya Pradesh and West Bengal may call for more nuanced approaches for development support. Madhya Pradesh's poor health development performance is driven primarily by deficient conditions of access to care given health needs, whereas in West Bengal the major development bottleneck refers to insufficient protection of residents against the financial consequences of health care payments. Central government policies may then be designed and targeted to the most pressing issue in each state, and donors may wish to adopt support mechanisms focused on non-financial aspects (e.g. technical assistance on service delivery geared toward more equitable access to available health services by the poorest residents).

Some of these policies and support mechanisms could be designed based on success stories from other Indian states. Arunachal Pradesh, for instance, is among the top 25% states in terms of health development, with good performance both on the access and financial protection dimensions, despite an income level similar to West Bengal and much lower than Madhya Pradesh. Although Arunachal Pradesh may still require extra financial support from donors so as to maintain and expand health coverage for its residents, closer scrutiny of specific health policies managed locally may offer valuable lessons for other states on how to translate available resources for health into broader coverage more effectively. Analyses like these, complemented by more detailed case studies, may help national and international agencies allocate their scarce resources by targeting support to specific bottlenecks in selected states.

4. Discussion and Conclusions

The aim of this study is to suggest an operational methodology to measure health needs and constraints across countries, based on information broader than national income and relevant to assess levels of national development in health. Composite indices aggregating a few underlying indicators, such as the "strict" and "extended" indices discussed here, can be helpful to communicate broad results and draw attention to trends in health development performance. However, such an endeavour will always require the analyst to make simplifying methodological assumptions and the analyses will always be subject to practical limitations.

In particular, the policy insights offered by our proposed health development indices are limited by actual cross-country data availability on aspects related to coverage of necessary health services (at all levels of care) and degree of financial protection from health care payments. We acknowledge, for instance, that comparisons of the share of pooled health spending across countries may not necessarily reflect money well spent or the degree of protection against inefficient health spending. However, to the extent that the degree of efficiency in health spending can be captured by comparing national health expenditures and the corresponding benefits obtained in terms of population health, the joint examination of our measures of access to care (which include population health status proxied by DALYs lost) and financial protection (through shares of pooled health financing) through the "strict" health development index should incorporate some relevant information on how efficient a country is in translating pooled health financing into better outcomes. Thus, perhaps the first lesson from our analytical work is the urgent need for standardized data collection procedures specifically designed to allow cross-country comparisons over time. National-level surveys will remain the main source of data for analyses of aspects such as financial protection, and, since cost is a major determinant of the interval between national surveys, it seems important for international agencies to intensify current efforts to support regular data collection in LICs.

Subject to the data limitations above, our simulations offer potentially useful policy insights. First, our proposed approach does better than simple measures of GNI pc to assess and compare national health development levels. In general, country rankings in the health development scale vary substantially when the conditions of access to care and financial protection in health are explicitly considered through our "strict" index, compared to GNI rankings. Several u-MICs and l-MICs fall many positions in the rankings due to poor performance on access and financial protection, ranking in the bottom half of the development scale implied by our "strict" index. The indices also reflect adequately known progress made by some countries in system coverage given health needs.

The decomposition of changes in ranking between a GNI criterion and our health development indices sheds light on other important aspects for health policy. The decomposition of the "strict" index into its access and financial protection components is able to provide leads on where the major bottlenecks for health development lie. Moreover, our sub-indices can help identify those country cases where there is a need for external support to fill in gaps in domestic ability to maintain and expand current health coverage levels, offering preliminary insights into specific support modalities (financial or non-financial) that may be more efficient to promote health development in a particular setting. Accounting for financial constraints through the "extended" index leads, for example, to noteworthy differentiation between many African and Asian countries with similar health needs, based on their domestic capacity to ensure adequate health system funding. In instances where countries enjoy a relatively good financial position, the case for external financial support may be weakened, pointing instead to support responses geared toward technical assistance and advocacy, rather than financial aid *per se*. Our indices are also able to flag cases where low ability to pay for health is a major hurdle for ameliorating low levels of health development. Finally, subject to data availability, similar analyses to the above can be conducted to help policy decision-making at the subnational level, as demonstrated for the Indian context.

We believe, therefore, that our methodological proposals can be helpful for policymaking in at least three broad informational fronts: to inform discussions around health resource allocation at the national and international levels; to inform programmatic choices and policy responses; and to inform priority setting by international donor agencies. With regard to the latter, we note that the primary aim of this study has been to contribute to the measurement of health needs and constraints across countries, based on information broader than national income. We nonetheless acknowledge that the issue of development assistance is a fundamental one and often linked to country classification mechanisms. In principle, our health indices could potentially be used as inputs within simple IDA-type allocation formulas, with alternative weights according to institutional preferences, or within more refined support allocation mechanisms such as capitation funding across and even within countries, for example with our "strict" index entered as a population risk-adjuster. This type of use for our proposed health development measures carries its own challenges of course. Some of these challenges are widely acknowledged in policy discussions, such as the potential for perverse incentives around indicator manipulation as countries seek to attract continued development support (Equitable Access Initiative, 2016). Although any approach based on measurement and country classification for aid entitlement is likely to be subject to perverse incentives to some extent, we believe that our guiding principle of selecting indicators mostly collected by international agencies through accepted mechanisms would help mitigate concerns about data manipulation. As such, the conceptual framework and health development measures proposed in this study could form the basis for discussions on new policies of national governments and international organisations to improve the health of populations.

Acknowledgments

This chapter has benefited immensely from comments received at several meetings organized by the conveners of the Equitable Access Initiative in Geneva and New York, as well as from participants of a seminar session at iHEA Milan 2015. We would also like to thank Raslan Alzuabi for excellent research assistance. All errors are our own. This work was supported by the GFATM on behalf of the convening partners of the Equitable Access Initiative (Grant Number 20155592).

Key Messages

- We propose a flexible approach to identify health needs and constraints in countries, based on indicators that are broader than national income and more relevant to assess national development in health.
- Our health development indices examine country performance under the overarching concept of health coverage, using indicators of access to care, financial risk protection and domestic financial constraints.
- Country rankings in the health development scale vary substantially when the conditions of access to care and financial protection in health are explicitly considered, compared to income per capita (pc) rankings.
- Beyond a simple reclassification of countries, the decomposition of changes in ranking between an income criterion and our health development indices also sheds light on where the main barriers to health development lie in each particular context.

References

Backman, G., Hunt, P., Khosla, R. et al. (2008). Health systems and the right to health: An assessment of 194 countries. The Lancet, 372: 2047–2085.

Equitable Access Initiative (2016). Equitable Access Initiative Report. https://www.theglobalfund.org/en/archive/equitable-access-initiative/ (Accessed: 30 August 2019).

Escobar, M. L., Griffin, C., Shaw, R. P. (eds.) (2010). The Impact of Health Insurance in Low- and Middle-Income Countries. Washington DC: Brookings Institution press.

Garrett, L., Chowdhury, A., Pablos-Méndez, A. (2009). All for universal health coverage. *The Lancet*, 374: 1294–1299.

Johnson, S., Kaufmann, D., Shleifer, A. (1997). The unofficial economy in transition. *Brookings Papers on Economic Activity*, 2: 159–221.

Moreno-Serra, R., Smith, P. C. (2012a). Towards an index of health coverage. Imperial College Business School Discussion Paper 2012/11. London: United Kingdom. http://spiral.imperial.ac.uk/bitstream/10044/1/10422/4/Moreno-Serra%202012-11.pdf (Accessed: 25 May 2016).

Moreno-Serra, R., Smith, P. C. (2012b). Does progress towards universal health coverage improve population health? *The Lancet*, 380: 917–923.

Moreno-Serra, R., Smith, P. C. (2014). Broader health coverage is good for the nation's health: Evidence from country level panel data. *Journal of the Royal Statistical Society: Series A (Statistics in Society)*. http://dx.doi.org/10.1111/rssa.12048 (Accessed: 25 May 2016).

Moreno-Serra, R., Thomson, S., Xu, K. (2013). Measuring and comparing financial protection. In: Smith P. C., Papanicolas I., Figueras J., *Health System Performance Comparison: An Agenda for Policy, Information and Research*. Berkshire (UK): Open University Press. pp. 223–254.

Saksena, P., Antunes, A., Xu, K., Musango, L., Carrin, G. (2010). Impact of mutual health insurance on access to health care and financial risk protection in Rwanda. Background paper 6, World Health Report 2010. Geneva: WHO.

UNDP (2015). Human Development Reports. http://hdr.undp.org/en/content/human-development-index-hdi (Accessed: 29 June 2015).

WHO (2008). *World Health Report 2008: Primary Health Care (Now More Than Ever)*. Geneva: WHO.

WHO (2010). *World Health Report 2010: Health Systems Financing: The Path to Universal Coverage*. Geneva: WHO.

WHO (2015). *Tracking Universal Health Coverage: First Global Monitoring Report*. Geneva: WHO.

Xu, K., Evans, D., Carrin, G. *et al.* (2007). Protecting households from catastrophic health spending. *Health Affairs*, 26: 972–983.

Case Studies

Application of Methods

Chapter 10

Supporting the Development of Health Benefits Packages (HBPs): Principles and Initial Assessment for Malawi

Jessica Ochalek, Gerald Manthalu, Dominic Nkhoma,
Finn McGuire, Alexandra Rollinger, Paul Revill,
Mark Sculpher and Karl Claxton

Abstract

In many low- and middle-income countries (LMICs), particularly those heavily dependent upon overseas development aid, a major tool for resource allocation decisions over the choice of health care interventions are health benefits packages (HBPs). These are a critical element to achieving Universal Health Coverage, but with no widely accepted method for their development; they have historically promised more than could feasibly be delivered given resource constraints. An analytical framework was developed to guide the design of HBPs and to support the revision of Malawi's essential health package (EHP). The framework is founded on an explicit and evidence-based assessment of health opportunity costs. This enables metrics of value to be reported which reflect the scale of the potential health impact of including an intervention in the package net of associated health opportunity costs, and of ensuring that it is fully implemented. It can be used to identify interventions that are "best buys" for the health care system. It also provides a method for

265

quantifying the health opportunity cost of including other interventions, whether they achieve some other aims or are included in response to stakeholder or donor demands.

1. Background

In many low- and middle-income countries (LMICs), particularly those heavily dependent upon overseas development aid, a major tool for resource allocation decisions over the choice of health care interventions are health benefits packages (HBPs). These are intended to be used as central components of national health plans, to which both governments and their development partners providing additional funding can commit, and they detail which interventions are to be prioritized from the limited resources available. HBPs define a core set of interventions that are "best buys" for the health care system (i.e. those which provide the greatest value, however value is defined), and are a critical element to achieving Universal Health Coverage (Glassman *et al.*, 2016, 2017).

Malawi's two previous HBPs, called essential health packages (EHPs), introduced in 2004 and 2011 (Ministry of Health, 2004, 2012), both promised more than could feasibly be delivered given the budget. This resulted in interventions being nominally included in the package but unavailable in practice (Malawi Ministry of Health, 2017). A new analytical framework was required to identify and to prioritize interventions. This would use available data to guide decisions about the interventions providing the greatest benefit to population health (consistent with the aims of health spending (Culyer and Harris, 1997; Malawi Ministry of Health, 2017; Jamison *et al.*, 2018)), given what Malawi can currently afford to generate improvements in health.

This chapter highlights work requested by Malawian policymakers to support the development of HBPs. It was undertaken as a collaboration between researchers at the Centre for Health Economics (CHE) in York, United Kingdom and individuals in the Ministry of Health, Malawi. The analytic framework is described in detail in a published journal article (Ochalek *et al.*, 2018), and is summarized here. The results of this work provided evidence that was used by the Ministry of Health in Malawi and the EHP Technical Working Group (TWG) to revise the EHP to inform the 2017–2022 Health Sector Strategic Plan (Malawi Ministry of Health, 2017). This work highlights the potential impact that can be achieved through practice-oriented research.

2. Methods

A framework was developed that was grounded in the principles of cost-effectiveness analysis (CEA). By using CEA and putting health maximization at the centre of the EHP, a package that results in the greatest gains in overall population health at a given budget can be determined (Sculpher *et al.*, 2017). Such a package will account for burden of disease by prioritizing interventions according to the population health gains as measured by the net health benefit — i.e. net disability-adjusted life years (DALYs) averted.[1,2] This accounts not only for the per patient cost and health benefit (i.e. cost-effectiveness) of each intervention, but also the size of the patient population that stands to benefit and the opportunity cost associated with each intervention. The opportunity cost is the benefit that could have been achieved if the resources had been spent on a different intervention.

However, a package that maximizes health may not be realistic or even desirable for three reasons, which can all be explored further using the framework. First, the budget is not the only constraint under which a health care system operates. Constraints to implementing interventions exist both on the supply- and demand-sides. For example, on the demand-side, constraints may include lack of perceived benefits of care and difficulty in getting to clinics due to poor road infrastructure. While on the supply-side, constraints may include lack of equipment, lack of trained staff, supply chain bottlenecks, lack of beds, water and electricity shortages (Kazanga, 2015).

---

[1] Net health benefit is the health benefit of an intervention net of its health opportunity cost i.e.: DALYs averted — cost/estimate of marginal productivity of the health care system.

[2] Health gains are quantified using DALYs averted, a generic measure of health that incorporates both mortality and morbidity (Salomon *et al.*, 2012).

Second, donors, who fund approximately 70% of the health care system in Malawi, may impose constraints through funding arrangements. Although HBPs can be used to align the objectives of various stakeholders in the health care system, donor funding arrangements may reflect a different set of objectives to those of the government. Finally, health maximization is unlikely to be the only objective policymakers themselves wish to achieve with the EHP. Additional objectives might include, for example, enhancing financial protection for vulnerable individuals and reflecting the contribution of health gains to key groups in the population to society more generally, such as net contributions to the economy.

The cost imposed by these constraints and/or additional objectives can be valued in terms of health benefit forgone (i.e. in terms of DALYs averted), net health benefit forgone or, equivalently, the financial value to the health care system forgone.[3] The latter tells us something about the value of spending to reduce or to remove constraints, whether specific to programmes or across the health care system as a whole. Take, for example, schistosomiasis mass drug administration. Only 13% of the eligible patient population receive it, resulting in 3,088 DALYs averted. Were it fully implemented, 23,754 DALYs would be averted. At the best estimate of health opportunity cost available at the time, 2015 US$61 per DALY averted,[4] schistosomiasis mass drug administration would avert on net (i.e. net of the DALYs that could have been averted had the resources required been spent on another intervention) 12,562 DALYs as compared to 1,633 DALYs averted on net at the level to which it is actually implemented. This provides evidence that an additional 10,929 DALYs stand to be averted on net from scaling up from actual levels of implementation to 100%. That is equivalent to a 2015 US$670,393 value to the health care system, which is the maximum that could be spent to scale up schistosomiasis mass drug administration from 13% implementation to 100% (on top of the cost of delivery) for scale up to be a cost-effective use

---

[3] The financial value to the health care system is the benefit of an intervention net of its opportunity cost measured monetarily or equivalently; net health benefit (see footnote 1) multiplied by an estimate of the marginal productivity of spending on health gives the monetary value of net DALYs.

[4] This estimate is drawn from the range of estimates from Woods *et al.* (2016) and Ochalek *et al.* (2015).

of resources.[5] The mean actual implementation level among all interventions included in the initial analysis reported in Ochalek *et al.* (2018) is 46%, with a range of 1–100%. Aggregating the financial value of removing constraints across all interventions gives the value of investing in health system strengthening to reduce or to remove constraints that are common across interventions.

Considering the health opportunity costs (i.e. losses in terms of net health benefit or financial value to the health care system) associated with different constraints is also useful when considering donor funding arrangements. Consider a scenario increasingly common across LMICs — donor-matched funding for a specific intervention. Where matched funding is tied to an intervention that is not cost-effective, its inclusion in the EHP will necessarily incur a cost. The cost of such an arrangement is simply the difference in the aggregate health gains associated with a health maximizing package and those relating to the package where the donor-specified intervention is included and displaces one or more of the interventions in the health maximizing package. The extent of any health opportunity cost will depend on the details of the donor offers, and the analytical framework provides a means of establishing the health impact and can provide an essential support for negotiation. In the context where a donor proposal includes a constraint that imposes considerable health opportunity costs, refusal of the offer may be entirely reasonable. The framework's estimates of the health opportunity costs the proposal would have imposed provide a valuable basis for explaining the decision to stakeholders.

The benefit of being able to value these losses explicitly is that it enables transparent decision-making. It may be the case that, in an effort to reflect an additional objective to health maximization, a given intervention would be included in a final package that would not have been if the only aim was to maximize health. The necessary cost of including that intervention (i.e. what is displaced as a result of including

---

[5]This assumes constant returns to scale on the cost of delivering the programme. Where scale-up costs are nonlinear, the maximum that should be spent scaling up from one level to another of coverage can be calculated. For example, 13% (14%) coverage to 14% (20%) is the difference between the financial value to the health care system (HCS) of the intervention at 14% (20%) coverage minus the financial value to the HCS at 13% (14%) coverage.

it), can be weighed against the value of including it. Take, for instance, the objective of equity, which is an oft-stated aim of policymakers. Quantifying the value of improving equity as part of the analysis is difficult given the lack of universally agreed values, both in terms of what constitutes equity and the trade-offs between equity and health gain ("aversion to inequity" parameters). However, decision-makers may have some idea of how much they think it might be worth, which can be compared against the cost in terms of overall population health. This latter quantity helps to make explicit the value judgements behind policy and thus to keep decision-makers accountable.

All of this relies on good data on the costs and effects of each intervention, and the patients that stand to benefit from each and realistic coverage levels. The best available data were used; however, there are limitations both in terms of the quality of the data and its comprehensiveness.

3. Findings and Discussion

The framework developed identifies interventions that are "best buys", defined here as those that generate the most gains in population health and should be at the core of the HBP. It provides a method for quantifying the health opportunity cost of including other interventions, whether they achieve some other aims or are included in response to stakeholder or donor demands. In Malawi, "best buys" included interventions for HIV prevention, TB prevention and treatment, maternal and neonatal health and malaria prevention and treatment. By identifying specific interventions that generate the most gains in population health, the framework can also be used to align donor preferences to those of the Ministry of Health. This chapter highlights a selection of key questions that can be answered using the framework, which is also useful in considering whether to expand (or to contract) the scale of the HBP and other questions.

Crucially, the framework is not intended to be used to define a list of interventions to include in the HBP. Instead, it should be used to support a decision-making process within the Ministry of Health. Indeed, policymakers need to be able to interact with the analytical framework in a number of ways. These include clearly setting out the scope of decisions that are being addressed — in particular, the emphasis to be placed on selecting interventions for the HBP, making investment decisions for intervention-specific implementation activities and system strengthening, and providing a basis for negotiation over funding proposals from donors. In addition, there is a key role for decision-makers in identifying a wider set of objectives that might be relevant to decisions other than gains in population health. How this process was undertaken in Malawi is described in Ochalek *et al.* (2018).

The analysis showed that constraints inhibit the full implementation of many interventions, signifying potentially large gains from improving health systems. The less that is spent to reduce or to remove constraints, the more budget is left over for delivering programmes; however, given relatively low levels of implementation across all interventions, it is clear that there is a good argument for spending on health system strengthening. Additional data on the costs and benefits (i.e. cost-effectiveness) of removing different constraints is required to maximize implementation improvements from health system strengthening.

The interventions included in the analysis were limited to those for which data were readily available on the costs and effects of each intervention, the patients that stand to benefit from each, and realistic coverage levels. As such, there may be interventions that result in large health gains and should be considered "best buys" that are not included in the analysis. This further underscores the role for a decision-making process. Policymakers may be well-placed to provide data inputs, such as the cost of delivery of particular interventions. Going forward, to support resource allocation decisions, the Ministry of Health and partners will need to establish suitable processes for continually seeking the best available evidence for Malawi to populate and update the library. In the longer term, it should be hoped that more of this evidence is generated within Malawi rather than having to rely on secondary sources drawn from health care systems that may differ in important ways for Malawi. Indeed, the HBP framework can help to prioritize where new information in Malawi would be most valuable.

Key Messages

* The framework developed is founded on an explicit and evidence-based assessment of health opportunity costs. This enables metrics of value to be reported which reflects the scale of the potential health

impact of including an intervention in the package net of associated health opportunity costs, and of ensuring it is fully implemented.

• Despite data limitations, health benefits packages (HBPs) can be used to define a core set of interventions that are "best buys" for the health care system (i.e. those which provide the greatest value, however value is defined). These are a critical element to achieving Universal Health Coverage (Glassman *et al.*, 2016, 2017).

• A decision-making process is required to enable policymakers to interact with the analytical framework. This has a number of advantages including clearly setting out the scope of the decisions being addressed and making judgements about the trade-offs between health gains and other objectives.

References

Culyer, A. J., Harris, J. (1997). The rationing debate: Maximising the health of the whole community. *British Medical Journal*, 314(7081): 667–672. Available at: https://www.jstor.org/stable/25173929.

Glassman, A. *et al.* (2016). Defining a health benefits package: What are the necessary processes? *Health Systems & Reform*, 2(1): 39–50. Available at: http://www.tandfonline.com/doi/full/10.1080/23288604.2016.1124171 (Accessed 11 November 2016).

Glassman, A., Giedion, U., Smith, P. (eds.) (2017). *What's In What's Out: Designing Benefits for Universal Health Coverage*, Washington D.C.: Center for Global Development.

Jamison, D. T. *et al.* (eds.) (2018). *Disease Control Priorities: Improving Health and Reducing Poverty*. Washington D.C.: World Bank.

Kazanga, I. (2015). *Equity of Access to Essential Health Package (EHP) in Malawi: A Perspective on Uptake of Maternal Health Services*. Trinity College Dublin.

Malawi Ministry of Health (2017). *Health Sector Strategic Plan II 2017–2022: Towards Universal Health Coverage*. Available at: http://www.health.gov.mw/index.php/policies-strategies?download=47:hssp-ii-final.

Ministry of Health (2004). *A Joint Programme of Work for a Health Sector Wide Approach (SWAp) in the Republic of Malawi. 2004–2010*. Lilongwe. Available at: http://gametlibrary.worldbank.org/FILES/466_Health Sector SWAp Malawi.pdf (Accessed 1 April 2016).

Ministry of Health (2012). *Malawi Health Sector Strategic Plan 2011–2016.* Lilongwe.

Ochalek, J., Lomas, J., Claxton, K. (2015). *Cost Per DALY Averted Thresholds for Low- and Middle-Income Countries: Evidence From Cross Country Data.* York. Available at: https://www.york.ac.uk/media/che/documents/papers/researchpapers/CHERP122_cost_DALY_LMIC_threshold.pdf [Accessed February 16, 2016].

Ochalek, J. *et al.* (2018). Supporting the development of a health benefits package in Malawi. *BMJ Global Health*, 3: e000607.

Salomon, J. A. *et al.* (2012). Common values in assessing health outcomes from disease and injury: Disability weights measurement study for the Global Burden of Disease Study 2010. *Lancet (London, England)*, 380(9859): 2129–43. Available at: http://www.ncbi.nlm.nih.gov/pubmed/23245605 (Accessed: 19 November 2015).

Sculpher, M. J. *et al.* (2017). How much health for the money? Using cost-effectiveness analysis to support benefits plan decisions. In: Glassman A., Giedion U., Smith P. C., eds., *What's In What's Out: Designing Benefits for Universal Health Coverage.* Washington D.C.: Center for Global Development.

Woods, B. *et al.* (2016). Country-level cost-effectiveness thresholds: Initial estimates and the need for further research. *Value in Health*, 19(8): 929–935.

Chapter 11

Modelling and Economic Evaluation to Inform WHO HIV Treatment Guidelines

Paul Revill, Andrew Phillips, Jeffrey W. Eaton
and Timothy B. Hallett

Abstract

International organizations influence national-level health sector priorities by affecting how much funding is available for health care delivery within countries and how that funding is used. The setting of guidelines for the management of diseases (e.g. for malaria, child health, nutrition) by the World Health Organization (WHO) exerts particular influence. Guidelines typically provide syntheses of evidence on clinical efficacy and effectiveness and make recommendations for health care best practice. However, for the most part, they do not well inform the allocation of limited available health care resources. Consequentially, they risk encouraging national and international decision-makers to divert resources away from areas of greater potential gains in population health. In this case study, we reflect upon efforts to incorporate economic evidence into the development of the WHO HIV Treatment Guidelines. We describe how the WHO has incorporated economic insight into these and other guidelines. However, even in this case, the processes currently followed for guideline development can limit the extent to which recommendations can draw upon economic evidence. Changes in the way WHO Guidelines are developed and interpreted, and how evidence is used to inform decision-making at the country level, is therefore required. We give our thoughts on what these changes could be.

275

1. Background

The World Health Organization (WHO) produces guidelines for disease management covering a wide range of health conditions (e.g. HIV/AIDS, malaria, child health and nutrition) (WHO, 2014). The guidelines are intended particularly to inform policy and practice in low- and middle-income countries (LMICs) without other established mechanisms to review and synthesize often complex and diffuse sources of evidence (e.g. through use of established health technology assessment processes (HTA)). Guidelines effectively represent "global public goods" that are available for mandated bodies in each country to use and adapt when formulating their own policies. It is intended there are additional processes through which recommendations are tailored to specific contexts. However, the advice of WHO is highly esteemed, and there is typically the perception that close-to-direct adoption of international recommendations is wise or necessary — not least for the receipt of development assistance, upon which the health systems in many countries largely depend (McRobie *et al.*, 2018).

WHO has established processes for the development of its guidelines (WHO, 2014). A Steering Group — convened by WHO and comprised of external experts — provides general oversight, whereas a Guideline Development Group — comprised of experts in the clinical field, programme managers, patient representatives and other stakeholders — produces the core content. An External Review Group, including other relevant stakeholders, reviews the process and recommendations. Content is centered around synthesizing evidence to answer "PICO" questions (in which the population of interest, interventions/comparators and outcomes are all pre-specified) and a recognized approach is followed (known as "GRADE" — Grading of Recommendations Assessment, Development and Evaluation). This leads to recommendations that one or more interventions are deemed effective with a certain level of evidence — i.e. GRADE is used to assess the quality of evidence and recommendations are made by the committees based upon their deliberations (WHO, 2014).

Given the pervasiveness of resource scarcity in all health care systems, but especially in LMICs, where annual per capita national health budgets can be US$50 or less (WHO, 2018), the extent to which morbidity and mortality can be reduced by the health care system is primarily limited by resource constraints rather than lack of existence of proven effective drugs and other technologies. Thus, the guideline-setting process is *de facto* often addressing policy issues that are essentially economic in nature — how to spend limited resources amongst a wide range of health care claims that cannot all be feasibly met. However, in almost all cases, they have focused on evidence of clinical effectiveness (although panels are also encouraged to consider intervention feasibility, acceptability, equity and resource use). With a few exceptions, there has generally been very little use of economic criteria used in guideline formulation or even advice on how recommendations could be translated to countries that vary in the availability of resources (Easterbrook, 2014). This raises fundamental questions as to the purposes of guidelines, whether and how economic evidence should be incorporated and how directly or not recommendations can be interpreted for country decision-making on adopting and funding interventions.

In recent years, in one disease area — HIV/AIDS treatment — concerted effort has been made to include evidence from economic evaluation studies into Guideline development. As part of their Consolidated HIV Treatment Guidelines in 2013 (WHO, 2013) and 2015 (WHO, 2016), as well as the 2017 Guidelines on the Public Health Response to Pre-treatment HIV Drug Resistance (WHO, 2017), the HIV Department of the WHO requested the HIV Modelling Consortium (www.hivmodelling.org) to provide consolidated evidence from a number of modelling and health economics research teams. This experience revealed the rigour with which current processes are followed, but also that there are limits in the extent to which policy recommendations draw upon economic evidence, with potentially adverse consequences for the health gains that can be attained from the limited resources available to country health care systems (Hallett *et al.*, 2014).

2. Economic Evaluation in WHO HIV Treatment Guidelines

As part of development of the 2013 HIV Treatment Guidelines, epidemiological modellers and health economists from the HIV Modelling

Consortium were asked to provide cost-effectiveness evidence on two prominent PICO questions:

(1) When should individuals infected with HIV begin treatment (in the form of antiretroviral therapy (ART))?
(2) How should individuals receiving ART be monitored for disease progression and treatment switching?

Rather than basing analyses on a single model, evidence was drawn from a diverse set of models to assess consistencies or discrepancies in modelling results.

Overall, there was remarkable consistency in the central findings across models. Clinical evidence from the HTPN 052 trial (Cohen *et al.*, 2011) had suggested that earlier ART initiation reduced the individual risk of morbidity and mortality. Mathematical modelling and cost-effectiveness analyses, which incorporated these mortality and morbidity consequences and the effects of ART in reducing HIV transmission at the population level, concluded that, in countries with high ART coverage, expanding treatment eligibility for HIV positive adults up to the higher threshold being considered (CD4+ cell counts up to 500 cells/μl) was likely to be cost-effective (Eaton *et al.*, 2013, 2014). Earlier ART initiation was taken up as a recommendation in the guidelines.

For the second question, modelling showed that more sophisticated forms of patient monitoring (i.e. routine viral load monitoring, instead of more basic clinical or CD4 monitoring) would confer some benefit to patients. However, at the then costs of delivery, viral load monitoring would unlikely represent good use of limited health care resources in most countries. What was deemed clinically effective for patients did therefore not appear to be cost-effective, as assessed when considering other claims upon limited available resources (Keebler *et al.*, 2013, 2014). The panel considered this information, but recommended routine viral load monitoring nonetheless.

For the 2015 HIV Treatment Guidelines, the HIV Modelling Consortium was again asked to design and present analyses that would be useful to the development of the guidelines. The questions were different this time. Instead of modelling being used to provide evidence on the cost-effectiveness of particular policies that were quite narrowly defined around clinical choices (using PICO questions), the task was to inform how whole treatment programmes could be redesigned in ways to better meet population health needs. For this round of guidelines, the questions were as follows:

(1) Among whom are HIV-related deaths occurring and what can be done about this?
(2) How may patient monitoring enable more efficient ART delivery approaches?

For the first question, modelling was used to analyze and extrapolate from HIV population cohort studies in sub-Saharan Africa. It was found that HIV-related deaths mainly occurred among HIV-infected persons not on ART, either because they had not been diagnosed and linked to care or had disengaged from ART programmes (Barnabus *et al.*, 2015). These analyses indicated that greater priority should be given to facilitate diagnosis, entry to care and retention. Moreover, deaths from disengaged patients were expected to increase in coming years, so the modelling highlighted where additional research and new intervention design could be valuable. Modelling was therefore used to take a wider perspective, although it did not, in this instance, formally include an economic assessment.

Following the recommendation for viral load monitoring in 2013 and its subsequent scale-up, the second question aimed at determining how HIV treatment programmes, recognizing their features, could be redesigned to more efficiently meet the challenge of vastly increasing patient numbers. Instead of patients receiving clinical assessments and picking up drugs every one to two months, as was the norm, one option was the introduction of *differentiated care*, whereby stable patients would receive less frequent assessment (e.g. six-monthly or annually) and take home a longer supplies of drugs. Given that viral load testing provides the most definitive indication of which people do not require frequent clinic visits, it was found to be cost-effective if used in this way to support differentiated care. Viral load testing using dried blood spots, which is much easier and cheaper to transport than plasma, was found to be adequate for these purposes (Revill *et al.*, 2015; Philips *et al.*, 2016).

3. Implications and Discussion

Despite the findings of the 2013 and 2015 modelling studies having potentially profound consequences for HIV treatment programmes, they were not necessarily a natural fit within the WHO Clinical Guidelines — structured around PICO questions and based upon assessment of evidence using the GRADE approach.

Economic analysis requires the comparison of the relative merits of alternative policies or interventions that, as a result of resource constraints, cannot all feasibly be delivered. It brings together evidence on clinical effectiveness, costs and opportunity costs into an integrated framework. Since costs and opportunity costs differ by setting, economic analysis is inherently context-specific. When combined with epidemiological modelling, it can address the big questions of programme design in a particular setting, illustrating also the consequences of other supply-side health system features or patient interactions with care that fundamentally affect the health produced from health care provision.

In contrast, the WHO Guidelines begin with clinical questions, framed as PICO questions, for which the GRADE process is used to assess evidence. Within this framework, evidence from randomized control trials specifically is valued most highly. At the culmination of the guideline-setting process, recommendations for policy choice and intervention uptake are made by the guideline development group. The recommendations they can choose are that an intervention is or is not "recommended", or it is recommended conditional on some other factors. Arguably, this is sometimes done with too little consideration given for context and the knock-on effects of such a change. Although such evidence on clinical effectiveness can be used as an input to economic analysis, it alone is far from sufficient. Whereas WHO Guidelines have been successfully applied to guide choices of what is clinically effective, something that may generalize reasonably well across settings, it is ill suited to inform economic choices.

If WHO Guidelines are to provide useful guidance for countries, then new approaches must be found. If the routine incorporation of economic evidence into guidelines is not feasible any time soon, the limitations of guideline recommendations must be clearly stated — that they are not sufficient to be directly interpreted for policy formulation whenever this has resource implications. Instead, alternative or additional processes that consider economic criteria are absolutely necessary. This could include the routine incorporation of economic evidence within the WHO decision-making processes, permitting varying recommendations for the very different epidemiological and resource contexts countries face. However, this would require substantial investment to ensure the necessary capacity and data are available. But such capacity is only ever likely to grow if the routes through which analyses can feed into policy deliberations are first made clear (i.e. WHO will need to show how economic evidence can be consistently used in the making of recommendations).

Another approach to setting priorities altogether may, however, in our view, enable even better decision-making. This would be for the WHO and other international organizations to contribute to empowering locally accountable officials to determine policies reflecting the contexts and values held within their own jurisdictions. This can be facilitated by the international community synthesizing and supporting the provision of relevant evidence — clinical, epidemiological and economic. However, ultimately, it will require processes that can better account for the consequence of programmatic factors and resource constraints locally. In an ideal world, and one which we believe the global community should aim to move toward, the analyses themselves would, in the main, also be produced locally. Again, this would require substantial and long-term investment in capacity and data.

A group of stakeholders has deliberated how international organizations, especially WHO in its formulation of guidelines, can better assist countries in resource prioritization (Working Group on Incorporating Economics and Modelling in Global Health Goals and Guidelines, 2019). The Working Group, co-convened by the Centre for Global Development, Thanzi la Onse programme at the University of York and the HIV Modelling Consortium, gave two sets of recommendations. Firstly, to empower countries to develop and analyze appropriate evidence to set health priorities for their populations (e.g. through investment in local analytic capacity). Secondly, to strengthen the WHO guidelines program to inform resource allocation (e.g. by establishing clear and robust principles, methods and standards for economic evidence to be included within WHO guidelines). The current WHO Guideline development processes are insufficient for formulating policies with resource implications, and other approaches specifically oriented toward this objective must be developed.

Key Messages

- Country-level decisions about health policy and implementation are typically as much economic in nature (i.e. concerning the allocation of scarce health care resources) as they are about choosing interventions on the basis of clinical effectiveness alone. In many LMICs, there is some reliance upon international organizations for both funding and guidance.
- WHO Guidelines hold particular influence by informing countries on disease management for a wide range of conditions. Established processes are followed to assess evidence on which interventions are likely to be *effective*; but if policies are then formed without due consideration of the consequences of *resource use*, there can be adverse outcomes due to inadvertent drawing of resources away from other more impactful health care investments.
- HIV/AIDS treatment is an area in which efforts have been made to incorporate evidence from the modelling and economic evaluation studies into WHO Guidelines. This highlighted, amongst other things, that what is *effective* is not always *cost-effective*, and that some of the greatest causes of HIV-related mortality and morbidity might be better addressed through supporting appropriate patient engagement in care, rather than a more limited focus on choices of clinical interventions alone.
- Although the value of contributions from modelling and economic evaluation to inform global health priorities is recognized, the current approaches followed in the development of WHO Guidelines are not oriented to the formal consideration of economic criteria. Steps are now being taken by WHO and its partners so that, in future, guideline recommendations may hopefully better contribute to policy decisions on resource allocation taken at the level of countries.

References

Barnabus, R. V., Bendavid, E., Bershteyn, A., Boulle, A., Eaton, J. W., Ford, N., Hallett, T. B., Hontelez, J. A. C., Klein, D. J., Olney, J. J., Phillips, A. N.,

Reniers, G., Revill, P., Slaymaker, E., Zaba, B. (2015). Priorities for HIV Care in sub-Saharan Africa: A population perspective. HIV Modelling Consortium Report for the World Health Organization HIV Treatment Guidelines Development Committee. http://www.hivmodelling.org/projects/modelling-submitted-consideration-who-development-2015-arv-guidelines-revision.

Cohen, M. S., Chen, Y. Q., McCauley, M., Gamble, T., Hosseinipour, M. C., Kumarasamy, N., Hakim, J. G., Kumwenda, J., Grinsztejn, B., Pilotto, J. H. S., Godbole, S. V., Mehendale, S. *et al.* (2011). Prevention of HIV-1 infection with early antiretroviral therapy. *The New England Journal of Medicine*, 365: 493–505.

Easterbrook, P. J., Doherty, M. C., Perriens, J. H., Barcarolo, J. L., Hirnschall, G. O. (2014). The role of mathematical modelling in the development of recommendations in the 2013 WHO consolidated antiretroviral therapy guidelines. *AIDS*, 28(Suppl 1): S85–S92.

Eaton, J., Menzies, N. A., Stover, J., Cambiano, V., Chindelevitch, L., Core, A., Hontelez, J. A. C., Humair, S., Kerr, C. C., Klein, D. J., Mishra, S., Mitchell, K. M., Nichols, B. E., Vickerman, P., Bakker, R., Barnighausen, T., Bershteyn, A., Bloom, D. E., Boiley, M.-C., Chang, S. T., Cohen, T., Dodd, P. J., Fraser, C., Gopalappa, C., Lundgren, J., Martin, N. K., Mikkelsen, E., Mountain, E., Pham, Q. D., Pickles, M., Phillips, A., Platt, L., Pretorius, C., Prudden, H. J., Salomon, J. A., can de Vijer, D. A. M. C., de Vlas, S. J., Wagner, B. G., White, R. G., Wilson, D. P., Zhang, L., Blandford, J., Meyer-Rath, G., Remme, M., Revill, P., Sangrujee., N., Terris-Prestholt, F., Vassell, A., Doherty, M., Shaffer, N., Easterbrook, P., Hirnschall, G., Hallett, T. B. (2013). How should HIV programmes respond to evidence for the benefits of earlier ART initiation? A combined analysis of twelve mathematical models. Report for the Consolidated Clinical and Programmatic ART Guidelines Committees. HIV Department of the World Health Organizations. http://apps.who.int/iris/bitstream/10665/93524/1/WHO_HIV_2013.56_eng.pdf.

Eaton, J., Menzies, N. A., Stover, J., Cambiano, V., Chindelevitch, L., Core, A., Hontelez, J. A. C., Humair, S., Kerr, C. C., Klein, D. J., Mishra, S., Mitchell, K. M., Nichols, B. E., Vickerman, P., Bakker, R., Barnighausen, T., Bershteyn, A., Bloom, D. E., Boiley, M.-C., Chang, S. T., Cohen, T., Dodd, P. J., Fraser, C., Gopalappa, C., Lundgren, J., Martin, N. K., Mikkelsen, E., Mountain, E., Pham, Q. D., Pickles, M., Phillips, A., Platt, L., Pretorius, C., Prudden, H. J., Salomon, J. A., can de Vijer, D. A. M. C., de Vlas, S. J., Wagner, B. G., White, R. G., Wilson, D. P., Zhang, L.,

Blandford, J., Meyer-Rath, G., Remme, M., Revill, P., Sangrujee, N., Terris-Prestholt, F., Vassell, A., Doherty, M., Shaffer, N., Easterbrook, P., Hirnschall, G., Hallett, T. B. (2014). Health benefits, costs, and cost-effectiveness of earlier eligibility for adult antiretroviral therapy and expanded treatment coverage: A combined analysis of 12 mathematical models. *Lancet Global Health*, 2(1): e23–e34.

Hallett, T. B., Menzies, N. A., Revill, P., Keebler, D., Bórquez, A., McRobie, E. *et al.* (2014). Using modeling to inform international guidelines for antiretroviral treatment. *AIDS*, 28: S1–S4.

Keebler, D., Revill, P., Braithwaite, S., Phillips, A., Blaser, N., Borquez, A., Cambiano, V., Ciaranello, A., Estill, J., Gray, R., Hill, A., Keiser, O., Kessler, J., Menzies, N. A., Nucifora, K. A., Salazar-Vizcaya, L., Walker, S., Welte, A., Easterbrook, P., Doherty, M., Hirnschall, G., Hallett, T. (2013). How should HIV programmes monitor adults on ART? A combined analysis of three mathematical models. Report for the Consolidated Clinical and Programmatic ART Guidelines Committees. The HIV Department of the World Health Organizations. http://apps.who.int/iris/bitstream/10665/93523/1/WHO_HIV_2013.61_eng.pdf

Keebler, D., Revill, P., Braithwaite, S., Phillips, A., Blaser, N., Borquez, A., Cambiano, V., Ciaranello, A., Estill, J., Gray, R., Hill, A., Keiser, O., Kessler, J., Menzies, N. A., Nucifora, K. A., Salazar-Vizcaya, L., Walker, S., Welte, A., Easterbrook, P., Doherty, M., Hirnschall, G., Hallett, T. (2014). How should HIV programmes monitor adults on ART? A combined analysis of three mathematical models. *Lancet Global Health*, 2(1): e35–e43.

McRobie, E., Matovu, F., Nanyiti, A., Nonvignon, J., Abankwah, D. N. Y., Case, K. *et al.* (2018). National responses to global health targets: Exploring policy transfer in the context of the UNAIDS '90-90-90' treatment targets in Ghana and Uganda. *Health Policy and Planning*, 33(1): 17–33.

Philips, A. *et al.* (2016). Sustainable HIV treatment in Africa through viral load-informed differentiated care. *Nature*. doi: 10.1038/nature16046.

Revill, P., Hallett, T., Phillips, A. (2015). The costs and benefits of alternatives approaches to monitoring patients on antiretroviral therapy: Modelling and economic analysis. HIV Modelling Consortium Report for the World Health Organization HIV Treatment Guidelines Development Committee. http://www.hivmodelling.org/projects/modelling-submitted-consideration-who-development-2015-arv-guidelines-revision.

Working Group on Incorporating Economics and Modelling in Global Health Goals and Guidelines (2019). *Understanding the Opportunity Cost, Seizing the Opportunity*. Washington, D.C.: Centre for Global Development.

https://www.cgdev.org/publication/understanding-opportunity-cost-seizing-opportunity-report-working-group.

World Health Organization (WHO). Essential medicines and health products website. http://www.who.int/medicines/areas/quality_safety/quality_assurance/guidelines/en/ (Accessed: 4 December 2018).

World Health Organization (WHO) (2014). *WHO Handbook for Guideline Development*, 2nd edn. Geneva: Switzerland. pp. 1–179.

World Health Organization (WHO). Global health expenditure database. http://apps.who.int/nha/database (Accessed: 4 December 2018).

World Health Organization (WHO) (2013). *Consolidated Guidelines on the Use of Antiretrovial Drugs for Treating and Prevention HIV Infection: Recommendations for a Public Health Approach.* https://www.who.int/hiv/pub/guidelines/arv2013/download/en/.

World Health Organization (WHO) (2016). *Consolidated Guidelines on the Use of Antiretrovial Drugs for Treating and Prevention HIV Infection: Recommendations for a Public Health Approach*, 2nd edn. https://www.who.int/hiv/pub/arv/arv-2016/en/.

World Health Organization (WHO) (2017). *Guidelines on the Public Health Response to Pretreatment HIV Drug Resistance: Supplement to the 2016 Consolidated Guidelines on the Use of Antiretroviral Drugs for Treating and Preventing HIV Infection*, 2nd edn. https://www.who.int/hiv/pub/guidelines/hivdr-guidelines-2017/en/.

World Health Organization (WHO). Global health expenditure database. http://apps.who.int/nha/database (Accessed: 4 December 2018).

Chapter 12

Evaluating the 2014 Sugar-Sweetened Beverage Tax in Chile: Observational Evidence from Urban Areas

Ryota Nakamura, Andrew J. Mirelman, Cristóbal Cuadrado, Nicolás Silva, Jocelyn Dunstan and Marc Suhrcke

Abstract

An already large and growing number of countries — both rich and poor — are facing an enormous challenge to curb rising rates of obesity and diet-related ill-health, much of which affects lower socio-economic groups. Fiscal policy has the potential to influence consumption patterns toward healthier options (and raise government revenue for welfare-enhancing purposes), thereby contributing to the prevention of chronic diseases and to the reduction of the associated economic costs. Yet, there is a scarcity of empirical evaluations of diet-related fiscal interventions, and it is still uncertain whether these can be effective in improving population diet and health in a "real-world" context. Chile is one of the very few countries that have thus far implemented an explicit fiscal policy to improve healthier diets. In this chapter, we describe and discuss the results of our impact evaluation of the tax policy (Nakamura et al., 2018). Results were mixed, showing population average results that consistently indicated a decrease in the monthly purchased volume of the higher taxed sugar sweetened beverages (SSBs) (21.6% for the statistically preferred model), but also one that varied considerably in magnitude across different models, thereby reducing the confidence in this overall estimate. The reduction in soft drink-purchasing was most robustly evident amongst higher socio-economic groups and higher pre-tax purchasers of sugary soft drinks. There was no systematic, robust pattern in the estimates by households' obesity status.

This suggests that the policy may have been partially effective, though not necessarily in ways that are likely to reduce socio-economic inequalities in diet-related health. A longer term evaluation, ideally including an assessment of the consumption and health impacts, should be conducted in future research.

1. Introduction

Very few countries have thus far implemented an explicit fiscal policy to improve healthier diets. In October 2014, Chile implemented a tax modification on sugar sweetened beverages (SSBs) called the *Impuesto Adicional a las Bebidas Analcohólicas* (IABA), adopting a thus far unique design by increasing the tax on soft drinks above 6.25 g of added sugar per 100 ml and decreasing the tax for those below this threshold. In a recently published article (Nakamura *et al.*, 2018), we have evaluated the SSB tax, using a quasi-experimental design applied to detailed household-level grocery-purchasing data from 2011 to 2015. Here, we summarize the main approach, findings and implications of this study. Detailed results and supplementary material are available in the original paper.

While the research focused on Chile, it is of global relevance, across low-, middle- and high-income countries, as reducing the burden of non-communicable diseases (NCDs) has been widely recognized as an overriding global health priority and a necessary condition for sustainable development (WHO, 2014). Diet-related health problems account for a large and growing share of the NCD burden worldwide, causing substantial human suffering and adverse economic consequences (Bloom *et al.*, 2011; Suhrcke *et al.*, 2006). The situation is of particular concern in Latin America and the Caribbean — a region that has been predicted to reach the highest levels of overweight and obesity worldwide by 2030 (Kelly *et al.*, 2008). Chile appears to be in a particularly challenging situation, as, for instance, illustrated by the fact that, in 2014, the country topped the worldwide ranking of per capita daily SSB consumption, while also recording the highest growth rate of SSB consumption in the 2009–2014 period (Popkin and Hawkes, 2016).

Fiscal policies have the potential to promote healthier consumption patterns, thereby contributing to the prevention of chronic diseases and their associated economic costs. They may also lead to increased government revenue that could in turn be used for welfare-enhancing purposes. Yet, we do not really know with confidence whether fiscal policy really *does* have the intended effects, as only preciously few countries have thus far introduced such policies. What little such evidence exists — from Mexico (Colchero *et al.*, 2016), Denmark (Smed *et al.*, 2016), Hungary (Bíró, 2015) and Berkeley, California (Silver *et al.*, 2017) — does indicate some early success though.

Since 1960, Chile has had a tax on non-alcoholic drinks called the IABA, or "additional tax on soft drinks" (Escalona, 2014) — an *ad valorem* tax that had been fixed at 13% since 1976. In March 2014, the Parliament announced a modification of IABA. At that point, the plan was to focus on a tax increase (by 5%) for all soft drinks containing any added sugar. At a later stage, but still ahead of the October 2014 implementation, it was decided to reduce the tax rate by 3% for low sugar items. In October 2014, Chile implemented the tax modification. The tax affects any non-alcoholic beverages, or soft drinks, to which colourants, flavorings or sweeteners have been added. For beverages above an added sugar concentration of at least 6.25 g per 100 ml, the tax was increased from 13% to 18%, while for those below this threshold the tax was decreased from 13% to 10%, creating effectively an 8% tax difference between these beverage groups. Measured against the WHO recommendation of implementing an at least 20% tax incentive, this may be considered a comparatively small incentive, even if not much smaller than other actual tax rates (e.g. in Berkeley or Mexico) (Colchero *et al.*, 2015).

For other beverages without flavor, sweeteners or colourants (e.g. plain mineral water) there was no tax prior to the reform and no additional taxation was introduced. These tax rates were applied in addition to the existing value-added tax (VAT) of 19%, and no other major policies were implemented around the same time that would influence the purchasing and consumption of soft drinks.

Apart from a slightly lower tax incentive, there are other ways in which the nature of the Chilean tax differs from those implemented elsewhere. For example, in Berkeley and Mexico, the size of the tax amount increases linearly with the volume of the relevant sugary drink (as defined in the policy). The Chilean tax, on the other hand, set a threshold of sugar content and applied either a tax rate increase or decrease to products above or below the threshold. The simultaneous tax increase and tax decrease makes Chile a unique case.

Our research set out to examine the impact of the IABA tax on: (1) the volume of soft drinks purchased and the amount of sugar from soft drinks purchased — both at population level and across different subgroups, (2) on the price of soft drinks and (3) on the shopping patterns of consumers, including the frequency of purchases of soft drinks and the use of price promotions. The full account of the results is available in Nakamura *et al.* (2018). Here, we focus on (1) and (2).

We used detailed household-level food purchasing data collected by a leading commercial research company (Kantar WorldPanel) for the period from January 2011 to December 2015, drawing on raw data from 2,836 households living in cities (and representative of the urban population of Chile). The data include detailed transaction records of the take-home purchases of products in select categories, focusing on the category of non-alcoholic beverages (excluding coffee, tea and dairy products). The data also include information on relevant household characteristics (i.e. socio-economic status, region of residence and (self-reported) BMI of all household members).

We complemented the Kantar WorldPanel data with relevant nutritional information on sugar content for all products that account for the top 90% of sales of all soft drinks in the Kantar WorldPanel data.

All soft drink products were coded into the following three categories based on the sugar content threshold set out in the IABA policy: (1) non-taxed products (non-sugary, non-flavored, non-colored products), (2) low-taxed products (containing equal or less than 6.25 g of sugar per 100 ml) and (3) high-taxed products (containing more than 6.25 g of sugar per 100 ml). We calculated the monthly volume of the purchased items for these three categories and hereafter refer to them as: "no-tax", "low-tax" and "high-tax".

We constructed a monthly, household-level panel dataset to analyze the impact of the IABA policy on the volume of soft drinks purchased. Finally, we also linked the Kantar WorldPanel data with information for regional unemployment and temperature. For unemployment, we used the database provided by the Chilean National Institute of Statistics (Encuesta Nacional de Empleo, 2017); and for temperature, data were obtained from the Center for Climate Research and Resiliency (Datos de Temperaturas Medias, 2017).

2. Methods

We employed a quasi-experimental approach to evaluate the impact of the tax policy. Since the tax policy was implemented nationwide at a single point in time, the entire Chilean population was exposed to the policy and there are no direct comparison groups for the evaluation within Chile. Our empirical approach therefore relies on the time series variations before and after the tax implementation in October 2014.

We used a fixed-effects regression approach (Aguilar *et al.*, 2016), the key assumption of this approach being that, after controlling for households' (time-invariant) unobserved characteristics and the general time trend and seasonality of the outcome variables, any remaining changes in the purchasing of soft drinks in the post-tax period will be attributable to the tax. If there are other factors that are time-varying and affect the outcome variables that are unaccounted for, then the estimated impacts will be biased. For details of the empirical approach, we again refer to Nakamura *et al.* (2018). We estimated the following linear model with household fixed effects:

$$\log Y_{it} = \beta_i + \tau Post + x_{it}\varphi + f(t) + \delta_{month} + \varepsilon_{it}, \quad (1)$$

where $\log Y_{it}$ is the log of per capita volume of items purchased by household i at period t. If a panel household did not show any record of purchasing of soft drinks for a given month, the outcome variable for the household was imputed as zero. The household fixed effect is represented by β_i, which captures household time-invariant unobservable characteristics that may affect purchasing of soft drinks. "Post" is an indicator variable taking a value of 1 if the purchase is made on or after 1 October 2014, and

0 otherwise. The vector x_{it} includes the temperature and unemployment rate for a household's region of residence. Temperature controls for the variation of demand for soft drinks due to climate, whereas the unemployment rate controls for the variation of macroeconomic conditions. The term f(t) is a function to control for a general time trend. We used a flexible approach to polynomial modelling, and the Akaike Information Criterion (AIC) was employed to select the order of the polynomial with the best fit. In this study, we selected a polynomial of order 4, i.e. $f(t) = \alpha_1 t + \alpha_2 t^2 + \alpha_3 t^3 + \alpha_4 t^4$, where α_1, α_2, α_3 and α_4 are parameters, and t is centered at October 2014, when the policy was implemented, taking a value of zero. The term δ_{month} represents the month of the year effects, which captures seasonality. Finally, ε_{it} is the idiosyncratic error term. The within-household impact of the tax policy is represented by the parameter τ.

To explore the sensitivity of the results to other modelling approaches, we complemented the above fixed effects regression approach with a difference-in-difference (DiD) approach. This approach uses previous time periods of the treated population as a comparison group and thus diverges from a standard DiD approach that uses two distinct groups. A similar methodology has been employed in a previous evaluation of the impact of a SSB tax in Mexico (Colchero *et al.*, 2016).

3. Results

3.1. *Volume of soft drinks purchased*

Based on visual inspection of the unadjusted trends in the volume of the relevant soft drink categories before and after the tax implementation (see Nakamura *et al.*, 2018, Figure 1), it is hard to detect a clear overall time trend based on pure visual inspection alone (except the no-tax soft drinks, which show a trend increase). Hence, the need for more fine-grained regression analysis (see Table 1 for the results of the main regression analyses).

Based on the principle of including the time polynomial that minimizes the AIC, the main results included up to a fourth order time polynomial. The results indicate a barely significant decrease in the

Table 1. Results from fixed-effects volume regression model (outcome in log ml).

		SES		
	All	**Low**	**Middle**	**High**
All soft drinks				
Point estimate	−0.060*	−0.043	−0.067	−0.057
Standard error	0.024	0.045	0.041	0.039
Proportionate change	−5.8%*	−4.2%	−6.5%	−5.5%
Pre-tax mean outcome (ml)	7341.40	6567.39	7217.27	8100.41
High tax soft drink				
Point estimate	−0.244***	−0.129	−0.179*	−0.376***
Standard error	0.044	0.073	0.076	0.078
Proportionate change	−21.6%***	−12.1%	−16.4%*	−31.3%***
Pre-tax mean outcome (ml)	3544.84	3524.01	3715.24	3427.45
Low tax soft drink				
Point estimate	0.030	−0.188	0.200	0.073
Standard error	0.062	0.114	0.119	0.094
Proportionate change	3.0%	−17.1%	22.1%	7.6%
Pre-tax mean outcome (ml)	2627.91	2059.60	2422.93	3275.52
No tax soft drink				
Point estimate	−0.105	−0.068	0.083	−0.270**
Standard error	0.054	0.088	0.102	0.092
Proportionate change	−10.0%	−6.6%	8.7%	−23.7%**
Pre-tax mean outcome (ml)	337.77	180.59	286.84	512.31
Sugar				
Point estimate	−0.164***	−0.093	−0.145**	−0.225***
Standard error	0.029	0.05	0.051	0.049
Proportionate change	−15.1%***	−8.9%	−13.5%**	−20.1%***
Pre-tax mean outcome (ml)	368.85	443.51	382.14	366.94
Number of households	2836	1120	963	1138
Number of observations	113,044	36,443	34,010	42,591

Notes: The number of households in each SES group does not add to the total households due to movement between groups. Proportionate change = exp(point estimate) − 1. *$p < 0.05$, **$p < 0.01$, ***$p < 0.001$.

volume of all soft drinks purchased, but a highly significant decrease on the monthly purchased volume of high-tax soft drinks by 21.6% (i.e. the implied proportionate effect, with the point estimate: −0.244 and standard error: 0.044). This corresponds to a reduction of 766 ml per person per month for an average household (the mean of pre-tax volume is 3,544.8 ml per person per month). The change in purchasing is also reflected in the significant 15.1% decrease in the amount of sugar purchased via soft drinks (point estimate: −0.164 and standard error: 0.029). By contrast, we detected no significant change in either the volume of low-tax items or in the volume of no-tax items purchased. The alternative DiD regression approach largely confirms the results from our preferred fixed-effects approach (see Supplementary Material in Nakamura et al., 2018). In an assessment of the announcement of the tax, we found no significant changes in all, high-tax, no-tax and sugar-purchasing, but we did see a decline in purchasing of low-tax soft drinks (see Nakamura et al., 2018).

For both high-tax soft drinks and the amount of sugar purchased, the overall change in volume appears to be driven by a decrease in the purchasing among the middle and high SES groups, and in the high pre-tax purchasers, which saw a significant reduction in the volume of high-tax soft drinks. For the amount of sugar purchased, the reduction magnitudes were 13.5% for the middle SES group, 20.1% for the high SES group and 23.6% for the high pre-tax purchasers, respectively. This result was robust to the different measures of SES mentioned above (see Supplementary Material in Nakamura et al., 2018).

We further disaggregated the main analysis by splitting the sample into risk factor groups, according to either the mean BMI of adults in the households or the level of per capita purchasing of high-tax soft drinks before the tax. The reduction in purchasing of high-tax items is statistically significant in all BMI groups, and there was no systematic patterning in the magnitude of the effect across groups. For groups categorized according to their pre-tax purchasing volume of high-tax soft drinks, there was a significant reduction of similar size in the middle and highest groups and no statistically significant impact among those in the lowest group.

Further results explored the sensitivity of the point estimates to different choices of functional form of the time trend. All the models with the full sample indicated a reduction in the volume of high-tax soft drinks and the amount of sugar purchased, but the reduction was only statistically significant using higher order (fourth and fifth) polynomials, as well as a linear time trend. By SES subgroup, for the high-tax soft drinks, all models showed a significant volume decrease in the high SES subgroup and in the high pre-tax purchasers. In the low pre-tax volume purchasers, all the model specifications indicated a non-significant change for the high-tax soft drinks and the amount of sugar purchased. For the other subgroups, in both the volume of high-tax soft drinks purchased and the volume of sugar purchased, a significant decrease was found in some models, while no significant change was observed in other model specifications. For low-tax soft drinks, the full sample models indicated a non-significant change or a significant increase of up to 14.6% in the purchased volume.

Going beyond the analysis of the volume of soft drinks purchased, we also sought to understand some of the potential mechanisms behind the observed changes. In particular, we examined changes in price (not reported here) and in certain *shopping patterns*. We examined the association between the tax implementation and the number of days per month involving purchases of any soft drinks, i.e. the frequency of shopping trips. The frequency of shopping trips that included high-tax soft drinks decreased by 7.8%, and these changes are visible in all SES groups, though they are more significant and larger in the middle and high SES groups. The change in the frequency of shopping trips involving low-tax soft drinks was only significant for the high SES group, with a 5.0% reduction.

Furthermore, we explored whether one way for consumers to "cope" with the tax increase was to revert increasingly to the purchase of price-promoted items. Such behavior seemed to unfold both in relation to high-tax and low-tax soft drinks. We found a less than 1% increase in the use of price promotions, which appears to be driven by the high SES group for high-tax items.

4. Discussion

Evaluating the SSB tax policy in Chile, we find that despite the tax incentive being comparatively small, there are signs that purchasing of

SSBs with higher sugar content has been reduced among the high socio-economic groups of the population. The overall, population-level effect, however, is much less clear.

The results suggest that the Chilean tax policy may have been partially effective, though not necessarily in ways that are likely to reduce socio-economic inequalities in diet-related health. Longer term evaluations are needed to analyze the policy effect on purchasing of SSBs in the long run as well as to evaluate the impact on health outcomes. The evaluation did not involve a randomized design, hence the degree of truly causal interpretation of the results will be limited.

While the reduction in purchasing of soft drinks seen in Table 1 is fairly widespread across SES groups, it is of note that in terms of the volume of high-tax items purchased, the magnitude of reduction was larger for the high SES group than for the middle SES group and statistically insignificant for the low SES group. This may be surprising to those that expect the response to be greatest among those with the tightest budget constraints, i.e. those among the lower SES group. On the other hand, theoretical considerations also predict that the higher and middle SES groups could be better placed either to make cost-minimizing purchasing decisions, and/or to better absorb and act upon the information conveyed by the tax change (i.e. that certain beverages are deemed unhealthy) (Cutler and Lleras-Muney, 2010). While many price elasticity studies, including one in Chile, show that individuals or households at lower incomes are more elastic than those at higher incomes (Green et al., 2013), other studies — especially some that use randomized designs — reject the commonly expected pattern in favor of a more even responsiveness across socio-economic groups (Blakely et al., 2011; Nederkoorn et al., 2011).

Disaggregating the analyses by the obesity status of the household, we found that all groups responded to the tax by cutting down their purchasing of high-tax soft drinks. When disaggregated by volume of high-tax soft drinks purchased in the pre-tax periods, all but the lowest category of high-tax soft drink purchasers significantly reduced the volume of high-tax items purchased. As is shown in Table 1, the baseline level of high-tax soft drink volume purchased was similar between the high and low SES groups, and within the group of high-tax soft drink purchasers, there was considerable representation of households from all SES categories. Disaggregating the results further by splitting the low-, medium- and high-volume pre-tax purchasers of soft drinks into low, medium and high SES groups, it was revealed that what may be driving the responsiveness within the high-volume purchasers was the responsiveness of the high SES groups (see Supplementary Material in Nakamura *et al.*, 2018). This is consistent with the greater overall change after the tax among the high SES group. However, again there is some degree of sensitivity of these results to the assumptions about the functional form of the time trend.

For the first time in a study evaluating SSB taxation that we are aware of, this work examined other behavioral responses. First, we showed that households decreased the frequency of shopping trips that included high-tax soft drinks and, perhaps as a way of coping with the tax, households modestly increased the use of price promotions.

Finally, the SSB tax was only a minor part of a major tax reform, thus having limited public visibility, and those who have better access to information such as those in higher SES groups, may have been aware of the SSB tax and reacted to it by reducing purchases upon implementation. We explored time series data of internet searches for soft drink- and tax policy-related themes, as a measure of public interest and information-seeking behavior, as retrieved from Google Trends. A higher frequency of internet searches for the related keywords (though subtle) was observed immediately after the policy announcement and implementation. It may therefore be possible — though difficult to test formally — that access to media and information sources, which tend to be more frequently used by the higher SES groups, might partially explain the differences in purchasing of SSBs across SES groups after the tax implementation.

4.1. *Implications for future research*

Future research would benefit in particular from

(a) increasing the sample size in the data used,
(b) analyzing the actual interrelationship between beverage-intake responses and food responses, and
(c) from examining the impact on consumption (rather than merely purchasing) and health outcomes.

As for (a), due to the relatively limited variations of purchasing from the less than 3,000 households, the within-household estimates of the changes in soft drink-purchasing for the full sample and certain sub-groups could be subject to a degree of uncertainty (and larger standard errors), depending on the functional forms assumed for the time trend in the regression models. Further data collection would likely reduce the uncertainty and increase the precision of the estimates.

As for (b), in this study, we were not able to examine the extent to which the tax policy was associated with the purchased amount of the *overall* sugar contained in all foods and beverages. For instance, it could be the case that those who reduced sugar from soft drinks also increased sugar from confectionaries. However, we did not have information about the sugar content of food products. Future research should explicitly consider the nutrient information of food items as well as of soft drinks, and examine the role of the SSB tax in overall sugar intake from beverages and foods. SSB intake accounts for about one-quarter of the total sugar consumed by the Chilean population (Cediel *et al.*, 2017), implying that a more broad-based sugar tax (also covering added sugar in solid foods) or even a tax on energy-dense and ultra-processed foods more generally, may be more effective in improving diet-related health outcomes. In this context, modelling the anticipated health impacts of different tax strategies in Chile would be a relevant future direction for research.

In terms of (c), the real interest of such research should ultimately be in assessing actual beverage (and food) consumption effects, as well as the impact on health outcomes (or relevant risk factors).

4.2. Implications for policy

Previous studies focused on evaluating the impact of the excise tax on purchases and found some significant short-term reductions (Colchero *et al.*, 2016; Silver *et al.*, 2017). Our study evaluated an *ad valorem* tax and also found some signs of a significant reduction in purchases. This might imply that the nature of the tax — specific rate tax or *ad valorem* tax — would not critically affect the effectiveness of the tax policy. However, in judging the full "success" of the tax policy and in considering future potential improvements, it needs to be borne in mind what the ultimate purpose of a corrective tax should be, from an economic perspective, to help increase the price of SSBs, so as to align their full "social costs", which include costs on society, economy, health and environment, with the costs that are perceived by the individual. Such social costs could entail the costs of future collectively funded extra health care costs to treat diet-related diseases or the future health problems not anticipated by the individual consumer. With this in mind, it is hard to argue against the notion that the higher the added sugar content in a given beverage, the higher the social costs associated with the consumption of this beverage will be, and hence the higher the taxed amount should be. In light of the current threshold nature of the Chilean SSB tax, those that consume SSBs with particularly large amounts of added sugar (i.e. well above 6.25 g /100 ml) are not discouraged more than those who consume SSBs just above the threshold. Similarly, those who consume SSBs just below the threshold are encouraged to increase consumption. Although we did find that the amount of added sugar from soft drinks purchased did decrease overall, it is still far from clear that this tax design is best suited to maximize the population's health and social welfare.

The robust sub-group results for the high SES groups suggest that the policy may have been partially effective, though not necessarily likely to reduce socio-economic inequalities in diet-related health, given that the higher SES groups cut down on sugary drinks-purchasing and the lower SES groups do not. This could also imply that the financial burden of the tax is predominantly carried by the latter, increasing the chances that the policy will have regressive financial impacts. Ultimately, policymakers will need to decide whether the expected gains in diet-related health for the higher SES groups would compensate for the potentially increased inequities in diet-related population health.

References

Aguilar, A., Gutierrez, E., Seira, E. (2016). Taxing to reduce obesity (Updated 9 June 2016). pp. 1–39. Available at: http://cie.itam.mx/sites/default/files/cie/15-04.pdf.

Bíró, A. (2015). Did the junk food tax make the Hungarians eat healthier? *Food Policy*, 54: 107–115.

Blakely, T., Mhurchu, C. N., Jiang, Y., Matoe, L., Funaki-Tahifote, M., Eyles, H. C. *et al.* (2011). Do effects of price discounts and nutrition education on food purchases vary by ethnicity, income and education? Results from a randomised, controlled trial. *Journal of Epidemiology and Community Health*, 65(10): 902–8.

Bloom, D. E., Cafiero, E. T., Jane-Llopis, E., Abrahams-Gessel, S., Fathima, S., Feigl, A. B. *et al.* (2011). *The Global Economic Burden of Non-Communicable Diseases*. Geneva: World Economic Forum.

Cediel, G., Reyes, M., da Costa Louzada, M. L., Steele, E. M., Monteiro, C. A., Corvalan, C. *et al.* (2017). Ultra-processed foods and added sugars in the Chilean diet (2010). *Public Health Nutrition*, 1–9.

Colchero, M. A., Salgado, J. C., Unar-Munguia, M., Molina, M., Ng, S., Rivera-Dommarco, J. A. (2015). Changes in prices after an excise tax to sweetened sugar beverages was implemented in Mexico: Evidence from urban areas. *PLoS One*, 10(12): e0144408.

Colchero, M. A., Popkin, B. M., Rivera, J. A., Ng, S. W. (2016). Beverage purchases from stores in Mexico under the excise tax on sugar sweetened beverages: Observational study. *British Medical Journal*, 352: h6704.

Cutler, D. M., Lleras-Muney, A. (2010). Understanding differences in health behaviors by education. *Journal of Health Economics*, 29(1):1–28.

Datos de Temperaturas Medias (2017). Santiago, Chile: Centro de Ciencia del Clima y la Resistencia.

Encuesta Nacional de Empleo (2017). Chile: Instituto Nacional de Estadísticas.

Escalona, E. (2014). Historia de los impuestos al consumo en Chile desde 1920 y al valor agregado. *Revista Estudios Tributarios*, 10: 9–49.

Green, R., Cornelsen, L., Dangour, A. D., Turner, R., Shankar, B., Mazzocchi, M. *et al.* (2013). The effect of rising food prices on food consumption: Systematic review with meta-regression. *British Medical Journal*, 346: f3703.

Kelly, T., Yang, W., Chen, C. S., Reynolds, K., He, J. (2008). Global burden of obesity in 2005 and projections to 2030. *International Journal of Obesity*, 32(9): 1431–1437.

Nakamura, R., Mirelman, A., Cuadrado, C., Silva, N., Dunstan, J., Suhrcke, M. E. (2018). Evaluating the 2014 sugar-sweetened beverage tax in Chile: An observational study in urban areas. *PLoS Medicine*.

Nederkoorn, C., Havermans, R. C., Giesen, J. C., Jansen, A. (2011). High tax on high energy dense foods and its effects on the purchase of calories in a supermarket. An experiment. *Appetite*, 56(3):760–5.

Popkin, B. M., Hawkes, C. (2016). Sweetening of the global diet, particularly beverages: Patterns, trends, and policy responses. *The Lancet Diabetes & Endocrinology*, 4(2):174–86.

Silver, L. D., Ng, S. W., Ryan-Ibarra, S., Taillie, L. S., Induni, M., Miles, D. R. *et al.* (2017). Changes in prices, sales, consumer spending, and beverage consumption one year after a tax on sugar-sweetened beverages in Berkeley, California, US: A before-and-after study. *PLoS Medicine*, 14(4): e1002283.

Smed, S., Scarborough, P., Rayner, M., Jensen, J. D. (2016). The effects of the Danish saturated fat tax on food and nutrient intake and modelled health outcomes: An econometric and comparative risk assessment evaluation. *European Journal of Clinical Nutrition*, 70(6): 681–686.

Suhrcke, M., Nugent, R. A., Stuckler, D., Rocco, L. (2006). *Chronic Disease: An Economic Perspective*. London: The Oxford Health Alliance.

WHO (2014). *Global Status Report on Noncommunicable Diseases*. Geneva: World Health Organization.

Appendix 1

Supply-Side Cost-Effectiveness Threshold Estimates for All Countries

Country	GDP pc, 2013	Woods *et al.* (2015) threshold range, 2013 US$	Threshold as a % of GDP	GDP pc, 2015	Ochalek *et al.* (2018) threshold range, 2015 US$	Threshold as a % of GDP
Albania	$4659	$702–2612	15–56%	$3,945	$2087–3338	53–85%
Algeria	$5361	$1012–3743	19–70%	$4,206	$4086–6485	97–154%
Armenia	$3505	$387–1801	11–51%	$3,489	$954–1422	27–41%
Azerbaijan	$7812	$1901–5051	24–65%	$5,496	$1345–1954	24–36%
Bangladesh	$958	$30–427	3–45%	$1,212	$114–165	9–14%
Belarus	$7575	$1895–4857	25–64%	$5,740	$3113–4967	54–87%
Belize	$4894	$584–2503	12–51%	$4,879	$2935–4808	60–99%
Benin	$805	$20–414	2–51%	$762	$171–223	22–29%
Bolivia	$2868	$250–1474	9–51%	$3,077	$2106–3053	68–99%
Botswana	$7315	$1621–4839	22–66%	$6,360	$2097–3411	33–54%
Brazil	$11208	$2393–7544	21–67%	$8,539	$6048–9318	71–109%
Bulgaria	$7499	$1720–5025	23–67%	$6,993	$4067–5952	58–85%
Burkina Faso	$684	$17–379	2–55%	$590	$138–182	23–31%
Burundi	$267	$3–137	1–51%	$277	$99–131	36–47%
Cambodia	$1007	$44–518	4–51%	$1,159	$189–276	16–24%
Chad	$1054	$31–540	3–51%	$776	$124–165	16–21%
Colombia	$7831	$1370–5518	17–70%	$6,056	$7067–11459	117–189%
Comoros	$815	$19–452	2–55%	$717	$233–311	33–43%

(Continued)

(Continued)

Country	GDP pc, 2013	Woods *et al.* (2015) threshold range, 2013 US$	Threshold as a % of GDP	GDP pc, 2015	Ochalek *et al.* (2018) threshold range, 2015 US$	Threshold as a % of GDP
Congo, Dem. Rep.	$484	$5–230	1–47%	$456	$54–69	12–15%
Cote d'Ivoire	$1529	$61–737	4–48%	$1,399	$205–268	15–19%
Dominican Republic	$5879	$937–3675	16–63%	$6,468	$2731–4045	42–63%
Ecuador	$6003	$858–3191	14–53%	$6,205	$4479–6965	72–112%
El Salvador	$3826	$422–1967	11–51%	$4,219	$2573–3832	61–91%
Eritrea	$544	$9–280	2–51%	$544	$112–147	21–27%
Ethiopia	$505	$10–255	2–50%	$619	$167–221	27–36%
Gabon	$11571	$3164–7218	27–62%	$8,266	$2275–3047	28–37%
Gambia	$489	$12–252	2–52%	$472	$247–326	52–69%
Georgia	$3605	$366–1850	10–51%	$3,796	$743–1044	20–27%
Ghana	$1858	$104–951	6–51%	$1,370	$371–491	27–36%
Guatemala	$3478	$360–1788	10–51%	$3,903	$1226–1726	31–44%
Guinea	$523	$9–269	2–51%	$531	$111–145	21–27%
Guinea-Bissau	$564	$9–256	2–45%	$573	$52–68	9–12%
Guyana	$3739	$348–1924	9–51%	$4,127	$1566–2147	38–52%
Honduras	$2291	$149–1177	7–51%	$2,529	$1707–2530	68–100%
India	$1499	$115–770	8–51%	$1,598	$264–363	17–23%
Indonesia	$3475	$472–1786	14–51%	$3,346	$535–778	16–23%
Jordan	$5214	$872–3432	17–66%	$4,940	$4917–8771	100–178%
Kazakhstan	$13610	$4485–8018	33–59%	$10,510	$3734–5809	36–55%
Kenya	$1246	$32–519	3–42%	$1,377	$491–647	36–47%
Kyrgyz Republic	$1263	$58–649	5–51%	$1,103	$644–973	58–88%
Lebanon	$9928	$2420–6416	24–65%	$8,048	$4704–9105	58–113%
Macedonia, FYR	$4838	$824–3246	17–67%	$4,853	$3373–6335	70–131%
Madagascar	$463	$9–235	2–51%	$402	$66–87	16–22%
Malawi	$226	$3–116	1–51%	$372	$124–164	33–44%
Malaysia	$10538	$3481–6192	33–59%	$9,768	$4396–7314	45–75%

(*Continued*)

Country	Woods *et al.* GDP pc, 2013	Woods *et al.* (2015) threshold range, 2013 US$	Threshold as a % of GDP	Ochalek *et al.* GDP pc, 2015	Ochalek *et al.* (2018) threshold range, 2015 US$	Threshold as a % of GDP
Mali	$715	$17–368	2–51%	$724	$69–93	10–13%
Mauritania	$1069	$46–550	4–51%	$1,371	$272–360	20–26%
Mauritius	$9203	$2248–5945	24–65%	$9,252	$3560–5442	38–59%
Mexico	$10307	$2410–6749	23–65%	$9,005	$5723–8730	64–97%
Moldova	$2239	$148–1151	7–51%	$1,848	$1570–2353	85–127%
Mongolia	$4056	$543–2085	13–51%	$3,968	$1394–1949	35–49%
Morocco	$3093	$316–1590	10–51%	$2,878	$927–1484	32–52%
Mozambique	$605	$8–294	1–49%	$529	$189–244	36–46%
Namibia	$5693	$791–2958	14–52%	$4,674	$3142–5014	67–107%
Nepal	$694	$22–357	3–51%	$743	$206–291	28–39%
Nicaragua	$1851	$118–937	6–51%	$2,087	$1830–3674	88–176%
Niger	$415	$5–213	1–51%	$359	$88–118	25–33%
Nigeria	$3006	$239–1545	8–51%	$2,640	$214–291	8–11%
Pakistan	$1275	$87–669	7–52%	$1,435	$133–175	9–12%
Panama	$11037	$3042–6869	28–62%	$13,268	$11003–17101	83–129%
Paraguay	$4265	$484–2179	11–51%	$4,081	$3401–5797	83–142%
Peru	$6662	$1114–4383	17–66%	$6,027	$3836–6531	64–108%
Philippines	$2765	$256–1421	9–51%	$2,904	$672–987	23–34%
Romania	$9499	$2467–5875	26–62%	$8,973	$5382–7838	60–87%
Rwanda	$639	$13–323	2–51%	$697	$211–277	30–40%
Senegal	$1047	$34–544	3–52%	$900	$284–371	32–41%
South Africa	$6618	$1175–4714	18–71%	$5,724	$2480–3334	43–58%
Sri Lanka	$3280	$453–1686	14–51%	$3,926	$1281–2090	33–53%
Swaziland	$3034	$288–1559	9–51%	$3,200	$1505–2351	47–73%
Tajikistan	$1037	$37–533	4–51%	$926	$323–449	35–48%
Tanzania	$695	$18–357	3–51%	$879	$231–305	26–35%
Thailand	$5779	$1181–3943	20–68%	$5,815	$4069–6507	70–112%
Togo	$636	$13–327	2–51%	$560	$117–153	21–27%
Tunisia	$4317	$678–2592	16–60%	$3,873	$2763–4730	71–122%
Turkey	$10972	$2950–6861	27–63%	$9,126	$7446–13032	82–143%

(*Continued*)

(*Continued*)

Country	GDP pc, 2013	Woods *et al.* (2015) threshold range, 2013 US$	Threshold as a % of GDP	GDP pc, 2015	Ochalek *et al.* (2018) threshold range, 2015 US$	Threshold as a % of GDP
Uganda	$572	$11–293	2–51%	$705	$117–154	17–22%
Ukraine	$3900	$487–2005	12–51%	$2,115	$1059–1626	50–77%
Uzbekistan	$1878	$138–965	7–51%	$2,132	$985–1426	46–67%
Venezuela, RB	$14415	$3724–9151	26–63%	$12,265	$3618–5540	29–45%
Vietnam	$1911	$144–982	8–51%	$2,111	$1198–1813	57–86%
Yemen, Rep.	$1473	$83–757	6–51%	$1,406	$202–267	14–19%
Zambia	$1845	$68–768	4–42%	$1,305	$417–575	32–44%

Notes: Estimates for some countries are missing where national gross domestic product per capita estimates are missing.

Results from all countries from Woods *et al.* (2015) and Ochalek *et al.* (2018).

Appendix 2

Economic Evaluation of Social Care Interventions and Informal Care in Low- and Middle-Income Countries — Online Survey

UNIVERSITY *of York*

Methods considerations in the economic evaluation of social care or long term care interventions in LMICs

Social care interventions and informal care are increasingly recognised as an emergent issue in low- and middle-income countries (LMICs). This survey seeks to gather information on whether, and how, agencies in LMICs conduct economic evaluations of social care interventions (also termed long-term care interventions), and whether, and how, informal care is considered in health technology assessment. This survey comprises nine questions

- five on general context
- two on social care interventions
- two on informal care
- there is space at the end to add your comments

The results of this survey will inform a discussion paper titled '*Methods considerations in the economic evaluation of social care interventions in low- and middle-income countries*' for the International Decision Support Initiative (iDSI). The intention is to disseminate the results of this study at scientific meetings and through papers in peer-reviewed journals.

This research is being conducted by:

- Rita Faria — Centre for Health Economics, University of York
- Helen Weatherly — Centre for Health Economics, University of York
- Alex Rollinger — Centre for Health Economics, University of York
- Bernard van den Berg
- Aurelio Mejia — Instituto de Evaluación Tecnológica en Salud
- Pritaporn Kingkaew — Health Intervention and Technology Assessment Programme

Please be assured that no information provided in this survey (including the names of individuals or organisations), will be referred to in this paper, without the prior consent of the individual who provided this information.

If you have any questions about the survey or research study, please contact Rita Faria (rita.nevesdefaria@york.ac.uk) or Alex Rollinger (alex. rollinger@york.ac.uk).

Background information

Social care interventions are being defined as services which help people with their daily activities and meet their non-medical personal needs. These interventions help people live independently and safely when they can do so on their own. Examples of social care interventions include:

- Personal care: in which people receive help with activities of daily living, such as bathing, dressing, using the toilet, eating, and moving around;
- Provision of special equipment and telehealth: such as personal alarms, rails, stair lifts, walking frames etc.;
- Befriending services: where people with loneliness issues are assigned a befriender who provides friendly conversation and companionship on a regular basis over a long period of time (see here for an example).

These interventions, and often health care interventions, can have implications for the provision of informal (or unpaid) care. Informal care refers to the help provided to people by family and friends who are unpaid. Tasks include: help with personal care; help managing affairs (e.g. transport for medical appointments; help with medicines; help with managing finances); and assistance in taking care of the house.

Context

Details on you, your country, and organisation.

Please be aware that the information you provide in this section will be kept strictly confidential and anonymous and we will not link any comments with specific individuals or organisations in any subsequent publications.

Your name:

Your email address:

What is your country?

What is your organisation?

Does your country have official guidelines for conducting health technology assessments (HTAs) or pharmacoeconomics studies (PES)?

O Yes
O No

If yes, what is the perspective recommended for the type of costs included in the evaluation?

☐ No perspective is recommended
☐ Societal perspective
☐ Health care perspective: health care costs only
☐ Health and social care perspective: health care costs and social care costs (such as costs of care homes and personal services)
☐ Other

If you selected 'Other', please define 'other'.

```
┌─────────────────────────────────┐
│                                 │
│                                 │
└─────────────────────────────────┘
```

If you selected 'Societal perspective', what costs does the societal perspective include?

☐ Health care costs
☐ Social care costs (may not be relevant if social care is funded by the health care service)
☐ Other public sector costs
☐ Private out of pocket costs
☐ Informal care costs
☐ Productivity costs
☐ Other

If you selected 'Other public sector costs', please indicate which ones.

```
┌─────────────────────────────────┐
│                                 │
│                                 │
└─────────────────────────────────┘
```

[f you selected 'Other', please indicate which ones.

```
┌─────────────────────────────────┐
│                                 │
│                                 │
└─────────────────────────────────┘
```

If you indicated that your country does have official guidelines for conducting HTAs or PES, what are the preferred measures of outcomes?

☐ The official guidelines do not specify a preferred measure of outcome
☐ Health outcomes
☐ Other outcomes

If you selected 'Health outcomes', please indicate which ones (tick all that apply).

☐ Quality-adjusted life years (QALY)
☐ Disability-adjusted life years (DALY)

☐ Life years
☐ Other measure of health

If you selected 'Other outcomes', please indicate which ones.

┌─────────────────────────┐
│   │
└─────────────────────────┘

What type of interventions does your organisation evaluate? In evaluation, we include:

— conducting studies
— evaluating submissions conducted by others
— commissioning studies

☐ Drugs
☐ Medical devices, such as hearing aids or compression stockings
☐ Diagnostic tests or techniques (tests to identify diseases)
☐ Surgical procedures, such as repairing hernias
☐ Health promotion activities, such as interventions to stop smoking
☐ Social care interventions (services which help people with their daily activities and meet their non-medical personal needs, such as: personal care, provision of equipment; and befriending services, among others)
☐ Others

If you selected 'Others', please define 'others'.

┌─────────────────────────┐
│   │
└─────────────────────────┘

Are some social care services funded by the public sector (nationally or locally) in your country?

○ Yes
○ No

Social care interventions

Social care interventions are services which help people with their daily activities and meet their non-medical personal needs, such as: personal care; provision of equipment; and befriending services, among others.

Has your organisation ever evaluated a social care intervention?

O Yes
O No

If 'Yes', then please provide examples and, if possible, the report or the link to the report.

```
┌──────────────────────┐
│                      │
└──────────────────────┘
```

Do your official guidelines for conducting the HTAs or PE studies include special mention to social care interventions?

O We do not have official guidelines
O Yes
O No

If 'Yes', then please detail the guidance of your official guidelines on social care interventions.

```
┌──────────────────────┐
│                      │
└──────────────────────┘
```

Informal care

Informal care refers to the help provided to people by family and friends who are unpaid. Informal care tasks include help with personal care, help managing personal affairs (e.g. transport for medical appointments, help with managing finances) and assistance in taking care of the house.

Do your official guidelines for conducting HTAs or PE studies give guidance on the inclusion of informal care?

O We do not have official guidelines
O The official guidelines do not mention informal care
O The official guidelines advise that informal care should <u>not</u> be considered
O The official guidelines advise that informal care should be considered but <u>do not</u> provide specific advice on how to do so
O The official guidelines advise that informal care should be considered <u>and</u> provide specific advice on how to do so

---

If you selected the final option, what is the advice on the consideration of informal care?

O Impact on informal care should be considered in the deliberations but it is not taken account as a cost or as an outcome
O Informal care should be valued monetarily by measuring the time spent in informal care and assigning a unit cost
O Informal care burden should be included in the health outcomes, such as QALY decrement or an increase in the DALY burden
O Informal care burden should be measured with specific outcome measures, such as carer quality of life
O Other

Is a particular method for measuring time recommend?

O Yes
O No

If 'Yes', please indicate which one.

Is a particular method for obtaining unit cost recommended?

O Yes
O No

If 'Yes', please indicate which one.

If you selected the third option, please indicate how informal care should be measured as an outcome.

Thank you for taking the time to complete this survey. If you have any additional comments, please detail them in the box below.

Supplementary Data — A New Approach to Measuring Health Development: From National Income Toward Health Coverage (and Beyond)

1. Further Results for the Computation of Health Development Indices

The full results for the computations of the health development indices described in the main text are shown in Table S1. All indices refer to year 2013, the most recent year available at the time of analysis. The first part of the table shows the GNI per capita and a corresponding "GNI index" calculated as described in the main text for the financial protection index; that is, normalized using the minimum and maximum values of GNI per capita observed in the entire sample between 1995 and 2013. Countries are ordered in a ranking (position) ranging from the lowest GNI per capita in 2013 to the highest GNI per capita in the same year. The second part of Table S1 presents the results for the computations of all our proposed health development indices and sub-indices for countries, as well as the corresponding ranking (position) of each country according to the "strict" and "extended" versions of the overall health development index.

Table S1 and all analyses in the main text and in this supplement refer to the results for the 165 countries with data on GNI per capita and for which at least the "strict" health development index could be calculated given data availability. The additional information required

Table S1. Full results of index computations.

| Country | GNI | | | Health development | | | | | | |
| | Position | GNI pc | GNI index | Sub-indices | | | Strict index | | Extended index | |
				Access	Fin. protection	Constraints	Position	Index	Position	Index
Central African Republic	1	586	0.002	0.216	0.549	0.033	12	0.344	3	0.158
Democratic Republic of the Congo	2	662	0.002	0.291	0.672	0.038	25	0.442	7	0.194
Malawi	3	726	0.003	0.330	0.883		55	0.540		
Burundi	4	747	0.003	0.296	0.797	0.053	39	0.486	13	0.232
Liberia	5	760	0.003	0.352	0.739	0.067	51	0.510	19	0.259
Niger	6	876	0.004	0.183	0.467	0.056	6	0.292	5	0.169
Mozambique	7	1072	0.006	0.259	0.936	0.090	42	0.492	22	0.279
Togo	8	1083	0.006	0.324	0.594	0.080	24	0.439	15	0.249
Eritrea	9	1129	0.006	0.284	0.452		13	0.359		
Guinea	10	1131	0.006	0.261	0.434	0.068	10	0.337	8	0.198
Madagascar	11	1326	0.008	0.337	0.698	0.073	38	0.485	18	0.258
Ethiopia	12	1333	0.008	0.224	0.645	0.070	15	0.380	11	0.216
Rwanda	13	1400	0.008	0.422	0.815	0.087	71	0.587	33	0.311
Burkina Faso	14	1444	0.009	0.328	0.667	0.096	34	0.468	21	0.276
Comoros	15	1447	0.009	0.475	0.548		50	0.510		

16	Guinea-Bissau	1456	0.009	0.179	0.566		8	0.318		
17	Solomon Islands	1498	0.009	0.549	0.966		127	0.728		
18	Gambia	1559	0.010	0.339	0.789	0.100	53	0.518	28	0.299
19	Uganda	1577	0.010	0.310	0.615	0.086	22	0.436	16	0.254
20	Mali	1587	0.010	0.213	0.397	0.102	5	0.291	9	0.205
21	Haiti	1653	0.010	0.302	0.702		30	0.461		
22	Sierra Leone	1697	0.011	0.267	0.385	0.089	9	0.320	10	0.209
23	Afghanistan	1703	0.011	0.242	0.260	0.074	3	0.251	4	0.167
24	Benin	1722	0.011	0.445	0.590	0.108	52	0.512	30	0.305
25	Chad	1847	0.012	0.136	0.388		1	0.230		
26	Senegal	2158	0.015	0.413	0.630	0.138	49	0.510	34	0.330
27	Papua New Guinea	2183	0.015	0.344	0.890	0.145	59	0.553	39	0.354
28	Nepal	2190	0.015	0.391	0.537	0.124	28	0.458	26	0.297
29	United Republic of Tanzania	2300	0.016	0.297	0.667	0.112	26	0.445	23	0.281
30	Kiribati	2337	0.016	0.444	0.999	0.132	96	0.666	45	0.389
31	Tajikistan	2417	0.017	0.584	0.397	0.106	37	0.482	25	0.290
32	Cameroon	2682	0.019	0.301	0.383	0.120	11	0.340	14	0.240
33	Kenya	2692	0.019	0.338	0.553	0.143	20	0.432	27	0.299
34	Vanuatu	2770	0.020	0.543	0.928	0.146	121	0.710	54	0.419
35	Sao Tome and Principe	2796	0.020	0.539	0.399	0.137	32	0.464	32	0.309

(Continued)

Table S1. *(Continued)*

Country	GNI Position	GNI pc	GNI index	Access	Fin. protection	Constraints	Strict index Position	Strict index Index	Extended index Position	Extended index Index
Cambodia	36	2812	0.020	0.478	0.401	0.125	23	0.438	24	0.289
Kyrgyzstan	37	2975	0.021	0.624	0.635	0.162	87	0.629	47	0.400
Côte d'Ivoire	38	2980	0.021	0.286	0.486	0.144	14	0.373	20	0.271
Bangladesh	39	3082	0.022	0.365	0.396	0.114	16	0.380	17	0.255
Mauritania	40	3255	0.023	0.392	0.536		29	0.458		
Lesotho	41	3278	0.024	0.222	0.856	0.308	21	0.436	44	0.388
Yemen	42	3491	0.025	0.383	0.257	0.126	7	0.314	12	0.232
Micronesia, Fed. Sts.	43	3537	0.026	0.647	0.905		143	0.765		
Zambia	44	3640	0.027	0.301	0.721	0.170	33	0.466	35	0.333
Sudan	45	3754	0.028	0.273	0.240	0.109	4	0.256	6	0.193
Ghana	46	3774	0.028	0.402	0.637	0.168	48	0.506	38	0.350
Honduras	47	3864	0.028	0.626	0.548	0.169	70	0.586	43	0.387
Marshall Islands	48	4278	0.032	0.476	0.876		92	0.646		
Nicaragua	49	4307	0.032	0.713	0.599	0.182	94	0.654	55	0.427
Lao People's Democratic Republic	50	4402	0.033	0.356	0.599	0.182	31	0.462	36	0.339

51	Pakistan	4680	0.035	0.370	0.449	0.163	17	0.408	29	0.300
52	Viet Nam	4906	0.037	0.706	0.505		75	0.597		
53	Republic of Moldova	5034	0.038	0.572	0.553	0.220	62	0.562	51	0.411
54	Tonga	5131	0.039	0.664	0.876		142	0.763		
55	Nigeria	5166	0.039	0.197	0.305	0.064	2	0.245	2	0.157
56	India	5180	0.039	0.403	0.416	0.170	18	0.409	31	0.305
57	Uzbekistan	5300	0.040	0.656	0.538		74	0.594		
58	Congo	5309	0.040	0.426	0.782	0.128	66	0.577	37	0.349
59	Swaziland	5407	0.041	0.274	0.894		45	0.495		
60	Samoa	5472	0.041	0.665	0.934	0.000	151	0.788	1	0.000
61	Bolivia (Plurinational State of)	5555	0.042	0.604	0.801	0.221	111	0.696	65	0.475
62	Guyana	5787	0.044	0.538	0.686		80	0.607		
63	Cabo Verde	5962	0.045	0.637	0.768	0.235	114	0.699	69	0.486
64	Bhutan	6705	0.052	0.537	0.745	0.180	88	0.633	52	0.416
65	Morocco	6776	0.052	0.597	0.414	0.295	47	0.497	53	0.418
66	Georgia	6799	0.052	0.580	0.379	0.293	35	0.469	48	0.401
67	Angola	6869	0.053	0.265	0.755	0.261	27	0.448	41	0.374
68	Guatemala	6895	0.053	0.468	0.480	0.198	36	0.474	40	0.354
69	Fiji	7002	0.054	0.562	0.790	0.292	97	0.666	78	0.506
70	El Salvador	7255	0.056	0.665	0.715	0.236	108	0.690	68	0.482

(Continued)

Table S1. (*Continued*)

Country	GNI Position	GNI pc	GNI index	Sub-indices Access	Sub-indices Fin. protection	Sub-indices Constraints	Health development Strict index Position	Strict index Index	Extended index Position	Extended index Index
Timor-Leste	71	7357	0.057	0.370	0.918	0.325	68	0.583	94	0.554
Jamaica	72	7377	0.057	0.699	0.749	0.223	124	0.724	50	0.409
Paraguay	73	7383	0.057	0.708	0.432	0.223	58	0.553	50	0.409
Philippines	74	7598	0.059	0.569	0.431	0.227	46	0.495	42	0.382
Belize	75	7614	0.059	0.675	0.737	0.302	118	0.706	86	0.532
Armenia	76	7891	0.061	0.649	0.451	0.279	56	0.541	58	0.434
Ukraine	77	8199	0.064	0.515	0.571	0.282	57	0.542	59	0.436
Sri Lanka	78	9177	0.072	0.703	0.534	0.242	82	0.612	61	0.449
Namibia	79	9212	0.072	0.445	0.929	0.337	91	0.643	80	0.518
Indonesia	80	9446	0.074	0.605	0.541	0.240	64	0.572	56	0.428
Bosnia and Herzegovina	81	9508	0.074	0.661	0.709	0.325	105	0.685	88	0.534
St. Vincent and the Grenadines	82	9695	0.076	0.662	0.826	0.345	134	0.740	99	0.574
Tunisia	83	9719	0.076	0.760	0.646	0.330	115	0.700	91	0.545
Albania	84	10004	0.078	0.642	0.483	0.304	61	0.557	62	0.455
Turkmenistan	85	10055	0.079	0.582	0.654		83	0.617		

Dominica	86	10117	0.079	0.689	0.730	0.343	120	0.709	95	0.557
Mongolia	87	10223	0.080	0.540	0.629	0.289	69	0.583	63	0.462
St. Lucia	88	10373	0.081	0.678	0.575	0.358	85	0.624	81	0.519
Ecuador	89	10385	0.081	0.658	0.549		77	0.601		
Egypt	90	10439	0.082	0.583	0.418	0.271	44	0.494	49	0.404
Grenada	91	10765	0.085	0.656	0.493	0.328	63	0.569	64	0.474
Peru	92	10819	0.085	0.695	0.650	0.310	100	0.672	82	0.519
Maldives	93	11103	0.087	0.880	0.624	0.285	136	0.741	90	0.539
Dominican Republic	94	11252	0.089	0.670	0.609	0.272	89	0.639	67	0.481
Jordan	95	11290	0.089	0.757	0.764	0.304	140	0.760	96	0.560
The former Yugoslav republic of Macedonia	96	11365	0.089	0.671	0.688	0.317	101	0.679	84	0.527
Libya	97	11377	0.090	0.768	0.702		130	0.734		
Colombia	98	11615	0.091	0.719	0.861	0.288	149	0.787	98	0.563
China	99	11747	0.093	0.735	0.660	0.256	112	0.696	75	0.499
South Africa	100	12134	0.096	0.397	0.929	0.408	81	0.607	87	0.532
Serbia	101	12353	0.097	0.560	0.620	0.362	73	0.589	76	0.501
Algeria	102	12486	0.099	0.732	0.748	0.501	135	0.740	119	0.650
Thailand	103	13050	0.103	0.668	0.887	0.341	146	0.770	104	0.587
Costa Rica	104	13134	0.104	0.813	0.766	0.311	152	0.790	101	0.579

(*Continued*)

Table S1. (*Continued*)

Country	GNI Position	GNI pc	GNI index	Access	Fin. protection	Constraints	Strict index Position	Strict index Index	Extended index Position	Extended index Index
Iraq	105	13234	0.105	0.645	0.634		90	0.640		
Montenegro	106	14453	0.115	0.639	0.572		78	0.604		
Suriname	107	14672	0.116	0.581	0.856	0.393	116	0.705	102	0.580
Barbados	108	14927	0.118	0.661	0.680	0.451	99	0.670	105	0.587
Bulgaria	109	15017	0.119	0.551	0.603	0.393	65	0.576	79	0.507
Brazil	110	15288	0.121	0.676	0.700	0.345	107	0.688	92	0.547
Gabon	111	15657	0.124	0.400	0.610		43	0.494		
Azerbaijan	112	15861	0.126	0.648	0.287	0.334	19	0.431	46	0.396
Mexico	113	15863	0.126	0.708	0.558	0.292	86	0.628	70	0.487
Botswana	114	16035	0.127	0.489	0.946	0.482	102	0.680	111	0.606
Mauritius	115	16221	0.129	0.673	0.534	0.409	76	0.599	85	0.528
Belarus	116	16284	0.129	0.509	0.680	0.366	72	0.589	77	0.502
Panama	117	16330	0.130	0.725	0.750	0.286	131	0.738	89	0.538
Lebanon	118	16491	0.131	0.725	0.656	0.372	109	0.690	97	0.562
Romania	119	17068	0.136	0.587	0.802	0.418	106	0.687	103	0.582

120	Venezuela, RB	17079	0.136	0.702	0.340	0.379	40	0.488	60	0.449
121	Turkey	18378	0.146	0.731	0.850	0.451	150	0.788	120	0.654
122	Uruguay	18697	0.149	0.671	0.829	0.437	139	0.746	114	0.624
123	Cuba	18712	0.149	0.686	0.930		156	0.799		
124	Antigua and Barbuda	19290	0.154	0.719	0.732	0.442	125	0.726	113	0.615
125	Croatia	19621	0.157	0.614	0.875	0.457	129	0.733	116	0.626
126	Kazakhstan	20305	0.162	0.577	0.536	0.392	60	0.556	73	0.495
127	Equatorial Guinea	20918	0.167	0.299	0.807	0.484	41	0.491	71	0.489
128	Chile	20959	0.167	0.774	0.682	0.468	126	0.727	117	0.627
129	Poland	21611	0.173	0.626	0.771	0.434	110	0.695	108	0.594
130	Latvia	21630	0.173	0.578	0.634	0.337	79	0.605	74	0.498
131	Bahamas	21656	0.173	0.639	0.697	0.428	98	0.668	100	0.576
132	Malaysia	21812	0.174	0.788	0.638	0.438	119	0.709	109	0.604
133	Hungary	22042	0.176	0.580	0.724	0.525	93	0.648	110	0.604
134	Russian Federation	22610	0.181	0.523	0.519	0.431	54	0.521	72	0.489
135	Lithuania	23912	0.192	0.569	0.673	0.773	84	0.619	125	0.666
136	Estonia	24635	0.197	0.602	0.810	0.468	113	0.698	112	0.611
137	Trinidad and Tobago	24990	0.200	0.588	0.574	0.622	67	0.581	107	0.594
138	Slovakia	25261	0.202	0.649	0.778	0.410	122	0.711	106	0.592
139	Portugal	25420	0.204	0.634	0.733	0.534	103	0.682	118	0.628

(Continued)

Table S1. *(Continued)*

Country	GNI Position	GNI pc	GNI index	Sub-indices Access	Sub-indices Fin. protection	Sub-indices Constraints	Strict index Position	Strict index Index	Extended index Position	Extended index Index
Czech Republic	140	26131	0.210	0.659	0.843	0.439	138	0.745	115	0.624
Malta	141	26757	0.215	0.728	0.684	0.629	117	0.706	128	0.679
Slovenia	142	27167	0.218	0.675	0.879	0.511	147	0.770	126	0.672
Cyprus	143	29165	0.234	0.874	0.535	0.610	104	0.684	122	0.658
New Zealand	144	31955	0.257	0.710	0.893	0.711	155	0.796	138	0.767
Italy	145	33757	0.272	0.667	0.819	0.647	133	0.739	132	0.707
Bahrain	146	35762	0.288	0.866	0.854	0.146	162	0.860	66	0.476
United Kingdom	147	36576	0.295	0.693	0.907	0.713	154	0.793	137	0.765
Oman	148	36741	0.296	0.838	0.877	0.229	161	0.857	93	0.552
Japan	149	36906	0.297	0.729	0.856	0.452	153	0.790	121	0.656
Ireland	150	37877	0.305	0.785	0.831	0.677	157	0.808	136	0.762
Finland	151	38914	0.314	0.651	0.814	0.653	128	0.728	131	0.702
Belgium	152	40222	0.324	0.657	0.830	0.742	132	0.739	134	0.740
Canada	153	41607	0.335	0.720	0.849	0.512	148	0.782	127	0.679
Australia	154	41796	0.337	0.727	0.808	0.701	144	0.766	135	0.744

Germany	155	43994	0.355	0.635	0.871	0.528	137	0.744	124	0.664
Austria	156	44022	0.355	0.689	0.842	0.665	141	0.762	133	0.728
Netherlands	157	45117	0.364	0.698	0.946	0.700	159	0.813	139	0.773
Saudi Arabia	158	52008	0.420	0.828	0.801		160	0.815		
United States of America	159	52097	0.421	0.671	0.882	0.551	145	0.769	129	0.688
Switzerland	160	55649	0.450	0.707	0.740	0.547	123	0.724	123	0.659
United Arab Emirates	161	59124	0.478	0.931	0.811	0.105	163	0.869	57	0.430
Luxembourg	162	60011	0.485	0.736	0.892	0.920	158	0.810	140	0.845
Singapore	163	75400	0.610	1.000	0.430	0.759	95	0.656	130	0.689
Kuwait	164	85119	0.690	0.932	0.843	0.181	164	0.886	83	0.522
Qatar	165	123282	1.000	0.954	0.916	1.000	165	0.935	141	0.956

Notes: Countries in ascending order according to GNI per capita. Position 1 = lowest ranked country (worst performance) according to the specific index. Lower positions (closer to 1) indicate worse performance, i.e. lower health development (according to the "strict" index) or lower health development and higher financial constraints (according to the "extended" index). See main text and Table 2 for definition of indicators and indices.

to account for the *constraints* dimension as currently defined means that the "extended" index could only be calculated for a smaller number of countries (141).

1.1. *Composition of quartiles of health development indices by world regions*

Figures S1 and S2 present composition analyses focusing on world regions for our proposed indices. Two-thirds of the group of countries with the lowest "strict" health development indices (quartile 1) are located in Sub-Saharan Africa. These countries also make up roughly one-third of the group in the second quartile of the "strict" index. Sub-Saharan African countries tend to concentrate in the bottom quartiles when the "extended" index is examined as well. Likewise, South Asian countries tend to belong to the first quartile both in the "strict" and "extended" versions of health development indices. Latin American and Caribbean countries, on the

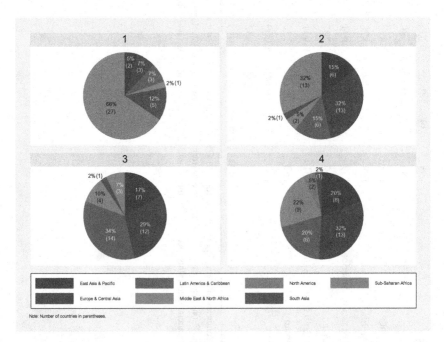

Figure S1.   Composition of the four quartiles of the "strict" index of health development, by world regions.

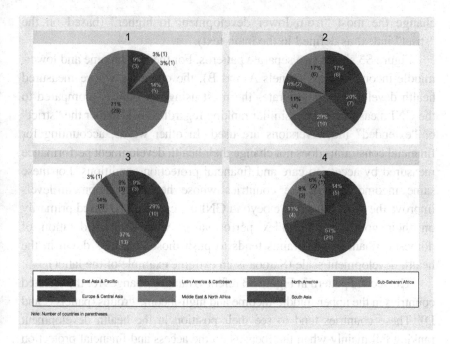

Figure S2. Composition of the four quartiles of the "extended" index of health development, by world regions.

other hand, generally exhibit higher levels of health development than their Sub-Saharan African and South Asian counterparts, being concentrated in the top two quartiles of the "strict" index. Accounting for financial constraints through the "extended" index has the effect of increasing the participation of Latin-American and Caribbean countries in the second quartile of health development.

1.2. Comparisons of changes in health development rankings for selected income groups and countries

We now perform an examination of changes in country rankings from GNI to "strict" and "extended" indices by income groups. We look at four country income groups: low-income, lower-middle-income, upper-middle-income and high-income (non-OECD). For each of these groups we select the three countries whose rankings change the most moving "from higher development to lower" as well as the three countries whose rankings change the most "from lower development to higher" (based on the "strict" index, as defined in the main text).

Figure S3 shows two separate patterns. For the low-income and lower-middle-income groups (panels A and B), the countries whose measured health development deteriorates the most using our indices (compared to the GNI measure) reach a similar ranking regardless of whether the "strict" or "extended" index versions are used. In other words, accounting for financial constraints does not change their health development performance measured by access to care and financial protection conditions. For these same income groups, the countries whose health development levels improve the most if we move beyond GNI per capita do so based primarily on their good "strict" index performance, whereas consideration of domestic financial constraints tends to push those countries down in the health development scale (Samoa is an extreme example of the latter).

The second pattern in Figure S3 refers to ranking changes for the selected countries in the upper-middle-income and high-income groups (panels C and D). These countries tend to see their position in the health development ranking fall mainly when the focus is on the access and financial protection dimensions; their relatively better situation regarding domestic financial constraints for health has the general effect of pushing measured development up. On the other hand, the countries in these groups that improve their levels of development when our indices are used do so based on particularly good performance in access to care and financial protection.

1.3. Decomposition of changes in health development rankings for selected income groups and countries

In Figure S4 we decompose the changes in health development rankings by income groups, using the four income groups and same country selection criteria as in the previous sub-section. In all income groups there are cases in which the significant fall in health development rankings from GNI-only to the "strict" index is driven mainly by particularly poor performance in the financial protection dimension. Examples are Afghanistan (panel A), Egypt (panel B), Azerbaijan (panel C) and Venezuela (panel D). In fewer instances does the access to care dimension clearly become the major determinant of the change in ranking, such as in Chad and Mali (panel A) and Equatorial Guinea (panel D). Finally, relatively good performance in the financial

Panel A: Low-income countries

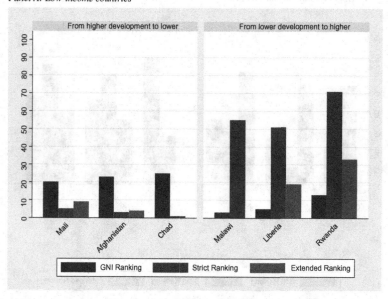

Panel B: Lower-middle-income countries

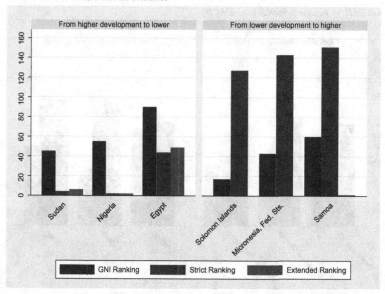

Figure S3. Changes in health development rankings using different indices, selected income groups and countries.

Note: The vertical axis denotes the country ranking according to the corresponding index. Lower ranking (closer to 1) = worse health development performance.

Panel C: Upper-middle-income countries

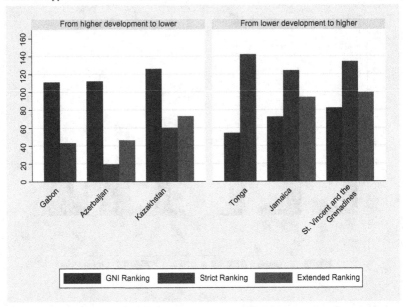

Panel D: High-income countries (non-OECD)

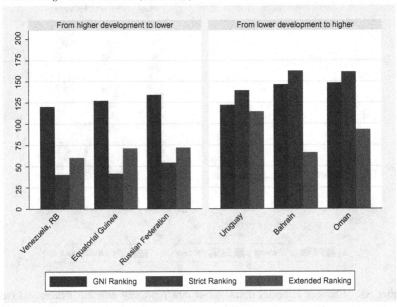

Figure S3.   *(Continued)*

Panel A: Low-income countries

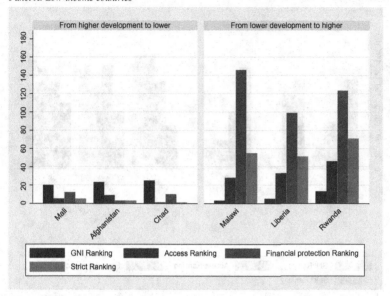

Panel B: Lower-middle-income countries

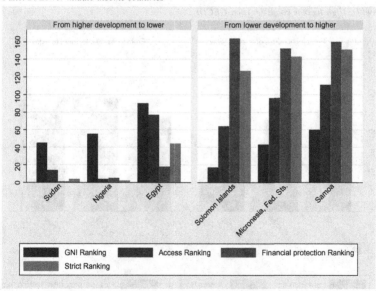

Figure S4. Changes in health development rankings using different sub-indices, selected income groups and countries.

Note: The vertical axis denotes the country ranking according to the corresponding index. Lower ranking (closer to 1) = worse health development performance.

Panel C: Upper-middle-income countries

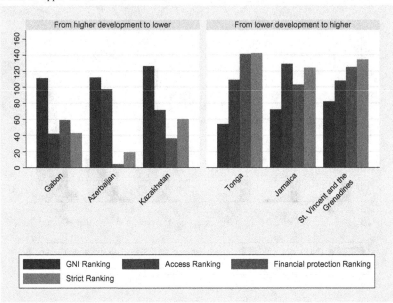

Panel D: High-income countries (non-OECD)

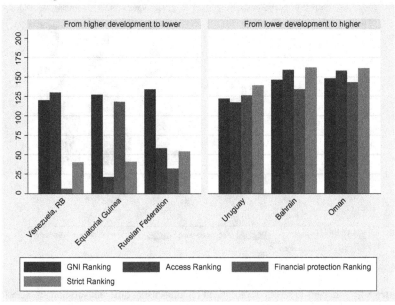

Figure S4. *(Continued)*

protection dimension constitutes, in general, the primary driver of the observed improvement in health development rankings according to the "strict" index for the selected countries in the low-income, lower-income and upper-middle-income groups.

1.4. *Broadening the definition and measurement of access: Equity and care quality aspects*

In the main text of the paper and above we have constructed measures of health development based on aspects broader than income per person, including health coverage and financial constraints, assessed by indicators widely acknowledged as relevant to assess national progress on health and for policy discussions in the area. Although we believe there are strong merits in relying on a parsimonious number of indicators that are reliable, valid, relevant, and can be easily understood and collected for most countries, a single framework will never capture all aspects of relevance for health development.

It is straightforward, however, to expand the sort of information included in the indices to offer a more complete picture of health development, provided the necessary country-level data are available. A very relevant case is the multi-dimensional nature of the access to care dimension. The current global health debate — around, for instance, the idea of universal health coverage as a key objective for health systems (WHO 2010) — makes frequent reference to *equitable* access to services, going beyond simple national averages. It also emphasizes the notion of access to services that are clinically effective, therefore making *quality of care* a crucial element within assessments of country development in health. Our theoretical framework is very flexible in that the evaluation of utility levels from health coverage can take into account concerns about equity in access by incorporating a set of weights based, for instance, on wealth levels (Moreno-Serra and Smith 2012). Quality deficiencies can be accommodated in our framework as an adverse impact on measured coverage and therefore health development.

In this sub-section we illustrate how our baseline analyses can be expanded to measure and compare levels of health development accounting for how equitable access to necessary health services is across countries, as well as the quality of care provided. To do so, we proxy equity in health service access by the skilled birth attendance ratio between the poorest and richest population quintiles of the wealth distribution. The assumption is that higher poor-rich skilled birth attendance ratios suggest more equitable access to necessary services in general in the country. The corresponding data source is the UNICEF *Childinfo* database (UNICEF 2015).

We are severely restricted by data availability for our choice of care quality indicator; we have been unable to identify more general indicators of care quality commonly used in country case studies — such as hospital readmission and avoidable mortality rates, or patient satisfaction measures — available for a reasonable number of developing and developed countries. We have obtained, however, data on the treatment success rate of new tuberculosis cases. These data are available for most countries from the *Global Health Observatory* (WHO 2015) and arguably offer a good approximation of quality standards at least in primary care.

A pragmatic way to incorporate the equity and quality information into our health development indices is to include the corresponding indicators directly within the access to care index. Following the same methodology described in Table 2 in the main text, we simply construct normalized sub-indices for the two extra dimensions, and the now expanded access to care index ("access+") is given by the normalized value of the geometric mean of sub-indices for skilled birth attendance (level), DALYs lost, skilled birth attendance poor-rich ratio, and the tuberculosis treatment success rate. We are able to calculate the "access+" index for 110 countries given the available data.

The main message from the new simulations is that using the "access+" index does not lead to wholesale changes in country rankings, compared to the ranking obtained using our original access index. Even though the distribution of the "access+" index shifts to the right relative to the original index, and its average value rises from 0.482 to 0.661, the average *change* in rankings is a deterioration of nine positions in a country's ranking, with a median decline of just three positions.

There are specific cases, of course, where changes are more significant. Figure S5 displays the results for the calculations of the

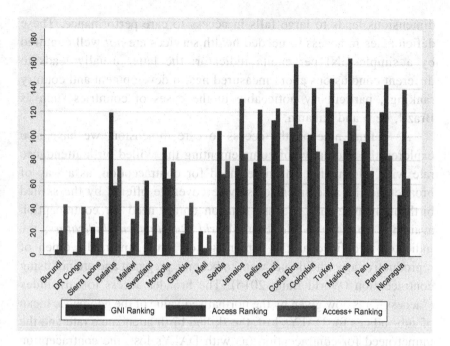

Figure S5. Changes in country rankings after adding equity and care quality indicators to the original definition of the access index, selected countries.

Note: The vertical axis denotes the country ranking according to the corresponding index. Lower ranking (closer to 1) = worse health development performance. The "access" index includes the skilled birth attendance rate and DALYs lost as indicators. The "access+" index includes the latter two indicators, plus the poor-rich skilled birth attendance ratio and the treatment success rate of new tuberculosis cases.

original "access" and "access+" indices for the 10 countries with the largest positive (improvement) and negative (deterioration) changes in ranking. Among the 10 countries on the left-hand side of the figure, Burundi and the Democratic Republic of Congo stand out as those whose rankings improve the most when the expanded definition of access is used, despite a still relatively poor performance on access to care (both countries are among the worst 40% performers).

Some interesting results are found among the countries on the right-hand side of Figure S5, those with the largest decrements in their rankings. Latin-American and Caribbean countries predominate among countries where the inclusion of the equity and care quality dimensions leads to large falls in access to care performance. These deficiencies in access to needed health services are *not* well captured by a simple GNI per capita indicator: the latter usually leads to different conclusions about measured health development and country rankings, particularly noticeable in the cases of countries such as Brazil, Peru and Panama.

As a final note on the access to care dimension, we have also explored the alternative of complementing the skilled birth attendance rate with information on unmet need for contraception, as a way of broadening the assessment of service coverage offered by the skilled birth attendance rate. We use data on unmet need for contraception available from the World Bank *World Development Indicators*; the indicator is defined as the percentage of fertile, married women of reproductive age who do not want to become pregnant and are not using contraception (World Bank 2015). The broader access to care index ("access+") is now given by the normalised value of the geometric mean of sub-indices for DALYs lost, the skilled birth attendance rate and the unmet need for contraception (as with DALYs lost, the contraception indicator enters the index computation as its inverse so that higher values denote better access).

We are able to calculate this new "access+" index for 120 countries given the available data. As before, Figure S6 shows results for the calculations of the original "access" and new "access+" indices for the 10 countries with the largest positive (left-hand side) and negative (right-hand side) changes in ranking. Once again some African countries (e.g. Guinea-Bissau, Swaziland and Nigeria) are among those with largest ranking improvements, despite a still low performance on access to care overall. Similarly to the previous analyses in this section, using the new "access+" index for health development assessments generally leads to different conclusions from using solely a GNI per capita criterion. This is evident among Middle-Eastern and North-African countries, many of which belong to the high-income or upper-middle-income categories but whose development performance tends to be much lower when the broader access to care index is examined (e.g. Oman, Libya and Qatar).

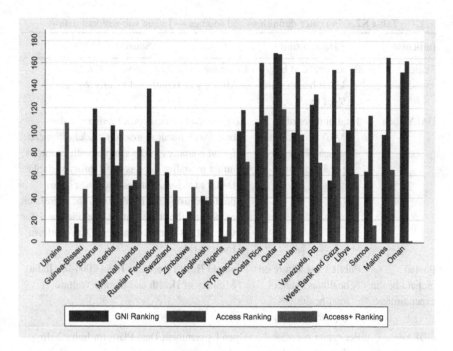

Figure S6. Changes in country rankings after adding the unmet need for contraception indicator to the definition of the access index, selected countries.

Note: The vertical axis denotes the country ranking according to the corresponding index. Lower ranking (closer to 1) = worse health development performance. The "access" index includes the skilled birth attendance rate and DALYs lost as indicators. The "access+" index includes the latter two indicators, plus the unmet need for contraception indicator.

1.5. Technical details of the computation of health development indices using Indian sub-national data

In the main text of the paper we use our proposed methodology to examine how health development performance varies across Indian states. The sub-national-level indicators used for this exercise are similar to the ones used for the cross-country analyses and are described in Table S2.

The conditions of access to necessary health services across Indian states are measured by the proportion of births attended by skilled health

Table S2. Indicator definitions and sources — Indian sub-national data

Indicator	Description	Source
Skilled birth attendance	Births attended by skilled health staff (% of total)	Coverage Evaluation Survey 2009. India Ministry of Health and Family Welfare
DALYs lost	Total number of DALYs lost for all causes, all ages (per 100,000)	Authors' own calculations. Predicted values based on a linear regression model estimated for all countries in the sample, with countries' infant mortality rates as explanatory variable. DALYs for Indian states have then been predicted using the results from the regression model and the states' infant mortality rates for year 2011 (Open Government Data Platform India, 2015)
Pooled prepaid health expenditure	Public expenditure on health as share of total health expenditure (%)	National Health Accounts India 2004-05. India Ministry of Health and Family Welfare
GDP per capita	Per capita net state domestic product at constant (2004–05) prices, Rupees, 2013–14	Open Government Data Platform India 2015 (https://data.gov.in/)

staff (% of total births in the most recent year). As for health needs, unfortunately data on DALYs lost are currently unavailable for Indian states. We predict the total number of DALYs lost for all causes in a given state based on a linear regression model estimated for all *countries* in the sample, with countries' infant mortality rates as the single explanatory variable (the regression has good explanatory power, with an R^2 value of 0.731). DALYs for Indian states have then been predicted using the estimated coefficients from the regression model and the observed state infant mortality rates for year 2011. Finally, the financial protection indicator is constructed as public expenditure on health as a share of total health expenditure.

The corresponding sub-indices and the "strict" health development index for each state are then constructed using the same methodology as

Table S3. Full results of index computations: Indian states

State	GDP Position	GDP pc	GDP index	Access	Fin. protection	Strict index Position	Index
Bihar	1	15506	0.000	0.314	0.085	7	0.163
Uttar Pradesh	2	19233	0.031	0.117	0.021	2	0.050
Assam	3	23392	0.065	0.169	0.119	5	0.142
Maharashtra	4	24042	0.070	0.685	0.068	12	0.216
Odisha	5	24929	0.077	0.130	0.112	3	0.120
Chhattisgarh	6	28373	0.106	0.270	0.095	6	0.160
Jharkhand	7	28882	0.110	0.353	0.247	16	0.296
Jammu and Kashmir	8	31054	0.128	0.438	0.502	21	0.469
Rajasthan	9	31836	0.134	0.244	0.164	10	0.200
Arunachal Pradesh	10	36019	0.168	0.531	0.586	22	0.558
West Bengal	11	36293	0.171	0.533	0.029	4	0.124
Manipur	12	37154	0.178	0.910	0.408	24	0.609
Meghalaya	13	41094	0.210	0.227	0.463	17	0.324
Andhra Pradesh	14	42170	0.219	0.438	0.083	9	0.190
Karnataka	15	45024	0.242	0.543	0.210	18	0.338
Tripura	16	47261	0.261	0.615	0.134	15	0.287
Punjab	17	49411	0.278	0.538	0.085	11	0.214
Mizoram	18	49963	0.283	0.548	0.822	25	0.671
Himachal Pradesh	19	54494	0.320	0.388	0.382	20	0.385
Uttarakhand	20	59161	0.358	0.430	0.287	19	0.352
Tamil Nadu	21	62361	0.384	0.787	0.079	14	0.250
Gujarat	22	63168	0.391	0.444	0.118	13	0.229
Haryana	23	67260	0.425	0.359	0.093	8	0.183
Madhya Pradesh	24	69584	0.444	0.000	0.088	1	0.000
Andaman and Nicobar Islands	25	72716	0.469	0.738	0.623	26	0.678
Sikkim	26	83527	0.558	0.606	0.762	27	0.679
Delhi	27	127667	0.920	0.636	0.824	28	0.724
Goa	28	137401	1.000	1.000	0.329	23	0.573

Notes: States in ascending order according to GDP per capita (in Rupees). Position 1 = lowest ranked state (worst performance) according to the specific index. Lower positions (closer to 1) according to the "strict" index indicate worse performance, i.e. lower health development. See main text and Table 2 for definition of indicators and indices.

in the cross-country case (see main text Table 2). Given data availability we are able to compute the indices for 28 states; the full results are shown in Table S3 and discussed further in the main text of the paper.

References

Moreno-Serra, R., Smith, P. C. (2012). Towards an Index of Health Coverage. *Imperial College Business School Discussion Paper* 2012/11. London, United Kingdom. http://spiral.imperial.ac.uk/bitstream/10044/1/10422/4/Moreno-Serra%202012-11.pdf (30 May 2019, date last accessed).

Open Government Data Platform India. https://data.gov.in (05 November 2015, date last accessed).

UNICEF. *Childinfo database.* http://www.childinfo.org (29 September 2015, date last accessed).

WHO (2010). *World Health Report 2010: Health Systems Financing: The Path to Universal Coverage.* Geneva: WHO.

WHO. *Global Health Observatory.* http://www.who.int/gho/database/en (29 September 2015, date last accessed).

World Bank. *World Development Indicators.* http://databank.worldbank.org/data (29 September 2015, date last accessed).

Index

World Scientific Series in Global Health Economics and Public Policy

(Continued from page ii)

Vol. 1   *Accountability and Responsibility in Health Care:*
         Issues in Addressing an Emerging Global Challenge
         edited by Bruce Rosen, Avi Israeli and Stephen Shortell

Forthcoming:

Social Capital and Health
         Dov Chernichovsky (Ben Gurion University of the Negev, Israel) and
         Chen Sharony (Ben Gurion University of the Negev, Israel)

Aging and Long Term Care: Global Policy and Organization
         Audrey Laporte (University of Toronto, Canada)

Healthcare Financing
         Winnie Chi-man Yip (Harvard)

The World Scientific Casebook Reference on Healthcare Reforms
         Peter Berman (The University of British Columbia, Canada &
         Harvard University, USA)

International Oral Healthcare Systems: Policy, Organization, Financing, Delivery
         Carlos Quinonez (University of Toronto, Canada)

Global Health Expenditures: Growth and Evolution
         Thomas Getzen (Temple University, USA)

Cancer Health Services Research: Improving Health Outcomes and Innovation
         Maarten J Ijzerman (University of Twente, The Netherlands)

Lectures in Financing and Delivery of Healthcare in Developing Countries
         Peter Berman (The University of British Columbia, Canada &
         Harvard University, USA)

Printed in the United States
By Bookmasters